THIRTY ROOMS TO HIDE IN

THIRTY ROOMS
TO HIDE IN

Insanity, Addiction, and Rock 'n' Roll
in the Shadow of the Mayo Clinic

LUKE LONGSTREET SULLIVAN

University of Minnesota Press
Minneapolis • London

Readers interested in seeing more about the Sullivan family,
including letters, photographs, and home movies,
may visit the website thirtyroomstohidein.com.

A prior edition of this book was published in electronic and print-on-demand formats.

The photograph on page 294 by Shelley Aubin. Photographs on page 300 by Susie Blackmun.
The illustration of the Millstone's gate light on title page courtesy of Tom Lichtenheld.

Published by the University of Minnesota Press
111 Third Avenue South, Suite 290
Minneapolis, MN 55401-2520
http://www.upress.umn.edu

Design and composition by Yvonne Tsang, Wilsted & Taylor Publishing Services

Library of Congress Cataloging-in-Publication Data
Sullivan, Luke.
Thirty rooms to hide in : insanity, addiction, and rock 'n' roll in the shadow of the Mayo Clinic /
Luke Longstreet Sullivan.
ISBN 978-0-8166-7955-3 (hc : alk. paper)
ISBN 978-0-8166-7971-3 (pb : alk. paper)
1. Sullivan, Luke—Health. 2. Orthopedists—United States—Biography.
3. Alcoholics—Family relationships—United States—Biography.
4. Mentally ill—Family relationships—United States—Biography.
5. Children of the mentally ill—United States—Biography. I. Title.
RD727.S85 2012
362.292092—dc23
[B]
2012017395

Printed in the United States of America on acid-free paper

The University of Minnesota is an equal-opportunity educator and employer.

20   19   18   17   16   15   14   13   12   10   9   8   7   6   5   4   3   2

Gone

A poem by my mother, 1981

You disappeared before they were born,
all of them—
except maybe the first
when you weren't quite gone
just beginning to go—
not over a cliff
with punctilious grace
leaving me most of a body to mourn;
not with somebody's gaudy wife
a flick of rue on your face
a farewell flourish on the MG's horn
and a monthly check
to prove your going was done.
No, you just disappeared
in bits,
like grain from a sack invaded by rats
a farmer finds
still standing in the corner,
empty.

Contents

Dr. C. R. Sullivan, Former Clinic Orthopedist, Dies

Dr. Charles R. Sullivan, 45, a former member of the section of orthopedic surgery of the Mayo Clinic, died Sunday morning unexpectedly in Augusta, Ga. Death was believed due to a heart attack.

He was born in Cincinnati, Ohio, April 27, 1921, and received the bachelor of arts degree in **Dr. Sullivan** 1943 from Ohio Wesleyan University. He received his medical degree from the University of Rochester School of Medicine and Dentistry after which he interned in the Strong Memorial Hospital of the University of Rochester. In July 1947 he entered the Medical Corps of the U.S. Navy in which he was a lieutenant, junior grade.

Dr. Sullivan came to Rochester in January 1951, as a fellow in orthopedic surgery of the Mayo Graduate School of Medicine. In 1945 he was appointed as an assistant to the staff of the Mayo Clinic and was appointed a consultant in orthopedic surgery a year later. He was certified as a specialist in orthopedic surgery in 1956 by the American Board of Orthopedic Surgery. He had recently resigned from the Clinic staff.

He was a fellow of the American College of Surgeons and a member of the Zumbro Valley Medical Society, the American Academy of Orthopedic Surgeons, the Orthopedic Research Society, the Society of Sigma Xi, and Phi Beta Kappa.

Dr. Sullivan is survived by his wife, the former Myra Longstreet whom he married Oct. 24, 1944, and six sons, Kip, Jeffrey, Christopher, Daniel, Luke and Collin.

Funeral services will be 10 a.m. Wednesday at the First Methodist Church in Rochester with the Rev. Winfield Haycock officiating.

Friends may call at the Towey Funeral Home after 7 p.m. Tuesday.

FUNERAL

Rochester, Minnesota, is a privileged white enclave of conservative Republicans nestled in the southeastern part of a Democratic state. It is the little town where kings come to fight cancer and presidents go for surgery. When Kennedy's best and brightest call for doctors, the phone rings here in Rochester's centerpiece, the gray marble slab of medicine that is the Mayo Clinic.

A few blocks away from the Clinic on Fourth Street is the First Methodist Church. In the sanctuary this hot July day, dressed in black, sit many of its good doctors, all friends of the forty-five-year-old surgeon who lies in the oak-and-brass coffin near the altar.

We six surviving sons of the doctor have been seated in the pew second from the front. The people sitting in the row behind us can see our shoulders heaving in sobs.

Er, no . . . wait a minute.

They hear our sniffling, yes, but at least one of the good Christians behind us has figured out that our runny noses and shaking shoulders are actually the result of an attack of wild but stifled laughter. Something hilarious has just happened in our pew, but from the undisturbed faces of most of the congregation, whatever it is that's so funny remains our secret.

Perhaps out of embarrassment for us, the good Christians turn away and look instead to the end of the pew where our mother sits. She is gazing up through her black mantilla at the sunrays pouring through the high stained glass windows. Her lips are moving. Perhaps they think she is praying, but she is not.

An hour earlier, my family was in a two-car motorcade driving through the July heat toward the church.

1

In front is the Towey Funeral Home's limousine, ferrying my mother and the two youngest; me, eleven, and nine-year-old Collin; we are wearing suits and ties mothballed since our last fidgety visit to church. Holding Mom's hand is her brother, Jimmy, in from Philadelphia to help settle affairs. The atmosphere in the car is appropriately solemn.

Thirty yards behind the limo, in the family car, are my four older brothers. The radio is up loud playing the Beatles number one song, "Paperback Writer," and all four boys are laughing their asses off.

Driving is the oldest, Kip, still sporting a California tan from his freshman year at Pomona College. Next to him is Jeff, a pale Minnesota seventeen, and in the back, the two middle brothers, Chris and Dan, fourteen and thirteen. All four are laughing so hard there is talk of slowing the car down so their raucousness won't be detectable from the limo ahead.

The laughing had started with a joke from Kip, the 1965 State High School Debate champion. He'd wondered whether, after our father's eulogy, the minister might allow "fifteen minutes for rebuttal."

Gales of laughter. Slapping of vinyl car seats. Wiping of eyes.

"We really ought to pull back," Jeff cautions.

Kip says, "Here's the cool part. Turn it up." And the elder two in front sing along with the Beatles in voices practiced from four years of performing in their own rock-and-roll band, the Pagans.

"It's a dirty story of a dirty man, and his clinging wife doesn't understand."

The car drops back forty yards. The storm of laughter passes. Deep breaths taken. A pack of Philip Morris Multifilter cigarettes is passed around.

They ride in silence for a mile. Chris turns to Dan beside him in the back seat and inquires, "So, does one hold applause until *after* the preacher guy or . . . what?"

He's teed up another joke to get the storm going again but the levity is short-circuited as their car pulls up in front of the church.

Stepping out on the passenger side, Jeff chirps, "Good turnout," as if the crowd gathering here under the noon sun is a party or celebration. The tears of laughter come again.

But now, as they approach an observant congregation, the four older brothers realize the need for decorum. They discover that casting their eyes downward not only looks appropriately mournful, it also keeps them from locking eyes with each other. Even a glance will set off the reflex, renew the conspiracy, the competition to assess the comic potential of the serious moment, to ferret out the absurdity, to nail the inappropriate remark that pops

Rochester's conservative adult bubble. Going through the church doors Jeff silently muses, "It'd be nice if they had a TV," and files the wisecrack for use later.

Finally all six brothers are together again, seated in the sanctuary a row back from the front pew, and the service begins. With eyes safely locked now on hymnbooks shelved behind the first pew, the conspirators relax, relieved to see they can finally exhale smoothly without the rippling diaphragms of remembered laughter. The attack passes as the minister guy drones on— somethin' about lambs of Jesus, somethin' about Trumpet of Gabriel.

Half-listening, Dan looks down at the foldaway kneeling pad and whispers, "Hey, check it out. A footstool." He folds it down, perhaps a little too quickly, and the squeak of the hinge is loud in the quiet heat of the church.

To the six boys the sound is a setup for a hundred unsaid jokes.

"Mind if I put the ol' dogs up for a spell?"

"Nice funeral. We should do this more often."

And when the laughter threatens to boil over, we realize it will be our unmasking. The good Christians will know they have infidels in their midst. Atheists! Even the name of that rock-and-roll band: the *Pagans!* And them, *laughing* at their own father's funeral.

But the dam holds. Maybe one or two of the congregation wonder what just happened on the family row up front, but most do not. To our relief, our mother doesn't notice either. She is looking fixedly up at the sunrays angling down through the stained glass windows that rise nearly four stories.

The ceremony ends. As the organist plays "Nearer My God to Thee," pallbearers begin to push the coffin containing the body of Dr. Charles Roger Sullivan slowly down the aisle.

As the coffin rolls past, each one of us realizes as if for the first time, "My father is in that box. He's dead. He's never coming back." And our tears of laughter are replaced with the other kind.

The Millstone in 1930.

THE MILLSTONE

Rochester, Minnesota, is a rich little town. The Clinic had been producing buckets of cash since the 1920s—and let it be noted here, 1920s money was *real* money. The large houses that began springing up around the Clinic were baronial estates built in a time when "cutting corners" meant cutting actual corners, like the edges of magnificent scrolled woodwork surrounding a home's five or six fireplaces. Many of these estates went up on the hills southwest of the Mayo Clinic, an area nicknamed "Pill Hill." Our home, however, was four miles out in the country.

You couldn't just pull into the driveway of the home my father purchased in 1954. That would be the cymbal crash without the drum roll. No, first you had to drive up into the hills and after turning off onto successively thinner and thinner roads, you came at last down a lane shadowed by fifty-year-old balsam fir trees that stood like bodyguards obstructing your view of the house until the last possible second.

And then . . . *then,* when you turned into the driveway between the giant stone gateposts, you'd had the proper warm-up for your first viewing of the great house we called the Millstone. This would be the part where the opening horns of Tchaikovsky's *Capriccio Italiane* would begin and the camera would crane up and pull wide to show the four acres of Minnesota summer that were the sovereign kingdom of the owners.

It wasn't the size of the Millstone and its grounds that made you want the house; it was the sense of stability to the thing. It had been there a quarter century by the time my father pulled into the driveway, and the ivy already clung to its sides; the red slate roof was veteran to a thousand Minnesota snowstorms, and the windows on the third floor looked down on you and said no matter how long you lived, the house would outlast you. Even as an owner, you only rented.

Half-timber English Tudor in style, with a mix of brick, stucco, and wooden accents, it featured a circular tower topped with an imperial cone, giving the overall effect of a castle masquerading as a family home.

My father came up with the name Millstone in a sour mood as he signed the first of many checks assuming ownership. In biblical times, of course, millstones (once they'd served their grinding purposes at the mill) were tied around the necks of condemned prisoners before they were pushed into deep water. Had it been my mother who'd named the house, she'd have christened it with a gentler, more poetic name—in fact, she did so, in two letters: "Green Gates" in one, "Meadowlark" in another.

Like many homes of English design, the rooms were small and you warrened your way from one to the next. Kip, seven years old when we moved in, often found himself calling to his mother from "somewhere" to ask "where he was." It was indeed a large house.

Sudden wealth is an idea America has grown used to, even bored with. But in 1954 it was still called without embarrassment the American Dream, and here at the Millstone it came true for my parents, Roger and Myra. Since moving to Rochester in 1950, the young couple had lived in a tiny farmhouse and now found themselves moving into a thirty-room mansion.

Back in the farmhouse they'd had only a few rooms to furnish, and so the first year at the Millstone saw rooms that were sparsely furnished or bare. But they had money now and Roger and Myra weren't ashamed to spend it. In 1954, they began living their American Dream without a trace of today's cynicism or self-consciousness. This was a time long before America became aware of its consumerism, its debt, and its profligacy. Myra and her hardworking husband had done their time. They'd scraped by on a medical student's salary, lived off the vegetables from the farm's garden, burned Sears catalogs in its furnace against the winter, taken the bus on their big night out, and split the entrée when they got there. Now after a year of residency at the best and most famous medical institution in the world, Roger had been asked to join the staff at the Mayo Clinic full-time.

They had arrived.

And that October 7, so did I, a bare month before we moved into the giant house.

"We acquired the home we will probably live in for the rest of our lives," wrote my mother in a letter to her parents, "and added another little boy to our wonderful family! There will surely never again be two such momentous events in such a short period of time in our family!!"

Other than Dad dying and our moving out of the Millstone, she was right.

In front of the haystack in the Low Forty, October 1962.
Front row, from left: Luke, Collin, and Dan. Back row: Jeff, Chris, and Kip.

SKELETONS IN THE CLOSET

❦

Forty years after we moved out of the Millstone, I'm sitting in my mother's study going through a box of old family photographs.

Was there some kind of national photo law in the 1950s?

"Okay, on 'three' I want everyone to look into the sun, squint hard, and make an ugly face, all right?"

It's likely that the proud fathers were all saying, "Look at the birdie," but in the pictures everybody is staring flat into a retina-frying supernova.

I squint back at the photos. I can see the details. They're right there in front of me, but no matter how I try to inhabit the moment captured there, it is a fly suspended in amber—I can see but not touch.

I want to stick my head through the black-and-white plane and look off to the left and to the right, to see what was happening before each picture was taken, what happened after. But each paper memory is frozen; every football hangs in the autumn air, forever an incomplete pass; every set of birthday candles forever *about* to be blown out. The photos are clear, but they don't show me what happened to my family in July 1966. They don't tell me who my father was, or what went on in the motel room where he died, or why it seemed perfectly normal to be laughing at his funeral.

After that day in the church pews, my brothers and I relived the hot summer of '66 many times. But in the years of reminiscing, the stories seemed to become shortcuts; they became what we *remembered* we remembered. We started to agree on things, to rehearse the history and over time the story of our father's death began to feel abbreviated, assembled by committee; like a JFK *Warren Report* in which each citizen could recount only his point of view—*a car backfired, a lady fell to the grass*—and the thing ultimately remained a mystery. On the cop shows, they'd call my father's death a cold case.

My mother enters the study. She's carrying some carousels full of my father's collection of photographic slides. As we talk, I begin to take them out and one by one arrange them in chronological order on the floor; this pile, 1950; that pile, '51. When I finish organizing, there on the carpet we see a graph; a mathematical goodbye letter Dad left for us to read forty years after his death.

The stack for 1950 is a tall column of Kodak moments, a foot high.

The stacks for 1951 through '54, not as tall.

'55 through '58, smaller still.

Until the last column.

One slide.

1962.

A hundred slides in 1950. And one in '62. It's as if Dad didn't move out of our lives all at once but packed a chair off in 1950, a desk in '53, bit by bit until '62, when he was gone, leaving this one last slide, which stands out in its solitude the way a goodbye letter stands out on the mantelpiece of an empty house.

Tellingly, it isn't a picture of us but of the house we lived in—taken in the summer of '62 and, from the look of the shadows' vertical drop, around noon. The bright sun throws the windows of its many rooms into shade, and I wonder what we were doing in there the moment the shutter snapped outside.

The photographic evidence examined, my mother and I discuss where else I might find pieces of my family history. Stories that haven't been rehearsed. Artifacts of my father's life that aren't already on display in the family museum.

All history, including family histories, involves archaeology of a kind—we uncover things. The archaeologist unearths bones, translates hieroglyphs; as does the family historian in his way, unearthing old photographs instead, reading old letters, old newspapers. We both try to reconstruct our ancient skeletons and if some parts are missing, we make guesses, piece together what we can, and step back to look at the thing. I have only these slides and photographs, which I've looked at many times. Maybe I can dig somewhere else; through some other box, through my brothers' diaries maybe, or the letters my mother's packed away. Perhaps then the shape of the dinosaur will begin to loom out of the mist.

I pick up the first thread and think, there's also that old photo album from my father's childhood. And the family films, there're those. Plus the notes from Dad's psychiatrist; nobody's ever asked to see *that* file, much less the medical examiner's report. Dad's doctor friends will probably remember things, too. There's even that police officer in New Ulm who arrested Dad. Is he still alive? And of course, there's Mom. She could retell the story. Maybe I'll just dig it *all* up with a noisy, smoking backhoe and sift through everything under a bright bank of klieg lights. Maybe then I'll be able to reach through the amber, to lean into the photograph, and All Will Be Revealed.

Forty years later, my mother still grieves the final years of her husband's life. She won't admit this, but I think she does. She won't talk about the old days without being asked and then her answers are short. "Why do you want to know such horrible things?" It almost seems to offend her, like I'm some reporter shoving a mike in her face. But she says she's willing to try.

"This remembering you're asking me to do isn't going to be easy," she admits. "Worse, it may not even be fair. The chance to get even by painting him meaner than he actually was will be tempting. He'll just have to take the chance that maybe he blew all hope of being remembered fairly."

There is some anger in her voice today. There is regret, too. And, strangely, some shame.

"I hate that something so *ordinary* happened to my marriage."

She says ordinary because what happened to her husband and to her family seems like a soap opera now. The shame is harder to understand. Perhaps she thinks she could've stopped it from happening. Not one of us six boys sees how, but she feels it nevertheless.

From her shelves, I bring down a scrapbook she made for Roger in 1945, right after they married. It's the story of their courtship written as a keepsake for her new husband, and it's the first time I've ever seen it. It's full of ticket stubs from ancient movies, matchbooks from restaurants long closed, hand drawings by an effervescent twenty-two-year-old girl, and the whole thing smells like it's spent a lot of time in a trunk.

She cringes at some of the writing. "Embarrassing!" she says, turning a page. "That letter was pretentious. Straining for effect."

"But I was only twenty-two," she says, softening. "I was probably trying to sound grown-up and judicious for my folks."

She turns to her desk and fiddles with the tape recorder I've set up. We're settling in to talk about the old days and about the girl who made the journal I'm holding.

Paging through this journal, the romance of Roger and Myra seems like an old black-and-white movie. They were two college students from the 1940s; they went on double dates to football games, met at the library between classes, and had real malteds at real malt shops. He, with his dark Irish good looks and brown eyes for the Florida girl to swim in; she, also dark haired, short like her mother, and a thin waist for the minister's son to put his arm around.

I press the record button and my mother begins to talk about those students and how they came to live with six sons in a house with thirty rooms called the Millstone.

Dr. Sullivan *(right)* and a colleague.

BONE DOCTORS

cᴊ℘

"He wanted to be the next Albert Schweitzer," Mom says, sitting now with a fresh cup of coffee. "He dedicated his career and life to a service so altruistic. He was going to be a medical missionary."

She'd met Roger in the fall of 1941 on a blind date at Ohio Wesleyan College. In the summer of '43, Roger went on to medical school in Rochester, New York, and Myra joined him there with plans for nursing school. But during her physical exams, Myra was told her X-ray revealed a "scar" on her lung and that it was likely to be tuberculosis. In its day, TB was the leading cause of death in the United States. And the cures—in 1943 anyway—included deflating the affected lung, removing it, or bed rest.

So my mother's blossoming relationship with Roger—her whole life actually—was put on hold and she returned to Florida to spend six months on her back in bed at a sanatorium (or "the San," as she called it in letters to Roger).

It was with these letters and with "long-distance telephone" that they kept alive the flame lit in Ohio; more, my mother says, on her initiative than his. When she finally joined him again in New York, they were married at a ceremony with only themselves and the minister in attendance. Barely a month passed before a follow-up X-ray suggested Myra's TB was not in remission and she went back to the Florida sanatorium, leaving Roger in New York to finish medical school.

So it was that the first year of my mother's marriage was spent on bed rest. With her new marriage on pause and her college education on stop, she continued to study, receiving books in the mail from an empathetic Ohio Wesleyan professor. In her bed that year she inhaled prodigious amounts of information, beginning what amounted to a lifelong self-guided PhD in English lit.

The year passed while Roger continued his surgical training in the navy's V-12 program at the University of Rochester School of Medicine. Finally in the spring of 1945, with a clean bill of health, Myra joined him there. After graduation she traveled with her young husband to his naval station in Portsmouth, Virginia.

It was here, actually, that Roger and Myra began their American Dream. The war in Europe was over. The country was about to coast into a long period of extraordinary prosperity and conservatism, and the future for young couples looked bright in a way America would never see bright again. The baby boom began, ground zero of which will perhaps one day be traced to my parents' bedroom. In four years, the first three of six sons were born: Kip in 1947, Jeff in '49, and Chris in '51—the second and third, results of leaves of absence from Truman's navy.

One year after his honorable discharge Roger landed a residency in orthopedic surgery at the famous Mayo Clinic and the family moved to Rochester, Minnesota. A fourth boy—Dan—was added to the crowded little farmhouse and then the booster rockets of Roger's medical career kicked in. In January of the year I was born, 1954, Mayo invited my father to become a full staff member and he received all the financial benefits that came with the position.

Even today, becoming a staff surgeon at Mayo is a bit like joining a secret society—a "Skull and Bones" with real skulls and real bones. Physicians have always had a mystique, back even to the days of medicine men. Doctors are just different. Their handwriting, a secret code, inscrutable to all but another doctor; their garb, blazing white and with a face mask no less. Few begrudge this breed the salaries they command. There's even the old joke about the doctor explaining his operating fee of ten thousand dollars and one cent: "The penny's for the surgery. The ten grand's for knowing where to cut."

Doctors do in fact know where to cut, and when they speak, we can *tell* they know because we hear the Voice of Authority. We nod as the doctor quietly tells us things, sometimes horrible things, and we doubt none of it. We nod as we listen in his small examining room or gather in a clutch outside his swinging emergency room doors. And when one of the chosen speaks—here at the Mayo Clinic—it is with the Highest Authority. This is, after all, the ivory tower of Western medicine, where you have traveled far to hear the definitive answer. And as you listen you nod yes.

I can hear this Voice of Authority today as I step into the parlor of the man who gave my father the job at the Mayo Clinic—Dr. Mark Coventry, chief of its Department of Orthopedics for nineteen years. He's nearly six feet tall, and a head of white hair adds to the regal bearing I remember as a child. He's retired now, and with children scattered across the country, we have the house to ourselves to conduct a sort of postmortem on his old friend and colleague, Dr. Charles Roger Sullivan.

In a chair in his study, Dr. Coventry (the medical mystique prevents me from calling him "Mark") has little trouble remembering details about my father.

"He was very good with people—witty, personable, intelligent. His performance was first-class in every way, so we of course asked him to stay on." In those days, Dr. Coventry recalls, "Orthopedists did everything. There wasn't the subspecialization there is now."

As I set up my tape recorder, he describes how my father began to specialize in children's orthopedics.

"I remember your father established a baseline for the curvature of the cervical spine, which was always poorly understood before his clinical research. One paper in particular he wrote on the curvature of the cervical spine in children is still quoted from considerably today."

There's pride in hearing that my father was an Authority. I get up to readjust the tape recorder and as I walk back to my seat, the Mayo doctor intones, "How long have you lived with that limp?"

It's been two years since I broke my right leg in a trampoline accident—a comminuted fracture below the knee that, when it happened, sounded like a broomstick snapping. It's precisely the kind of injury that might have been wheeled into Dr. Coventry's operating room had I been living in Rochester at the time instead of Minneapolis. When I explain I'd successfully completed nearly a year and a half of physical rehab, Dr. Coventry—in the Voice We Nod Yes To—says, "Well, obviously you haven't isolated the right muscle group and strengthened it."

He tells me to turn around and walk the length of the room again.

I obey.

When my leg first came out of the cast, I was startled at how the muscles had atrophied; I could almost wrap my hand around my thigh. But the sessions at rehab had brought back the girth and helped me walk again. As I limp back and forth across Dr. Coventry's living room floor, I tell him the stories about modern knee-replacement surgery I'd heard from the Twin Cities doctors; how I'll be a candidate for a full replacement one day, but until then, I inform him, my gait is the best that can be expected.

"The knee may well be replaced, but your problem is a muscle in the gluteus group, one you simply haven't isolated," says the Voice.

He reaches for a pad of paper and scribbles some of the famous hieroglyphs to pass on to my physical therapists—exercises to identify the weakened muscle.[1] As he does this, he tells me how the joint-replacement surgeries I'd just been kind enough to explain to him were developed by his team at Mayo back in the '60s. He tells me how the first hardware was forged, how they began work with polyethylenes, the medical-grade plastics that replaced their patients' tattered cartilage, and how they sank long metal tubes into the middle of femur bones.

As he talks I remember what my father told me when I asked what he did at work. "Well, it's sort of like carpentry," my father had said. "You have a saw and a drill and some screws and you make things fit together perfectly and that's all there is to it."

This skill—part *Gray's Anatomy*, part Black and Decker—fascinated me, as it did my mother. She often described my father's latest surgery in letters to her parents:

> Rog is on emergency this week. Last night he was in O.R. till 2 a.m. putting an arm back together that was mangled in a combine. Last week he did a hip pinning and put a "McLaughlin plate" on a woman with an intertrochanteric fracture. Tomorrow Roger must operate on the little daughter of friends of ours. She came in with a lump on her leg near the knee. Roger tried to break it as gently as possible, but had to inform Bill he must biopsy his daughter's leg tomorrow, not Wednesday. He doesn't see how it can be anything other than a fibrosarcoma—but he hopes he's wrong. If he's not, the child's leg comes off, mid-thigh. These fibrosarcs are so malignant that even a biopsy is done between tourniquets.

If there was a day when my father's skill shone most brightly it was when he operated on a family friend, Richard Plunkett, then president of the Rochester Savings and Loan. Like many gentlemen farmers living just outside Rochester, Plunkett kept horses and was a skilled rider. In July 1963 he was badly injured in a riding accident. When he arrived at the hospital, X-

---

1. Perhaps it's no surprise that Dr. Coventry's notes to my physical therapist prescribed precisely the exercises I needed. I was walking normally within six weeks.

rays showed his pelvic bone was in seventeen pieces. Years later, his daughter Pat told me that "before they wheeled him into the OR, he was given the Last Rites by a Catholic priest and was whispering to Mom what to do if he didn't make it.

"It was a long surgery," Pat remembered. "Your father wired my dad's whole pelvis back together. Dad still credits your father with his life."

In 2004, my brother Chris wrote to tell me he'd met an orthopedic surgeon from India at a party. "When I indicated my father had also been one," Chris wrote, "she asked where he'd practiced. I said the Mayo Clinic and the lights went on in her eyes. She said, 'Oh, you mean *the* Dr. Sullivan?'"

The Dr. Sullivan's career is in fact well documented. In the Plummer Building across from the Clinic is the medical library, and in its stacks are his papers: lots of information on him as a surgeon but nothing about him as a man. Before I leave Dr. Coventry's house, we begin to talk about Roger's private life; about those insane final weeks of June 1966.

"Perhaps you ought to contact the facility he was treated in," he suggests. "The man who was running it had been the head of our staff in psychiatry, Dr. Braceland."

I told him I'd already been in contact with the Institute of Living in Hartford, Connecticut. There are many strange things you can order over the phone, and your deceased father's forty-year-old psychiatric records are right up there. (The strangest is ordering a police report on the scene of a death. *"Um, yes, my father kicked the bucket in a motel in your precinct back in '66 and . . . um, University Motel, I think. . . . Yes, I'll hold."* Followed by: *"Moon Riverrrrr, wider than a mile . . ."*)

But Dr. Coventry knows plenty about the insanity. It was he who'd driven out to the Millstone to calm my father down on nights when his rage scared Mom enough to call for help. It was he who'd tried to keep my father from resigning so we wouldn't lose his family benefits and medical coverage. And it was he who drove to our house that Sunday morning to bring my mother the news of his death.

At the door, I ask him if he thought the death of Roger's mother six months prior to his own demise had anything to do with his final dissolution. The dry conclusion given by the Mayo physician is, again, the definitive answer.

"No. There's always something in life. You're never going to be free of those things. Roger simply couldn't handle his problem," said the doctor.

I nod yes.

The Rock in 1960. To see Irene the Church Monster,
turn this photo upside down and look at the "eyes."

GRANDMA ROCK SENTENCES
EVERYONE TO HELL

ഷ

For many years after our father's death my brothers and I unfairly laid all the blame for Dad's low self-esteem squarely in the frosty Puritan lap of his mother, Irene.

H. L. Mencken described Puritanism as "the haunting fear that someone, somewhere, might be having a good time." Irene rarely seemed to be having one, and certainly nobody standing near her did. She was a chilly woman who banged the Bible more than she did her husband, shamed her only child at every opportunity, and sucked all sense of hope and joy out of every room she ever entered. Hugging her was like putting your arms around a burlap bag filled with sticks; she didn't hug back, either. Nor did she laugh. Nor did she ever use the word "love" without accompanying it with the word "Jesus" in the same sentence.

If she's in hell now, she's the librarian.

She was cold like a rock and so we six boys nicknamed her "Grandma Rock."

Her husband was a Methodist minister, but none of us knew Grandpa Sullivan; he died in 1942. Later we became convinced he died early just to ditch Irene earthside and get a head start into eternity. The six boys and Mom weren't the only ones who didn't like Grandma Rock; even Dad finally admitted to it, though privately. A year before he died, he confessed to his psychiatrist that while he had at least *liked* his father, his mother was a different story:

> The patient said at this juncture, "I don't like my mother, as you can see from my scores on the Minnesota Multiphasic Personality Inventory." He went on to describe her as "a farm girl who taught school and married when she was 31 years old." [Pressed for more,] he said she's "good about church-going."

21

"Good about church-going"? If you were to ask any of Roger's sons about *their* mother, we'd say: "Loving. Encouraging. Smart. Funny." The best my dad could manage was the less-than-stellar "Good about church-going." *("Bob Eubanks? I'll take Bachelorette Number Three! Because she's 'GOOD ABOUT CHURCH-GOING!'")* Roger's other memories of life in Irene's household were equally effusive: "We always had enough to eat" perhaps being his most ringing endorsement:

> The patient remembers his mother as stern, rigid, and recalls guilt feelings concerning his pursuit of sexual information. He traced a history of being an only child who never felt close to his parents. Above all, the patient remembers a stern, religious environment in his childhood home. On one occasion when he was at a church summer camp, he recalls the atmosphere of the "old-time religious environment" got to him. He recalls crying and going to the altar in response to the evangelist's plea. On the way home that night, he clearly remembers his mother's disapproval and his feeling of resentment.

Grandma Rock offered her son a rancid little cup of her religion, and when he moved to drink from it, she shamed him—"for drawing *attention* to yourself walking up to the front of the church like that."

There are pictures of our father growing up in this religious meat locker, and in all of them he looks haunted. Standing there next to his prim mother, his eyes have that same look the prisoners of war had at the Hanoi Hilton press conference, blinking Morse code to the photographers. *("Am being tortured. Forced to stand next to her. Send help.")*

He'd confided to Myra that nothing he did was ever quite good enough for Irene. "If I brought home five As and one B, she'd say, 'Well, what are we going to do about this subject you do so poorly in?'"

Nothing about Roger was good enough, not even the pictures he took. During one of her Rochester visits he showed Irene some slides he'd taken of his boys and in the middle of his little slide show she interrupted: "Now Roger, everybody *knows* these are your children. You should take pictures of beautiful things. Like cathedrals."

Not only were Dad's children not beautiful, she even took issue with the names he gave them. Kip, the oldest, was named after my father's best friend at medical school. But the Rock insisted, "Nobody knows whom you named him after. You should name him after somebody famous, like John Adams and such." In a world full of sharp objects within easy reach, how this woman managed to die of just heart disease is a mystery for the ages.

Her visits to us in Minnesota were like flu season; something nasty was in the air, everybody felt vaguely shitty for a month, and when it went away we all felt better. When our mother's parents drove up from Florida, we'd all wait eagerly at the end of the driveway for the arrival of their Pontiac and its big grill full of strange Florida bugs. There'd be jumping up and down, cries of "What did you bring us?," and hugs given through the car windows even before the motor was turned off. But Grandma Rock's appearances were prissy, high-maintenance affairs heralded only by warnings from Dad about how to behave once she arrived. In a letter to her parents my mother described one such visit that happened during the last week of her pregnancy with Chris in August 1951:

> Roger's mother came to the hospital for a few minutes to see our new baby. I knew she'd have a few derogatory things to say so I was all primed to hold my tongue. And it was good strategy. When we got to the nursery window there were five or six little pink and bald-headed babies behind the glass cuddled up in their trundle beds. Then up rolled little Christie with that full head of hair. Grandmother Sullivan's first words on viewing her new grandson were: "Dear me. There's not much Sullivan in him." And then added in a sibilant whisper, "He looks like a *Jew*!" When my baby began waving his little arms and legs she said, "I'm afraid he's going to be nervous like you, Myra."

Given Roger's childhood home, it's not surprising that at college he recoiled at the sight of Myra's bright homemade Florida dresses on the drab Methodist campus, or that he was vexed by the brown ink she used in her class notebooks. *("Ink should be black.")* In my father's upbringing, if something wasn't black or quiet or pious it was an affectation that "nervous" people used to call attention to themselves. Perhaps he remembered his first and only religious ecstasy; how it led him to the front of that Ohio church revival, and how Irene scolded him for it.

"Walking up to the front like that. Are you so special?"

Years later, whenever the six of us gathered to look at slide shows of my father's old photographs, we played a game called "The Rock." To win, you had to be the first to spot the old shrew lurking in the back of a photograph and shriek, "It's the ROCK!"

For years, Chris was unable even to speak her name without automatically adding, "God exercise her soul." In fact, one winter night in the mid-1970s, Chris was out in the unheated garage scrounging in trunks for one of his old diaries. He came back in from the Minnesota snowstorm bearing a book. He held it out to me. It was Grandma Rock's Bible and it was cold. Very cold.

We liked the joke enough to refreeze the Bible out on the front step for subsequent presentations to the rest of the brothers.

The Rock pays a visit to the Millstone, 1956.

LITTLE CHRISTIANS,
ALL IN A ROW

clр

I do not know if all children are born atheists, but we six were.

Watching my mother try to get us to Sunday school an observer might have thought we were vampires being dragged out into the noonday sun to fry. We made the process of getting dressed and off to Sunday services such a whiny mess that, except for our father's funeral, few of us have any memories of sitting in a church at all. Photographic evidence, however, establishes that our parents succeeded at least once. And we have Grandma Rock to thank for that.

There is a family film taken in the summer of 1959 during one of the Rock's visits that shows the six boys wearing what appear to be Sunday school clothes. Grandma Rock was in town and Dad was putting on a show. (He never went to church, objecting even to the few times Mom took us to Sunday school. But if the Rock's broomstick was leaning against the Millstone, you can be sure come Sunday we were all in church.)

The scene in this 8 mm film begins with the entire family standing quietly at attention. We're in front of the Millstone, behind one of the two stone benches at the entryway—we're all silently staring at the camera. There is no laughter in the moment, no joy; it's a police lineup in Sunday school clothes. In the back row, with pursed lips, stands the Rock. *("It's the ROCK!")*

In the next scene everybody's gone and it's just twelve-year-old Kip standing there, wearing his suit and an impassive face. He holds his pose dutifully for five seconds, allowing, one guesses, the camera to drink in the full splendor of his church raiment. He then takes a smart quarter turn left, walks around the bench, toward the camera, and offscreen.

Cut to the second-born, Jeff, standing alone. It's the same routine: the expressionless face, the sartorial photo op, the quarter turn snap-to, the walk past the camera. And so it goes down the line even to little Collin, then barely two years old.

With the sound of the old projector keeping me company, I try to imagine what my father was hoping to capture in his camera that day; clearly, it wasn't joy. Then I wonder if I'm so cynical I can't accept this may simply be footage shot by a proud father of his children in a rare scrubbed-clean moment.

Maybe. But there's a sense to the scene that Dad had barked at us just before the film began to roll. *("Stand still!")* And there's something about how he ordered us all to take those glum little marches. Hut, two, three, four.

I begin to wonder if, as a child, Dad had been ordered to make this same religious perp walk in front of Grandma Rock's camera. Remembering those lifeless photos of Roger as a child leads me to the bookshelf again.

The photographs in my father's childhood album show events commonly associated with happiness—picnics, camping trips, outdoor gatherings—and yet not one person in any of the pictures is happy. The props are there: the canoe, the picnic basket, the lakeside cabin; all situations one might reasonably assume would yield at least one candid image of actual joy. But there sit Irene *("It's the ROCK!")*, the Minister, and Roger—all without expression. Perhaps this is simply the way people used to pose for photographs. But not *one* smile? Even on the outings? To make sure I'm not seeing things, I go through the album again and count the number of photos of Irene Sullivan. There are forty-one. She has an expression in four of them (the expression is technically a smile, but it bears more similarity to a paper cut). In all the rest she is a totem pole, a snow-covered gargoyle high on a church looking down on her little hell-bound congregation.

From the shelf I bring down another family heirloom, one I've never had the least bit of interest in—a collection of my grandfather Sullivan's sermons. Not one of the six of us has ever read more than a page of it, peppered as it is with evangelistic clichés: "For a man may be changed and reborn in the fiery furnace of God's wrath. . . . [A]ppeal against all forms of intemperance and debauchery . . . of the use of liquor and opium and other poisons . . . of immorality, adultery, of all social forms of sin, of worldly lust, impurity and perversion of nature." Growing up, Roger listened to these sermons and watched as his father's congregations nodded in rapt agreement that God was "vengeful," God was "jealous" and that God would send you to Hell if you did not tread straight and true on "the great moral highway."

Several pages into these nearly hundred-year-old sermons, I discover how Irene and the Minister may have divided the labor:

From the Rev. Charles W. Sullivan's sermons, 1917
A mother could predestine a child to a religious and moral life by her high idealism when he is born ... for she has him tied to her apron strings and almost perfectly under her control. He is the seed bed and if she is so determined she can plant that seed bed so thickly with religious and spiritual motives that it would almost require insanity or a moral revolution to tear up her work.

Like most households of the era, the raising of children was left to the women. Appropriately, the Reverend set out to save the world's souls, leaving Irene in charge of the seed bed of Roger's little soul, planting it "thick with religious and spiritual motives." The Reverend may have been the mastermind, but Irene was the axman.

Before I return the books to the shelf, I open the photo album again and turn to a last small picture of Roger, my father, as an eight-year-old. He too is dressed in his church clothes and sitting on a stone bench very similar to the one in our family film. He looks a little sad. The impression I get is that he believes Jesus loves him, but his mother, he's not so sure about.

There's a line from Camus: "After a certain age, every man is responsible for his own face." Passing blame back a generation seems to be an American pastime. When we find ourselves standing in front of the judge, we're all suddenly victims.

"Yes, Your Honor, I did in fact fill those vats in my basement with body parts, but I had a sad childhood and I'd like to leave, please."

Perhaps I am too hard on Irene. Her parents, Susannah P. Love and Frank Compton, may have been even worse. Following this line of reasoning, the blamestorming session leads logically to a bitter old *Australopithecus* spreading guilt and anger around Olduvai Gorge.

"Well, Thog, that isn't much of a bone tool you've made, now is it?"

But my father's monstrous behavior in his final years belongs on his bill, not Irene's. So too, then, do his acts of goodness, as do his early years when he was a loving father. With Irene-and-her-Bible as his mother, it's to my father's credit he was ever as good a man as he was. According to my mother, the man she met was a sparkling, funny, passionate, and gentle man. And if none of that counted, passing the son-in-law test with a character as formidable as Myra's father was an accomplishment worthy of a tattoo.

Roger didn't set out in life to be a father; he set out to be a missionary doctor. But when we happened along, he found great joy in raising a family. Irene hadn't frozen it out of him. He was capable of intense love. He also beat the odds coming out of Irene's meat locker with his creativity intact. He became an extraordinary photographer. Roger bought a Rolleiflex camera, built a darkroom in the basement of the Millstone, and produced hundreds of excellent portraits of his family (some are in this book). Chris and Jeff both remember many good hours with Dad in the red light of the darkroom, gently shaking pictures to life under the developing fluid, Dektol. Kip remembers how Dad carried him on his shoulders through the front door of the Millstone after Kip scored the winning goal for his hockey team.

"I can clearly remember how loving Dad could be with us in his healthier days," Kip says. "He loved tickling and kissing us almost to death, sledding with us in winter, and throwing the football around in summer. He was such an accurate passer I could have run around the Millstone yard all day long chasing his passes. I have one particularly good memory of sitting at the dining room table, getting ready to eat with all you guys. And when Dad came home, he went down the line stopping at each brother and kissing you on the cheek from behind."

Roger was different in the early days. We all were.

Dan and Chris in front of the Millstone, 1958.

LITTLE MONSTERS
IN EVERY ROOM

ʃ♩

Awag observed that a firstborn's birthday is enshrined with detailed memory: "Our beloved son entered the world at precisely 1:19 a.m. on Monday, the sixteenth of August, in the year 1947."

The next child's birthday is remembered as "January '49."

All the third gets is, "He was born, uhhh, the year the grocery store burned down, right?"

As the fifth son of six, I arrived late to a noisy party that had started years ago and, as neither firstborn nor baby, I was a face in the crowd. Collin, my only little brother, was born in 1957 and from that year forward we youngest four became known as "the little ones." Kip and Jeff retained their given names; all the rest of us were the little ones.

"Kip, will you please send the little ones outside?"

"Jeff, have the little ones brushed their teeth?"

By the time they were ten years old, Kip and Jeff had been dubbed lieutenants in Mom's army and were conscripted to help her with crowd control. But her toughest mothering years, Mom confided, were actually when she had just the first two—Kip and Jeff, as toddlers. Dad was still away with the navy then and she was left to keep two small boys from sticking forks in each other's eyes. It's been said that when there are just two children to watch, the parents can run a man-on-man defense; when the third is born they're forced to switch to zone. Mom was in zone defense from the get-go, and with six children—six *boys* no less—some might have advised her to just drop back and punt. Simply getting her brood from parking lot to store involved mapped-out plans on the level of the Allied landing at Omaha Beach. Yet in a 1957 letter, she seemed to shrug it off: "We made our way through the train station in the fashion of a paramecium—one child thrusting ahead and being held back physically, another child lagging behind and having to be coaxed forward verbally."

If it takes a village to raise a child, what sort of horizon-filling metropolis does it take to raise *six*? Raising only two boys as I am today, each evening finds me exhausted and wondering—marveling, really—"How did she raise six?" When asked, all Mom offers is an unsatisfying, "One at a time." Perhaps, like the forgotten pain of childbirth, one at a time is simply the best she can remember.

What I remember, however, is a constant sound of thunder.

We little ones thundered over the wooden floors of the Millstone, destroying everything in our path. Every object in our parents' new home was something for forty greasy little fingers to prod, pull out, bend in half, push in a brother's ear, or otherwise trash. Antiques became weapons; knick-knacks, missiles:

> I seem unable [wrote my mother] to impose much discipline on Luke. He has unscrewed every unscrewable screw in the house (from water faucets, radiators, door knobs, washing machine, and typewriter); he's squeezed out miles of toothpaste, shaving cream, Prell shampoo; he's lost six needles from the record player in the Rumpus Room, two sets of my car keys, and dozens of toothbrushes; he's cost us at least $200 in plumber's bills to recover tractors, Tinkertoys, tongue depressors, and apple cores from the toilet; he's spilled coffee, honey, boxes of straight pins, Grape-Nuts, poured gallon jugs of bleach into a $3.65 box of Tide, sugar into the flour bin, and all the checkers down the hole in the fireplace; he has been discovered stacking up the Irish Belleek china, leaning perilously out car windows at 45 mph, playing with kitchen matches, crayoning on the dining room wall, blowing into a full ashtray and, as you well know, he's had his taste of kerosene. The chances of his surviving into the hazardous 6-to-16 years seem remote.

Hurricanes have categories, as do tornadoes (the dreaded "F5"); even the armed forces assign a metric to the destructive power of their explosives. Little boys should be no different. Gradients could well have been calibrated to prepare our parents for the effect we would have on their belongings, and had such a system been in place, warning sirens would've been on full blast at the Millstone through most of the '50s. *(Cut to my poor mother telling the reporters, "Well, I guess it was a 'Level 3' by the time it hit our couch. And then it touched down near that new lamp, you know, the one we used to have by the fireplace?")*

Little boys have an ability to look into a thing and divine its weakest internal structures. In one eidetic blink we knew the precise spot to bend a thing—the exact coordinates to produce the most pleasing snapping noise, maximize the number of resulting pieces, and ruin a thing beyond all hope of repair. Destruction was an art.

Much of Myra's new home was built out of stone, which we could only deface temporarily; sometimes with mud, sometimes paint. Cast iron was another medium we found difficult to work in, and so the giant furnace in the basement and the radiators were all safe. Wood was an attractive canvas and gouging a specialty of ours. But even here we had difficulty as the Millstone was done in "combed oak"—a hard crenellated surface resistant to all but the most determined vandal. It was Jeff who finally cracked the code on wood. He'd seen Davy Crockett on TV throw a knife into a tree and, after some practice, successfully reproduced the same pleasing thunk on the back of his bedroom door. But as it turned out, our best work was done on the plaster walls of the long hallways in the Millstone. Frescoes in crayon and booger went up throughout the giant house with new exhibits opening weekly. Magic Marker was popular, but more memorable were some excellent studies done in fingernail polish.

Destruction was an art, one we pushed to a level critics might call metadestruction. When Mom locked something away from us, the lock itself became the new toy and we'd break that first, play with it, and then break whatever she'd locked away. If Mom roped off the vegetables in her garden, she simply provided a cool lasso to wrangle tomato plants with.

Each destructive act came with its own sound and our mother soon learned the signature noises associated with our various disassemblings. Crashing china was, for instance, an easy read but one heard after the fact. Harder to discern were the sounds of horrible things *about* to happen—the scrape-bump-rattle of a ladder being leaned against the china cabinet; the hollow slosh of paint cans being stacked; the brittle clack of framed paintings being arranged into a fort. Had my mother been able to catalog these sonic silhouettes she might still own many of her nicer things.

"My children," she wrote to her parents in 1961, "are being boys. Records turned on loud, wrestling on the floor, timing each other in dashes upstairs—oh, tell me, what do little girls do early on Sunday mornings?"

What little girls did we had no idea. We lived in our Man Village—a place without cleanliness or quiet, and where everything was eventually destroyed. Had my Dad owned an anvil we would've figured out how to destroy that, too. And the dirt. Oh, the dirt. Six pairs of feet tramping in from Minnesota's mudbottom Aprils moved the rich soil of the Midwest into the Millstone as steadily as if we'd shoveled it in through an open window. Wet clothes heavy with earth were peeled off at the front door before a mad dash to the bathtub to choke the drain with the leafy sludge that washed off us in viscous waves. Snips and snails and puppy dog tails were not what we were made of, as my poor mother could well attest as she cleaned up the bodily messes six boys left like slug trails through her deteriorating home: bathrooms splattered by little boys playing "sword fight" while peeing . . . critter carcasses brought in from the ravine for closer biological investigation . . . the smell of urine in a sink *("But the bathroom was so far away")* . . . and the sick.

Memory: Throwing Up

Sometime in third grade—

I'm in bed and I throw up.

I have the lower bunk; my little brother, Collin, is asleep overhead. I am drifting off to sleep and then Blap! just like that—the adventure begins.

Throwing up is still kinda scary. Scarier still, there in the dim light of my bedroom, is the pool of barf—the Thing from Beyond the Esophagus. It looks like a giant pancake of creamed corn, lurking there just below my pillow, making its plans. I back away, but the monstrosity cascades down the slope in the mattress created by my body weight and rolls toward me like a giant yellow amoeba. The more I crawl away from it, the faster it comes. Quick thinking is in order.

Plan Number One: Make a mad dash straight through it— "Splish, splash I was takin' a bath"—and leap off the bed. Nope. Can't touch the barf.

Plan Number Two: Call for Mom? No time.

Plan Number Three: Spider-Man!

Yes, that's it! I grab the slats under my brother's mattress overhead and lift myself up. Just as the Thing from Beyond the Esophagus rolls under me, I kick out, arch my back, and land lithely on the bedroom floor. It's then I notice how tightly my pajamas cling to my body, how much they feel like a superhero's costume. Wow, this is so great.

As my poor mother cleans up the defeated remains of my archenemy, I entertain her with a vivid recounting of my spiderlike agility.

"Luke barfed!" someone yells.

"He what? Lemme see!"

A sound of thunder on the stairs; never to bring help, no, only to rubberneck.

Assuming a child throws up, say, even just two times a year, my mother mopped up somewhere around 120 piles of emesis on her premises. Similar conservative calculations suggest that before the six of us were toilet trained, our mother changed some 30,000 diapers. Before the last boy left her household, Myra had also washed 78,000 socks and done some 473,000 dishes. This was the 1950s—before paper towels, before disposable diapers, before dishwashing machines. The Millstone may have been a magnificent house, but Myra was its charwoman. One could argue that even the assistant janitor in a Roman vomitorium had a better job than our mother—he was at least paid for his work and could do it without a crowd of little boys leaning around his knees for "a better look."

This was the 1950s.

Roger was never expected to wash one of those 473,000 dishes or 78,000 socks; that was women's work. There was never a single break for Myra over the two decades of raising six boys, not one night off. She never complained, though—this was the 1950s. This is how it was. She did, however, have one room where she could hide.

Above the main entryway of the Millstone, the balcony to Mom's library; above that, the conical roof of the attic.

A LIBRARY OF HER OWN

✒

During Roger's itinerant youth, his father took a pastorate at the Methodist church in Daytona Beach, Florida.

There in the same town, several miles away in the halls of Seabreeze High School, walked our other grandfather, the school principal. The clipped approach of his steps got the attention of students lingering outside classrooms, but it was his voice that ran Seabreeze High for thirty years. Long before there were public address systems, there was the booming, benevolent basso profundo of my maternal grandfather, Rubert James Longstreet.

Grandpa RJL began his career in education first as a teacher, then advanced to overseeing several schools in the district, and finally became supervising principal of the entire peninsula. This post included Daytona Beach's new high school—Seabreeze—and it was here he kept his office and here my mother graduated in 1941 as valedictorian. RJL retired in 1949 and though his beloved high school was demolished in the late 1950s, an elementary school in Daytona Beach stands today bearing the name "R. J. Longstreet Elementary School."

RJL had a classicist's love of knowledge and to the very end of his days continued to learn, study, read, and teach. He retired in the small town of DeLand nearby but continued as a professor of law at Stetson University. Just outside town in a little home on Lake Winnemissett, he kept a library of two thousand books—on ornithology, history, religion, science, and philosophy. On clear nights he fiddled with his new telescope to look at the moons of Jupiter and during the day continued to band birds to study their migrations. He was thrilled when told a pelican he'd banded as a young Audubon Society member in 1933 was retaken thirty-one years later a hundred miles to the north.

His love of knowledge, of books, and of learning was thoroughly transferred to his daughter. And though she was every bit the lifelong student her father was, she'd occasionally confess—even late in her life—that she felt "uneducated." Tuberculosis and marriage had disrupted her college career, and lacking the actual certificate, she felt her lifelong studies somehow didn't count. But she had an extraordinary education—self-made—one that began during her convalescences and continued throughout her life. As a reader, she was tireless. She ate information. She tore through books at a pace that would've made Evelyn Wood, the speed-reading queen, slam her book down and say, "Myra, can we just take a fucking *break*?"

She was never without a book. She grabbed one on the way to the hospital to have a baby. She had one in the car "for emergencies." She read while stirring Sani-Flush in the Millstone's toilets and while waiting to pick up her boys from school. If she didn't have a good book to read, she'd head to the library at night, even during a Minnesota winter.

Her education did not cost us a parent; she was a mother first, a student second. She read in stolen moments, in between breaking up fights or hosing our art off the walls. Throughout the house she kept books propped open to be read while she ironed or cooked or sewed. Taped to the refrigerator were definitions of new words to learn; to the front door, new titles to get at the library. She brought home children's books, too, and left them by our bedsides, in the basement playroom, on the porch, even on a reading rack in the bathtub. Her education suffused the whole house with the rustle of a university library—the turning pages of six boys reading books, the older ones writing in their journals.

And then there was her crown jewel—the Tower Library.

"Tower" makes it sound higher than it was; it was only the second floor. But it was the way the room commanded that whole rounded section of the Millstone—above the curved stone entryway and below the cone of the attic's red-slate roof—that gave it the feeling of a tower.

French doors opened onto a stone balcony and let morning light into the small oval room. It was in this room that my mother's love of learning flowered.

Myra believed, as her father did, that "books are the best wallpaper." So she began to paper the room, filling the shelves as her interests grew and took turns like a river, branching from philosophy to history, the Revolution to the Civil War, biography, astronomy—everything but "popular novels," which both she and her father disdained. Even the library's ceiling bore the imprint of her interests—there she carefully mapped out the constellations in pencil and labeled the stars.

In the middle of this room was her favorite place to write, an antique Betsy Ross desk; with drawers on both sides, it was a desk made to own the center of a room. In its drawers she stored the letters from her father and at this desk she answered them.

Their letters were written in the small blue composition notebooks, the same kind the old professor handed out in his classes before essay tests. They called their letters "Blue Books," and when a year's worth of them had collected on his desk in Florida and hers in Minnesota, Grandpa would gather and bind them by hand into green hardcover books. The complete set of their correspondence now stretches across thirty-seven inches of my shelf.

By the time our family moved into the Millstone, Myra and RJL were into their tenth year of weekly correspondence and subjects were well established. Family was first. But the letters were more than "the kids are fine." The two of them filled the Blue Books with such detail about their daily lives that even if long-distance telephone had been affordable, the sheer volume of information they exchanged would have moved through the wire like a goat through a python.

Following family life and daily events, the subject was books, old books in particular. The smell of old books, the delicious weight of them in one's hands, and the musings on who the previous owners might have been. History, biography, and literature formed the core of their interests, but they also studied Greek together, the daughter sending her weekly translations fifteen hundred miles to the professor with a three-cent stamp.

As the 1960s brought the nation's attention to space flight, the two of them studied astronomy to complement their breathless viewings of every liftoff from Alan Shepard to Neil Armstrong. The new decade also brought the centennial of the Civil War, and the two of them inhaled volumes on the great conflict. R.J. Longstreet and daughter were related to Confederate general James Longstreet (cousin, several times removed), and although Myra and the professor were both card-carrying liberal Democrats, their sympathies leaned to at least one Confederate, the often-maligned soldier whom Robert E. Lee called his "Old War Horse."

RJL, in a letter to Myra
Am moving along through Catton's This Hallowed Ground and the next few pages will have me back in Gettysburg. Shall be interested to see whether General Longstreet gets the blame again for not taking Little Round Top. Some day I want you to stand with

me on that summit. Let's spend at least two or three days immersed there in our favorite subject before it is too late.

The comforting smell of old books and the silence of Mom's library seemed to me an ideal place to set up my army men and conduct noisy large-scale wars. More than once, her prized editions on the Civil War served as fort walls, behind which I set up a motley band of soldiers, mixing cowboys and Indians, World War II soldiers, and the Blue and Gray. Like General Longstreet, I too sent my captured prisoners south—down the laundry chute to the distant basement.

Dan, Luke, and Chris, circa 1956.

FORTS, DEATH, AND BEDTIME

⚜

The Civil War was not my introduction to the whole idea of "sides"—
that had been formed by fighting with my brothers. But the fact that
grown-ups had once broken off into warring groups so clearly defined they
even had uniforms, well, this was fascinating: conflict institutionalized. On
top of that, these guys had forts. And *forts* were cool.

My very first forts were sculpted on my mother's dinner china. Fort
Mashed Potatoes was indeed a mighty structure, its high ground command-
ing the entire plate. Bristling with baby-carrot cannons and staffed by green-
pea army guys, it was impregnable to all but the Giant Fork.

Little boys who lived in the quiet Midwest of the 1950s were, of course,
under constant attack by armed hordes, and so forts had to be constructed
everywhere. A ring of pillows in your bed. A blanket over a card table. And
no matter where the fort went up, that outer wall was key—it separated
Them from Us. Inside the wall you had sovereignty. A room to hide in and
outlast any siege (provided you'd put up enough Kool-Aid and Hostess Sno
Balls).

Along with the idea of forts, the Civil War introduced serious weaponry.
Did cowboys and Indians have artillery? We think not. Bayonets? Please.
The *Monitor* and *Merrimac*? No and no. The Old West's dusty little skirmishes and scalpings were playpen fights, we thought, compared to battles
big enough to have names.

In a letter to RJL, Mom wrote about my nascent interest in the Great
Rebellion:

> In Luke's kindergarten class, we divided the children—three into the
> Northern group and two for the South. Luke Longstreet was tickled
> to be General Longstreet, saying "That really is me." I made battle
> flags for Chancellorsville, Manassas, and Fredericksburg. But history

dealt a hard blow to Luke and General Lee. They couldn't understand how they could win so many battles and yet lose the war. Luke said, "Let's do it over again next week and this time we win."

Seeing my interest in the Civil War, my mother poured in as much history as my little teacup would hold, but I was in it for the blood. Winning was everything. One side had to lose. Or more precisely, one side had to be "the Loser." In a just world, right beat wrong like rock beats scissors, and not being on the winning side set one's whole world crooked. Not winning an argument, unthinkable. Not winning a game of Civil War (or "Army Guys" as it came to be known), that was catastrophic. Perhaps worst of all was being shot by a soldier you had *already killed*. This was injustice itself.

In fact, the issue of authenticating death in all games of Army Guys was a sticky wicket given that our ordnance was invisible bullets fired from imaginary guns.

"You can't shoot me! You're already dead!"

"I was just wounded! You're the one who's dead!"

"How can I be dead? I didn't fall down."

Everyone knew that proper machine gun deaths were officially identified by a herky-jerky marionette dance and a full face-plant in the turf; this was agreed-upon play action. Our backyard version of the Geneva Accords required adherence to this agreement; otherwise, what did you have? A universe without rules, where any fool could just jaywalk through your hailstorm of hot lead? Unchallenged, such heresies lead to anarchy, as it did on occasion when someone would secretly switch from Army Guy rules to Superhero rules. *("The bullets bounced off me so I'm not dead.")* This kind of nonsense was shut down on the spot.

Army Guy rules were fairly specific, one of which required you to produce a realistic machine gun noise. In fact, having the best *rat-a-tat-tat* was another thing your side could win at. Individual bragging rights, however, went to the guy with the most realistic noise, a sound we each created with various success behind a spitty mist of grape-colored Kool-Aid.

If you were out in the open and you heard the *ack-ack-ack,* you were dead. Since losing was unacceptable, you made your peace with being killed by winning in the Best Death category. Nobody died as good as you. You flung yourself to the ground, overacting a death rattle that could be heard from the cheap seats, giving your first grader's take on the Greek playwright's timeless

"Oh verily, I am slain!" Your hands went to your stomach, your legs crumpled, and then stillness. Of course, death by grenade was even showier—the concussion flung you several feet to a boneless rag-doll heap of heroism. Tossing grenades was also a show because you had to pull out the arming pin with a manly yank of clenched teeth. The one drawback to grenades was that your opponent needed to actually see you throw it; otherwise your dramatics were for naught, and after several moments of silence on the battlefield you had to verbally inform your enemy of his demise. *("Hey, I tossed a grenade in there, you know.")*

Falling to the spongy green grass, that was death for us—your face to the Minnesota sky, the sunlight turning eyelid blood vessels into orange spiderwebs. There you lay, certain your showy death had given a sort of murderer's remorse to your assailant, and you waited until the battle ended or Mom called you in for sandwiches. To us, that's all death was—a brief midsummer stillness and then a sandwich.

Real death didn't exist yet. It certainly hadn't happened to anyone *we* knew; our grandparents were alive, our parents, even the family dog. Of course, we'd heard stories about Heaven during our few visits to Sunday school, but Heaven sounded like a cartoon—angel wings, halos, and harps and a bunch of other silly shit even we little ones didn't buy. Still the grown-ups seemed convinced this was the case and so we didn't press the point.

Death, too, was a cartoon. When you fell off a cliff like Wile E. Coyote, you didn't die—you became accordion shaped. Even on the grown-ups' TV programs, death was a pratfall. Shoot the bad guy on Sunday night's *Bonanza* and there was no blood, just a crumple to the ground followed by *Bonanza's* theme song and the credits rolling by.

We never gave death or Heaven a second thought, but those ending credits on *Bonanza*? They were horrifying. Because Sunday was a school night, school nights meant bedtime, and to little boys bedtime was in fact death.

Bedtime was the sudden, unexpected, and horrifying end of all things. Even though it came at precisely the same time every night, even though we received countdown warnings as the dreaded hour approached, when it arrived we never failed to be both shocked and outraged. *("WHAT?? But we're not even tired!")* Bedtime was so much like death we went through the same Kübler-Ross stages of acceptance.

Denial—*"It CAN'T be bedtime."*

Anger—*"Why do we even have bedtime?"*

Bargaining—*"If you let us stay up, tomorrow we'll go to bed after lunch."*
Depression—*"This is the worst thing that has happened since the dinosaurs."*
And finally, acceptance.

Bedtime was indeed death. Even the rituals were the same: the preparing of the body (the solemn washing of teeth, the funereal donning of pajamas), the readings, the occasional prayer, and finally the inevitable darkness. All that was missing were Hallmark sympathy cards arriving in the mail:

Our thoughts are with you during this difficult hour, when "Bonanza" is over at 8 p.m. Central Standard Time, and 9 p.m. Eastern.

Aside from the nightly horror of bedtime, the days of the early 1960s brought little that was truly life threatening. There was no terrorism on the nightly news, no anthrax, no AIDS, no buildings falling, no children disappearing. There was only the sunny back yard with games of Army Guys and Mom's sandwiches and the grass unreeling under your feet as you ran and ran and never grew tired.

Wait. There may have been one thing—Being in Trouble. That was scary. And you knew you were in trouble when Mom changed your name to "Young Man."

"And just what do you think you're doing, Young Man?"

That was bad, but Mom's punishments were swift and fair. Far worse was Being in Trouble with Dad.

Convicted murderers await execution at midnight, but you, Young Man, your hour of reckoning was always "When Your Father Gets Home." You had to wait. Since this was before you knew how to tell time, the hour of When-Your-Father-Gets-Home o'clock arrived when it arrived, with only the warning crunch of gravel in the driveway as his car pulled in. You ran upstairs to watch unseen from a high window as Dad entered the Millstone. You caught some of the muffled conversation down in the kitchen, certain you'd heard the phrase "limb from limb," and then listened for the inevitable thump of feet on the stairs. When at last the door to your room opened, there was nowhere left to hide but the fort inside your head. Dad's red face bent down within inches of yours and then came the huge wads of angry sound you could almost hear with your hair. With his spittle misting your black-framed 1960s glasses, the Alamo inside was as far away as you could get and it's there you waited for the final whack on the back of your head.

It wasn't particularly painful, the whack—just humiliating. It always came, and always with its signature phrase: "WHAT DO I HAVE TO DO AROUND HERE? KNOCK SOME HEADS TOGETHER?"

In the early days, that was the closest we little ones got to the furnace of Dad's anger, its orange flames not yet white with rage.

Dr. Sullivan in front of the Millstone, a year or two
before everything went to hell, probably 1956.

COLD WAR

&

For now, the thick walls of the Millstone were a safe place for my mother to raise six little boys. But beyond the gates at the end of the driveway the country drifted into a period of dangerous intolerance: the Cold War was getting into high gear and civil rights were more than a decade away. The 1950s were a combination of boredom, paranoia, racism, and sexual repression. If the Religious Right could travel back there today, they'd break the return switch and set up shop in Paradise. They had Russians to hate, generals to vote for, "Negroes" to fear, beatniks to laugh at, and church to go to on Sunday. Life was good.

Grandpa Longstreet, who'd voted Democratic in every election since Wilson, voted for Democratic nominee Adlai Stevenson in 1952 and served as the county campaign manager for him when he ran again in '56. My mother read widely to inform and support her political affiliations but took counsel in these matters from her father. RJL was of the opinion that "the General's" White House was fearmongering half the time and golfing the other.

The state of Minnesota was one of few Democratic stalwarts, with local heroes like Hubert Humphrey making a stand for civil rights at the '48 Democratic National Convention. "But Rochester and the Clinic were a Republican stronghold," my mother remembers. "Which is why the Democrats had to dig around to find people like me, you see. To stand in the reception line for Eleanor Roosevelt when she came through town campaigning for Adlai."

The little town was Republican, full of what Myra called "rabid Ike-men": men who'd survived the war and wanted now only to practice medicine and raise their families. World War II was over. They'd all paid their dues: some in combat, all in medical school. They were the best in the world at what they did, and the world needed what they did. Polio stalked the summer streets and cancer was warming up on deck.

The Republicans beat Adlai Stevenson twice—in 1952 and again in '56. During the months leading up to the elections, tensions grew between my father and mother. What began as dinner disagreements lasted until the dishes, and then until bedtime. Arguments about who was fit to serve in the White House devolved into who was fit to have an opinion. In October 1952, Myra wrote, "Rog and I have gotten into such violent arguments I am reminded of our Roosevelt–Dewey days."

When Adlai Stevenson's sister, Elizabeth Ives, campaigned for him in Rochester, my mother had the opportunity to tell her the story of the great divide in Sullivan family politics. When a local pol later suggested it was time to "get out and ring a few doorbells," Mrs. Ives interrupted, saying, "Everyone but Mrs. Sullivan. She has her work cut out for her at home."

Outnumbered in Rochester and overpowered at the Millstone, my mother sought more "ammunition," as she put it, from her father and brother, Jimmy: facts, figures, proof. To which Roger's reply would be, "You're not thinking for yourself." To which Myra responded by visiting the public library—"to get newspaper articles and read both candidates' speeches and some editorials." But no matter how she fortified her position, she gained no ground and by election time was writing, "Things are so tense in our house we hardly dare mention politics."

She began to keep her politics to herself. The Cold War had arrived in the Millstone.

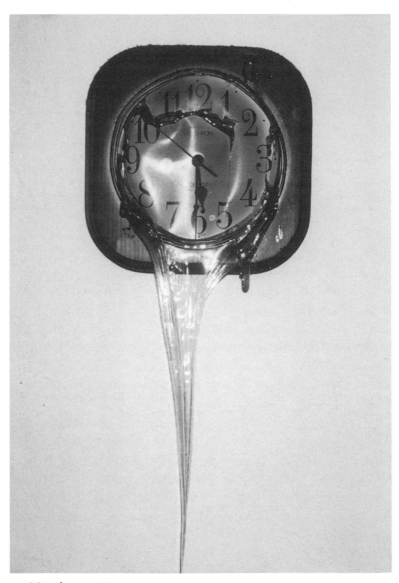

Metaphor at a crime scene, 1994.

FIVE O'CLOCK SHADOW

cJ(>

A few years ago, an arsonist nearly burned down my brother Chris's house. Neither Chris nor any of his family was there at the time, though the family hamster died. The morning after, Chris and I drove back to his house to examine the damage. When we pried away the firemen's temporary plywood door and entered, the smell of wet charcoal was strong. I watched Chris walk through the dripping cavern of his old bedroom, where ceiling insulation hung down like pink stalactites. As he looked for possessions worth salvaging I noticed a clock on the wall. Its hands had stopped at the height of the fire and its melted plastic housing had begun to droop like the timepieces in a Dalí painting. My reverie was broken when Chris handed me the first undamaged things pulled from the shelves—his collection of old family photographs and the diaries he'd been keeping since 1965. We packed them in boxes from the U-Haul store and carted them out to the trunk of his car.

Like everything else in the house that hadn't burned outright, his archives suffered smoke damage. Weeks later, when he opened the box, its contents still had the odor of a wet barbeque pit—so very different from the pleasant smell most old books develop as they sit on a shelf, preserving history. Chris sent his diaries off for the suggested ozone treatments, but even when he lent them to me months later, the smell of disaster and ruin wafted from the turn of every page; a strange sort of olfactory onomatopoeia, reading as I was the story told there of the ruin of Chris's childhood home. Like the clock on the wall, here too time was frozen; here too was damage.

As our father's anger began to burn in the Millstone, everybody near the heat suffered.

The clock on the wall of our childhood began to melt around five o'clock when Dad got home from work and poured a drink.

Five o'clock was when the tension began, when eggshells were spread up and down the hallways of the Millstone. In November 1958, a letter from my mother reads: "There are tragic overtones in our house today—and omens of catastrophe ahead. Jeff has lost Roger's transistor radio. So everyone in the house is trembling at the necessity of revealing the loss to Roger. There is sure to be donder and blitzen crashing over his head tonight—poor luck-less boy. . . . Few indeed (and bless you for it, Poppa) are the memories of my father in anger."

Five o'clock was when the arguments began. Argument isn't the right word because it suggests a back-and-forth, two voices. In the Millstone, it was only Dad's voice and it was angry. Mom didn't pick up the fight, and as we eavesdropped from the top of the stairs, it was like listening to a man yell at somebody over the phone—you heard only half the script and had to imagine what the other person was feeling.

It wasn't a sound you could hide from. The bass notes of my father's voice came through the walls of the Millstone, and though we little ones couldn't make out the words, even a dog knows when its owner is angry. Like dogs, we too assumed the anger was because of us, but what we'd done we had no idea. You crept away to a quiet room and you learned to handle things as best you could. You certainly couldn't approach the grown-ups with any kind of a problem. It could light another fire.

They say, "When elephants fight, the ants suffer." True, and when ele-phants drink, the ants are toe jam because we never knew which way to run. You might get Maudlin Dad, with the false cheer and boozy kisses. You might get Sulking, Silent, Sitting-in-his-study Dad, burning like a fuse to an unseen bomb. And if anyone said the wrong thing, *boom*—you had Angry Dad. Wrote Mom in a letter from 1958: "Thursday was Thanksgiving. A very pleasant day until nighttime, when the boys caught you-know-what from their father. He was sleeping on the couch and they made too much racket playing with the dog. So everyone was sent to bed about 6:15."

Arson investigators pick through rubble for clues to how a fire started. Perhaps this smoky diary has clues. Here, in Chris's handwriting: "Dad came home all mad today." Perhaps all the damage that came later can be traced to a short circuit in Dad's head, to the anger that smoldered in his study as he sat there after work nursing grudges and a drink: mad at Mom's politics, mad at the noise we made playing with the dog, mad at . . . at *things*.

Head X-ray: Roger in 1957

You say, "Don't mind if I do."

Why, yes, a whiskey would in fact be just the thing to take a fella's mind off that jackass who hogged two parking spaces in the lot this morning. Or the pretty nurse who batted her eyes at you during surgery. And now, here it is seven at night, you've finished ten surgeries, and you're supposed to what? Just go home?

So you say, "Don't mind if I do" to a few other residents milling about and you toss your bloody scrubs into the laundry hamper and three of you head out. You don't really know these men, but they say they're gonna toss a few back, so you go. You're soon settling on stools in the quiet of a small bar near the Clinic and, oh, you deserve to be here. You, after all, are a Mayo Clinic surgeon—the best and the brightest.

"Why, yes, barkeep. A martini is 'just what the doctor ordered.'" Laughs all around and then the mighty conversations begin.

"For Christ's sake, that kid who came in with a fibrosarcoma? Of the femur? Huge. Had to excise half a pound of good bone just to get the goddamn thing out. Should've taken the leg off, but it doesn't matter. She's dead by Christmas anyway."

The day's stories are remembered, told, and soon it's 8:30.

The other two leave but you stay for a few more. You buy a new pack of Winstons from the machine and now you're out in the parking lot. There's a nice fire in your belly now, a little spring to your step, and . . . oh, there's that asshole's car, the one who hogged two spaces. Maybe a little scrape o' the key is just what the shitbird deserves. You should do it. You really should.

But you don't key his car and as you drive the short four miles home you notice you're a little angry again; just at things in general. But it's more than that. It's just, well, the wife, you know? She'll probably have her nose in a book or be writing another one of those long goddamn letters to Mommy and Daddy.

Jesus.

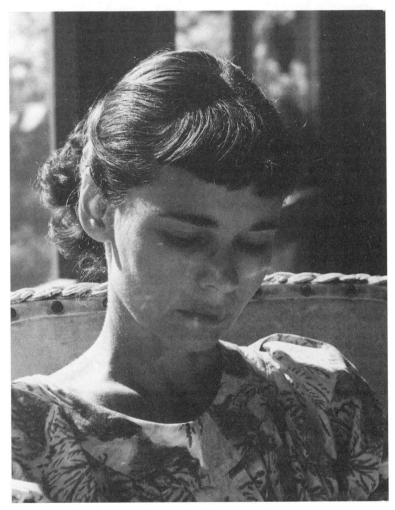

Myra and the short hairstyle she hated, circa 1957.

SHIT GATHERS IN
GENERAL AREA OF FAN

∂l∫

"You-know-who came home in a foul mood tonight."

That sentence, in one of Mom's 1958 letters, was the lump in the breast, the iceberg off starboard bow.

In 1958, the term "chemical dependency" didn't exist. "Boozer" might have. "Party guy," definitely. But "alcoholic"? "Chemically dependent"? Forget about it. Alkies flew under the radar. You could smack the wife, wreck the car, take a shit in the neighbor's birdbath, and as long as you showed up for work on time all anybody did was roll his eyes.

"Having a delicious highball or two is a great way to unwind," read the magazines. Even today when drinkers get shitfaced and do horrible things, people give them yards and yards of slack. But in the 1950s and '60s, America was an especially confused culture on the subject of drunkenness. Dean Martin slurred his way to prime time and all the dads in suburbia laughed while pouring another one. Drunk jokes are still common; and they're *funny:*

> So this drunk staggers into the church, okay? He sits down in the confession booth but says nothin'. The bewildered priest coughs to attract his attention, but the man says nothin'. The priest knocks on the wall a couple of times in a final attempt to get the man to confess. The drunk replies, "No use knockin', buddy. There's no paper in this one either."

Couple the cultural confusion about alcohol with a woman's place in 1950s America and you have something like checkmate. My mother didn't see checkmate coming and even if she had she couldn't have done a thing about it. Mention to Roger that his drinking was starting to scare her? It wasn't in the realm of possibility.

As I sort through Mom's letters, I wonder exactly when Roger became an alcoholic. Was it the drink Mom mentions in a letter on January 30, 1958: to "unwind" after his boss cut the time he needed to prepare a presentation on pediatrics?

Perhaps it was the one he poured on May 30, 1956: the night she wrote about how he came home angry at a medical technician in the operating room. I picture Roger putting the stopper in the neck of the bottle, then maybe popping it off again to pour that extra half inch over the ice, talking over his shoulder about how the idiot technician didn't move fast enough and this is an *operating* room, for crying out loud.

Maybe it was his very first drink.

The one on that marvelous night twelve years ago. You remember, in medical school, back when the war was over and Irene was no longer just down the hallway listening for heresies, and it was just you and Mack and Kupe and Tunk, you all had your booth at the Town Taverne and—damn—the wine really warms your chest from the inside out, doesn't it, though? And the words, they just come so fast and easy and everybody seems so happy and Jesus how you laughed and you all fit in so well and the cigarettes tasted better and even though it was late you didn't wanna go you didn't wanna stop you just wanted more of that same good feeling and more and more of it.

Going through the photos and letters, I begin to realize that trying to carbon-date the exact hour of the monster's appearance is futile. It wasn't a moment anyway, but the slow dawn of a long era. Alcoholism crept into the Millstone so quietly no one noticed. In fact, as I reread Mom's early letters I begin to see where she was writing about Roger's alcoholism without realizing it.

Mom writing to her parents, January 30, 1958
I seldom see Roger lose his patience with Clinic policy or pronouncements but he came home last evening in a monumental rage. His time to prepare for the presentation of his paper had been worse than halved! He goes to Chicago early to set up an exhibit he has planned but now has to be back Tuesday. His exhibit and paper prove a theory of his that the blood supply to the talus is not through a single artery but several. Says Roger, "It simply stands to reason. God wouldn't have made it that way!!"

My mother says she thinks it was 1958 when bottles gradually began to appear on that shelf in the kitchen. Gradual also was the appearance, in my mother's letters, of my dad's souring temperament. She mentions a bit of snappishness here, an angry moment there. Reading the letters again, the pattern seems clear, but at the time it wasn't. The first attacks were mostly put-downs, jibes at Mom's character calibrated to make her feel bad about herself. If Mom bought a new Erroll Garner album of jazz piano it was, "Why did you waste money on *this*?" Everything she did that wasn't house-keeping was cause for eye rolling, derision, or contempt. Perhaps the worst thing was that, for a long time, Myra believed him. In a letter to her father, she wrote, "Call me a crazy fool if you like—I am! What poor man other than Roger has to suffer a wife who takes horseback riding lessons and string bass lessons, and builds model ships! Poor Roger."

Poor Roger also expressed contempt for Myra's love of reading, a sub-ject he would return to again and again: "Why are you wasting money on books?"

Looking back today, Mom says, "Even my Greek studies were seen as further proof of my inadequacies. And my beautiful instrument, the cello? Given up to avoid more recriminations from you-know-who. He was unap-peasable. In college days when I wore my homemade Florida dresses and big white pearly button earrings, he was embarrassed that his roommates called me 'El Gitano'—the Gypsy. But then by 1957, I was disapproved of for wear-ing my hair in a *conservative* bun."

When the bun wouldn't do, she acquiesced to a shorter hairstyle in front, confessing in a letter, "I hate it—but my husband likes it—so what else can I do?"

I go back through the family photographs and find the September '57 shot of Mom in the shorter hairstyle. For the first time, I discern she was angry when the picture was taken. When I show her the picture, she says, yes, she remembers trying to ignore Dad and his camera, looking down at her book, embarrassed at having to pose like a shorn prisoner of war. When I mention I've had trouble figuring out exactly when Dad's drinking went nuclear, she says, "I'm not sure, but one incident does come to mind."

She was pregnant with Collin when she had her first look into the lupine eyes of Roger's true rage—which would make it 1957. In the summer of that year my parents hosted a Mayo Clinic party at the Millstone. The festivities were winding down to a very late end and at 2:00 a.m. only a single guest remained, drinking and talking loudly with Roger. She doesn't remember his name, only that he was the kind of saloon fixture who'd quickly show up on my father's radar ("*I hail from Texas. Where the 'hail' you from? HA-HA-*

HAAAA!"): the too-hard laugh, the high-and-tight haircut, the florid skin of the veteran drinker. With five of his children sleeping upstairs and his pregnant wife standing right there to hear it, Roger began telling this sodden stranger what a horrible wife Myra was. She stood there puzzled, then insulted, then sick at hearing lies so cheerfully shared with this bar-stool tumor: "She's frigid, Bob. Won't have sex. Don't make the mistake I did, Bob. Don't marry a woman like this."

It was the eyes, she said, the eyes that were the worst. There was nobody back there anymore; not a person anyway but something else, a sort of predatory cunning that peered out and looked for things it disagreed with, looked for things to FUCK WITH.

One night she was just about to lead her four youngest boys upstairs for the customary bedtime story. Dad walked out of his study where he'd been drinking since five o'clock. He stood at the foot of the stairs and calmly put his leg out across the staircase, blocking her ascent.

"You are not going to turn those boys into sissies by reading them to sleep," he told her. "Let them go to sleep on their own."

No further explanation. No discussion. Just the eyes.

It wouldn't be until May 1964 that Myra would write openly to her parents about how life really was at the Millstone. For now, instead of saying, "Roger came home drunk and yelled at the kids," she wrote. "The kids caught you-know-what from their father." She wasn't ready to open the furnace door and let them see into the Millstone, to witness their daughter burning. So she said nothing.

But Myra's parents picked up on some of the trouble at the Millstone anyway. Myra and RJL had planned a trip in 1958. Mom was to visit her parents in Florida. It was a trip talked about in their letters, planned there, and warmly anticipated. Then Grandpa RJL received a Western Union telegram from Minnesota—a dozen apologetic words glued in a strip on yellow paper: "FORGIVE ME. HAVE BEEN TOO HASTY. SOMETHING MAY YET WORK OUT. — LOVE MYRA."

In 1959, she guardedly mentioned to Roger renewed plans for another trip to Florida. Surprisingly, he agreed but then began to sulk, sitting alone in his study. Later, as the drink took effect, his eyes would get the look and he'd rage.

"How in God's name do you think we have the money for this? For you to run off and see Mommy and Daddy? Huh? You make me buy this goddamned

house and fill it with kids just so you can go waltzing off?? Grow up, will you? Just GROW UP!"

Rage is different from anger.

Rage is the inferno firemen don't even try to put out. There's no talking to rage. Anger is explosive; rage is nuclear. Rage is the end of hope— Armageddon. In this new nuclear landscape Myra realized fighting back meant unleashing her own anger, which, in the parlance of the times, was "mutually assured destruction." All she could do was keep silent. Anything she said in her defense would only escalate the attack. She just had to wait it out.

By morning the rage would be gone, but Roger's silence and the way he slammed the door on the way to work made it clear any trip to Florida would cost more than money. At the Clinic he was still the charming, brilliant doctor and giver of care to all. Back at home his wife was sending yet another telegram with another excuse just vague enough to finally prompt Professor Longstreet to call his daughter "to see if everything was all right up there."

Being a somewhat worse liar on the phone than in a telegram, Mom would backpedal a bit and say, "Roger thinks with money as tight as it is perhaps it's best to wait." (No mention of the nuclear rage, the fallout.) "But don't worry, we will work something out."

No matter how Myra tried to spin it, RJL suspected things at the Millstone were not entirely right. Still, as thin as her excuses were, at least she kept the cops from looking in the trunk.

Mom's final letter from the '50s, New Year's Eve, 1959
And so another year has passed, and on the whole it has been a good one. 1959, the last of another decade ends jubilantly! My only cause for remorse is my weakness in exposing you to unnecessary alarm and helpless concern [regarding the canceled trip]. For which forgive me. The 1940s were a fateful ten years, bringing college days, tuberculosis, marriage, and two children before their close. The 1950s brought a mighty economic improvement, our beautiful home, and four more sons. Life has been lavishly kind to me these twenty years. God (and the politicians of this world) willing, "the best is yet to be."

Professor R. J. Longstreet in class.

The Millstone basement fallout shelter, with the
four-hundred-pound "portable" TV at center.

CYCLOPS AND THE FALLOUT SHELTER

The Millstone sat on its hill in Minnesota for nearly thirty years before the first television was carried across its threshold, or lugged, rather. In 1958 Dad brought home the single heaviest object ever to exist in the house—a "portable" TV. If I owned the thing today I could string a purple rope around it and charge people admission just to cool off in its shadow. The old black-and-white was as portable as a box of anvils and was moved probably twice in all the time we owned it.

My brothers and I, of course, met it at the door as if it were an honored guest, and we became without knowing it the first generation of kids to grow up bathed in the bouncing light of television. At first, we watched mostly Westerns: *Gunsmoke, The Rifleman,* and *Bonanza.* But their themes of righteousness and gunfire soon bored us and we discovered the cartoons, which showed almost exclusively on Saturday mornings. *Rocky & Bullwinkle* was a favorite.

Kids then were no different from kids today. We would watch the thing for hours, our jaw muscles slowly relaxing until our mouths hung open and the tops of our tongues dried out. The blank looks on our faces and the crap we spent hours watching gave chills to intellectuals like Mom and Grandpa. They were both convinced television represented the death of Western culture.

But it was the news programs on TV that finally hooked old RJL. Although he was a man who loved the printed word, even he could see television was the best way to follow the returns during a presidential election. And when JFK ran against Richard Nixon in the fall of 1960, Grandpa did the only thing any self-respecting book lover could do. He rented a television for the week.

Myra was the first of the two to give in and actually buy a television. In a 1960 letter she admits to Grandpa, "It must now be told we are the owners of a television set," and she goes on to explain how "our two big boys are spending Saturday afternoons away from home to watch football games and Luke and Danny are too frequently going down the hill to the May-nards' to watch cartoons there."

With the Millstone having fallen, Grandmother Monnie, as we called her, had less of a job getting old RJL to capitulate. She had no scholarly revulsion for television and simply wanted something to watch while she knitted.

Eventually, a confessional Blue Book appeared in the mailbox at the Millstone in which Grandpa admitted he'd given in. From that day forward until his final letters in 1969, almost every letter from RJL had some guilt-ridden mention of his deepening relationship with television, a one-eyed monstrosity he dubbed "Cyclops."

Grandpa, August 1962
Here I sit before Cyclops—slowly declining in IQ, morale, and decent citizenship—and no rescue in sight. To entertain your mother, Cyclops portrays something styled "To Tell The Truth." I bet you never heard of it, much less endured it. I see the ad is for Geritol—must rush out and buy a bottle. In fact, I have now be-come so exposed to the art of Madison Avenue that I am well deter-mined never to buy anything that is advertised on TV.

Television alternately amused and galled RJL. He hated the commercials most of all. For a man who loved the English language, Madison Avenue's blithe disregard for grammar, clarity, and truth was often too much for the old man. And in the 1950s, advertisers could lie all they wanted. *"Not one single case of throat irritation due to smoking Camels,"* read one ad. *"Not a cough in a carload!"* claimed another for Old Gold cigarettes.

Up in Minnesota, we six boys watched the commercials, saw the grown-ups puffing away, and learned that inhaling the smoke of dried weeds rolled in paper was acceptable behavior; reserved for adults of course, but accept-able. It was on TV all the time; even sport stars extolled tobacco's virtues. *"Show us your Lark Pack! . . . I'd rather fight than switch! . . . Show me a filter cigarette that really delivers taste and I'll eat my hat!"* We let ourselves believe these commercials and one by one began to sneak cigarettes from Mom's purse and Dad's desk. Ultimately, four of us became addicted and it took us each about twenty-five years to pull free of nicotine's talons. (Mom quit in 1967.) The happy cigarette commercials seemed full of the same stuff that powered the Ozzie-and-Harriet America of the '50s—cheerful dishonesty.

Sexual repression, too, cut across the continent like a fault line and ran straight under Rochester, Minnesota. The tectonic plates—God and Jayne Mansfield's pointy breasts—ground against each other, but it would be years before the whole thing blew. In fact, to understand the Eros of the '50s, picture the vice president's wife, Pat Nixon, and then imagine the only "mood music" you can put on is Doris Goddamn Day.

Lies, sexual repression, public relations, and cheerfulness were the culture of the 1950s. There were the lies Joe McCarthy told about pinkos and lefties, in between his trips to the liquor store; there was the lie that radioactive iodine-131 wasn't contaminating the milk supply; that Gary Powers's U-2 was a "weather plane." There were the lies about thalidomide and DDT, the lies from Madison Avenue, and the lies from Hollywood. (America's macho hunk Rock Hudson? Gay.)

Then there were the lies about surviving an atomic attack. The government knew full well entire cities would turn to charcoal in the event of an attack. But they were still able to look us in the eye and assure us that the half-inch plywood laminate of our school desks was sufficient protection from fireballs of ten million degrees Fahrenheit. My brothers and I later wondered if the narrator of the 1951 Civil Defense film *Duck and Cover* occasionally had to stop while recording the script just so he could get the giggles out of his system and make it through the whole thing.

"And so, kids, when you see the flash, what do you do? That's right, like a turtle going into its shell, you duck and . . .

"CUT! Cut! Give me a minute here, guys. (Sound of laughter off-mike.) 'That's right, kids, desktops will save you.' Jesus, it's . . . never mind. Okay, sorry. Take Two."

While the Department of Defense rattled its sabers, its lapdog the news media hopped into action and began telling citizens it was their patriotic duty to be very afraid and to build fallout shelters. *("If you dig a deep hole and sit in it while we have our war you can come out later and the Commies will be gone. Maybe even the beatniks, too.")* To the neighborhood kids, fallout shelters were just cool new forts to play in. But for Kip and Jeff and any kid coming of age in this time of paranoia and public relations, there developed an underlying cynicism. Their lack of faith in seeing old age probably contributed to the creation of a whole generation of wiseasses. An honest appraisal of their likely early demise (and the attendant "Krispy Kritters" jokes) seemed preferable to the grown-up world's suppressed paranoia and billboard grins.

The paranoia began with the successful explosion of a Soviet thermonuclear device in 1949. It went up a couple of levels when East German soldiers strung barbed wire across Berlin in August '61. And by the Cuban Missile Crisis of October 1962, my mother and much of America were teetering on the edge of hysteria.

"We hear heavy planes flying south over our home here in Florida," wrote her father, RJL. "I suppose this is part of the concentration of forces in this area. One is roaring overhead as I write."

Writing back, Myra noted, "The Maynards' and the Weidmans' are the latest in our neighborhood to begin construction of atomic fallout shelters. The contractor who is building the Maynards' says he put in 50 shelters last month." So at a cost of six hundred dollars, Mom and Dad bricked over all the windows in the Millstone's basement and turned that bright play area we once called the Rumpus Room into a dungeon. It became the ultimate room to hide in—our atomic Alamo, where we would wait out the end of days as the world's grown-ups flung nuclear fire.

Memory: Dad Helps with Homework

Luke: Mama is at the sink and my brother Collin and I are sitting at the table having hot cocoa and Danny is doing his homework and Dad sees Danny's quiz from school about naming the twelve months, and Danny didn't get a good grade, so Dad makes him stand by the icebox and says, "SAY THE MONTHS OF THE YEAR" and Danny starts to cry and I look across the table at Collin and we're scared and Mom is at the sink and then Dad knocks Danny's head against the icebox "IT'S APRIL! HOW DID YOU GET SO DUMB? SAY THEM AGAIN." And then he grabs Danny's head and gives him all the answers while knocking his head against the icebox after each month.

Dan: "JANUARY!"—THUMP—feels his head hit the icebox . . . "FEBRUARY!" . . . hits the icebox again wonders what's happening . . . "MARCH!" . . . tries to see around Daddy thinks Mama Mama do something Mama but . . . APRIL!!" . . . April hurts . . . "MAY!" . . . brings his head back upright but it's like cocking a gun so maybe I won't bring it back up and maybe it . . . "JUNE!" . . . but, but . . . "JULY!" . . . can't look at the ceiling cuz he'll see tears, so look down . . . AUGUST!" . . . look down . . . "SEPTEMBER!" . . .

I am looking down, I am I am ... "OCTOBER!" ... all the guys are watching ... "NOVEMBER!" ... and I bet this doesn't happen ... "DECEMBER!" ... this doesn't happen to smart kids.

Twenty-three years after that day in the kitchen, my mother wrote a poem she titled "Peeling Carrots":

> Ice rattled in their father's drink
> when he shoved the boy against the door.
> At the table, two little brothers,
> motionless as baby rabbits, and their mother,
> quiet, peeling carrots at the kitchen sink.
> "January, February, March ..."
> the boy tries again, and in her head
> the mother whispers April, child, April.
> The father, his finger in the boy's face,
> mutters, "Dumb mother and you get dumb kids,"
> and strokes his necktie back in place.
> Silence darkens the kitchen. He waits,
> rattles the ice in his glass again.
> The other two stare at their plates.
> The mother's back feels the eyes
> of her child begging her to Mama
> Mama do something Mama.
> "January, February, March ..." he quails.
> Once again she holds the father still
> with her stillness
> and goes on peeling carrots with her fingernails.

Myra on the shore of Lake Winnemissett, in DeLand, Florida, visiting her parents, 1962.

HIDDEN BOOKS, HIDDEN LETTERS

℘

It always happens so fast.

Mom's making dinner and you're having a snack at the kitchen table maybe thinking about Spider-Man or Daredevil, and a rabid dog leaps gracefully up on the table and walks down the length, grinning through its foam.

Maybe something else will attract its attention, you think, maybe somebody will break from the pack and try for the woods. You freeze. You don't even move your eyes. You stare into the pattern on the plate, into the flowers, past the bee.

When Dad had a drink he became predatory. Some drunks get amiable, some maudlin, all of them stupid; but Dad attacked. He looked for something to piss him off and chewed until he drew blood.

One drink said, "Oh, sounds like somethin' Mama read in one of her books, am I right, boys?"

The second drink said, "Maybe you boys would've had your homework done if Mama wasn't writing to her *daddy* all day?"

By the bottom of the third drink he was taking street-fight swings at Mom's character: "MAMA WANTS TO VOTE FOR JACK KENNEDY BECAUSE HE'S SUCH A PRETTY MAN, ISN'T THAT RIGHT, MAMA? WHY DON'T YOU JUST GROW UP?!?"

Kip, 2006
One of the very first times I saw Dad drunk and abusive with Mom was right after the election in 1960. I was thirteen. It was in the kitchen. Mom was standing over the stove making soup. And Dad was drunk, berating and belittling her for voting for Kennedy. I remember Mom just looking up at the ceiling, stirring soup, and crying. Dad was using swear words and yelling at Mom for, God, what? An hour or so? I retreated upstairs to take a bath but left the door

to the bathroom ajar so I could hear the yelling from downstairs. It scared me. The next morning I remember asking Mom, "Are you guys gonna get a divorce?"

Most of us did not see the early years of abuse. Much of it happened late at night and down in the kitchen or living room, spots chosen by Mom because they were the farthest away she could get from the bedrooms of her six boys. She would sit on the couch in the living room and let him rage.

"It was usually a matter of just waiting," she says. "Waiting until he got that last drink in him and would simply tip over."

The rages flamed hotter and burned longer and over time Mom, like the caretaker of an old furnace boiler, learned tricks to keep him from exploding.

"When he really got going I would drop my eyelids halfway down," remembers my mother. "If I completely closed my eyes I got in more trouble, because it looked like I was asleep or was shutting him out. I found by closing my eyes halfway he wouldn't take it as insult and, for me, it was sort of like covering your eyes at the scary part of the movie."

Roger returned home every night and picked up where he'd left off, coming around to the same subjects again and again, pawing at his prey, searching for that smell to set him off.

"When he came home, I had my letters hidden away, my books put away." But no matter how safe she made the room he always found some purchase for his anger. It was always the same things: how "easy" Mom was with his money, the letters she wrote to Grandpa, the books she had her nose in, the trips she wanted to take to her parents. One autumn his preferred feeding spot was by the front door where we tied our shoes before school; none of us could lace up fast enough for the famous doctor, a failing he would point out with humiliating comments. When Mom recognized the pattern she bought us loafers.

Money was the big flashpoint. He'd worried about it for years. Even in 1953 Myra was writing, "Roger is in one of his recurring dumps, depressed about money and the lack of it. Says he sees no future for an extra dollar for pleasure for the next 15 years."

Yet it seemed his fretting was never that of a man but of a child whining, of wishing things were different, and demanding somebody fix things. Mom remembers, "He resigned any authority position long ago. Left every decision to me—even regarding little things like getting the snowplow to come or what to do when a teacher sent home a note about misbehavior. He'd say 'It's your problem.'"

The other land mine was "the trips to Florida." The plural "trips" makes too much of it considering that my mother visited her parents in Florida a total of three times after moving to Rochester in 1950. Yet every time she proposed a visit home, the night would end with Roger hoarse from drunken rage. The next afternoon he'd pick the subject back up and rage for hours until finally Mom would go to the train station downtown, cash in the tickets, put the money back in the bank, and show him the receipt. Roger would go back to the station the next day, buy *another* set of tickets, force Mom to take them, and then rave when she took the trip.

In 1961, another trip was canceled.

Mom, 2006
I approached your father that spring about my taking a few days to visit the Civil War battlefields of Chancellorsville or Gettysburg with Poppa. Roger's response was that whiny fretfulness which worked itself into wide-ranging wrath, no longer complaining about my proposed trip but, as usual, berating me with the battery of charges regularly leveled. I gave up the plan rather than face prolonged trouble before and after such a trip. I don't remember how I told Poppa that I couldn't make the Gettysburg trip. I probably sent a wire merely saying I couldn't go. No explanations. But this time my short note so troubled my folks they phoned our neighbor, Betty Hartman, to find out if I had been taken to the hospital or hurt in some way. I still hadn't the courage to tell my mother and father the real reason.

There was never enough in the bank for Mom to visit her parents, yet when Dad wanted a vacation, money wasn't an issue. Even here Dad found material for anger—Mom was scared of flying and preferred traveling by train. "I couldn't decide which was worse," she remembers. "To endure my own anxieties while flying or his psychotic ravings aboard the train."

There were other reasons to dread going on a trip with Dad. Away from the eyes of the family his vitriol and outrages went up a level. Mom remembers a night in a hotel room when Roger threatened suicide, saying he was going to jump out the hotel window if Mom wouldn't "change," wouldn't "grow up!" He went so far as to open the window and put his foot on the sill.

Even with the possibility of a similar episode, she left on another trip with him. It was probably better than keeping him near her boys.

In 1985, as part of an assignment in her writing class, Myra wrote this stream-of-consciousness essay about that trip.

Myra remembers the trip to Chicago

She sat there in that Chicago restaurant uneasy in the elegance, uneasy in the thought she'd probably have to find her way back to the hotel alone. He was cranking up toward another attack. One drink after another. The persuading her to go along with the drinks and her refusal only inflaming him, sending him to faster drinking and more vicious abuse. None of it new. All the same old stuff. That was the real nightmare: the having to hear the same things over and over again, knowing there was no way to protest, no words to deny, no logic to pursue, no way to stop him once he'd begun. Efforts to make him stop only angered him, made him talk louder, made him threaten more. Though only a few of his threats were ever carried out. Only his threats against her. A threat against a waiter or a train conductor or a passing driver or his boss or a neighbor . . . none of these threats were ever directly made, never carried out, only announced to her in his ripping voice, the ripping that tore into her and bled her and left her silent, screaming in her head to stop stop stop, staring straight ahead or half closing, unfocusing her eyes. The waiter had not brought that third drink fast enough, obsequiously enough. So he lashed out at her for over-tipping the waiter, and started in at the beginning of the record again, telling her what a total failure she was as a wife, as a mother, losing her mind she was, fast, and would soon have to have the children taken out of her care. Why wouldn't she grow up, for god's sake! Grow up! And on and on and on and on and the people at nearby tables beginning to listen, beginning to try not to listen, beginning to be annoyed at his monotonous voice. And when the meal came he just ordered another drink, threw it in himself, put down money which might cover the bill, came as near as ever to throwing the table over into her lap but hadn't the final guts for that much open defiance of the rest of the world; just of her. And left. Left as he'd left her many times before, often in strange cities. Left her again without a thought to her getting safely back to the hotel. Left.

She always carried extra money, hoping it would be enough. She paid the bill. There wasn't enough to get a cab back to the hotel. But if one doesn't get too far from the lake and the street where the hotel was, it's not too hard to find the way back alone, along Michigan Avenue. So she walked. Walked in the city with her country-girl fears alongside. Walked in the dark, fearing every footfall she heard behind, fearing every figure that approached. Huddled into herself, holding her hands so that any mugger could see she had no pocketbook to steal. Counting the blocks backward from how she'd counted them when they left the hotel . . . 19 . . . 18 . . . 17 . . . where he was didn't trouble her. She walked most of the way back to the hotel without thinking about him, except to hope he wouldn't be there when she got back. She wanted a quiet bath. A long bath to clean in. But first she had to get there . . . 12 . . . 11 . . . 10 . . . 7 . . . 5 . . . a lifeline from here to the hotel. She could take a taxi from here probably but still wasn't sure the few dollars in her pocket would be enough and a final humiliation from a cab driver she didn't need. She was afraid even of cab drivers here in Chicago after dark. She was a small-town girl and wasn't sure anything or anybody in Chicago was really safe. And yet, for these last few blocks, she was safe from him.

A photograph my father took in New York City
the night of November 22, 1963. Note the headlines.

ELEVEN TWENTY-TWO

◈

> It is 10:30 p.m. and I am tired. But before I leave this day, it is fitting I should
> write down its date, as it is one none of us will ever forget. So exhausted am
> I in mind and spirit I cannot find other words. Good night, my dear ones.
> I know how much this day's infamy has shaken you.
>
> —*Mom writing her parents, November 22, 1963*

My memories of JFK's assassination want to come in shivering from
the cold of a Minnesota November and stand by the big furnace in the
Millstone's basement. It's been turned on since October, and you can see the
flame in its belly through the slots in the iron door, roaring orange to send
steam up four floors to distant radiators.

Outside in the valley, thin not-quite-winter snow blows through the
fields of cut cornstalks. In the yard, our secret summer places are abandoned;
June's bicycles are in the garage, July's toys in the bushes under a layer of
leaves and frozen crust. Even October's color has flown south. Everything
about November 1963 is in black and white, like the news shows on the television set in Dad's study.

Down at the school in Mrs. Maus's fourth-grade classroom—up on
the wall above pictures of Pilgrims, Indians, and turkeys—is the intercom
speaker. From here our principal, Mr. Patzer, announces, "Boys and girls,
I'm sorry to say that the president of the United States has been shot and
killed. There will be a period of national mourning and school will be dismissed for the rest of the day."

There is a cold quarter-mile walk home with brothers Collin and Danny,
up the steep hill and past the Hallenbecks'. Soon we are clomping into the
Millstone, peeling parkas and dropping mittens. Roger and the oldest three
are out of town—on a sightseeing vacation in New York City—and so we
call for Mom, breathless to tell her the news. She answers from Dad's study,
where we find her in front of the TV. There are no cartoons, no commercials,
just the man with the black glasses sitting at the desk with the phone on it

and talking in that voice adults use when something really bad is happening and they don't want you to feel the way they feel.

It's not until we've been in the study for a while and seen the look in Mom's eyes that we realize something big and terrible has happened. The country's father was suddenly gone and the world wasn't as safe a place as it was at lunchtime in the gym.

By bedtime, a light snow is falling.

Jeff, 2006

On November 21, 1963, the night before it happened, Dad and we three oldest boys had gone to New York City, just to visit. Did the usual stuff—top of the Empire State Building, toured NBC, watched the taping of a TV show, *The Match Game.*

That evening the four of us were at dinner in a little restaurant. Dad was across from me and I remember it was a tense dinner. I think Kip and Dad were having one of those discussions that bordered on an open argument. Dad was boozing and I remember he said none of us should "get nervous and start masturbating." There were other demeaning remarks, but that's the one I remember. Somehow, Dad became so irritated with Kip he suddenly told Kip and me to just go; go off and do whatever we wanted. Dad got up, took Chris and left. I remember watching them cross the busy New York street and disappear.

The next morning, the twenty-second, Kip was too pissed off at Dad to stay any longer and left for Minnesota. Dad, Chris, and I took a subway downtown to see the Statue of Liberty. It was there on the train someone told us JFK had been shot.

We never went out to the Statue of Liberty. Instead we stood along the wrought-iron fence in Battery Park listening to someone's radio. That night, Dad went out and took pictures of Broadway. All the advertising lights were off, restaurants were closed, and there was very little traffic.

Kip, 2006

I was sitting in a plane at O'Hare when the captain announced Kennedy was dead. A stewardess standing a few feet up the aisle instantly dropped her face into her hands and began to weep.

Mom, November 26, 1963

I write this date and there is too much and nothing to say. This is the day after his funeral. The ranks have closed up and we move on. This has been such a shattering event it has left a scar and we are changed by it. No one of us is the same person we were last Friday noon. I am still dazed—I cannot write about it—yet we talk of nothing else and think of nothing else.

Kip was alone in Chicago when he heard the news. Once home, he climbed into the car and we never spoke (other than our mutual "Have you heard?") and continued listening with horror to the radio.

Roger called from New York City about 3:00 to say he and the other two were leaving—that there was no longer any pleasure in being there. They were on a subway when someone gave them the news—they had only moments before they left NBC where they had been watching the news being hung in great sheets. One of the newspapers they brought home was an "Extra," printed and on the streets before 2:00 EST, with the giant headline "JFK SHOT" and the "news" that Johnson too was wounded.[1]

As you, we sat for long unbroken hours watching the TV. From 7:00 in the morning until late in the evening for three uninterrupted days. Even my Republican husband was crying several times that dark weekend.

But as Montaigne wrote: "No one dies before his hour: the time you leave behind was no more yours than that which was lapsed and gone before you came into this world. Whenever your life ends, it is all there. The utility of living consists not in the length of days, but in the use of time." Wherein I find some comfort.

---

1. The issue of the *New York Post* that my father brought home (vol. 163, no. 6) reads, "Vice President Johnson apparently was also shot, but was able to walk to the hospital."

The six of us on the bed in our parents' room. From left: Kip, Jeff, Chris, Dan, Luke, and Collin.

FUN AT THE FOOT
OF THE VOLCANO

♪♪

1963: COLDEST WINTER SINCE 1927.

—Rochester Post-Bulletin

We had no Nine Eleven to compare with Eleven Twenty-Two but looking back, similarities exist. The exact freeze-frame answer to the question, "Where you were when you heard?" The empty feeling the adults must have had when returning to work, picking up useless tools from wooden desks that no longer mattered really.

As my mother wrote, "There is too much and nothing to say." The murder of JFK painted America black. Yet on that very day—November 22, 1963—something good happened too, an ocean away. On that day in England, Parlophone Records released *With the Beatles,* the second album by a new "pop" group. And on February 8, 1964, the band flew to the United States on a Pan American jet to save the entire country.

It was Kip who first brought home the Beatles' American album *Meet the Beatles.* I remember seeing the Capitol Records logo going around the spindle, that gristly hiss as the needle found the outside groove, and then in the opening two seconds all six of our lives changed. Because there was Paul McCartney timing the opening of "I Saw Her Standing There" with his British numbahs—"one, two, three, FAH!"—and everything changed.

"Happiness, too, is inevitable," wrote Camus, and when Paul hit "FAH!" so it was. Happiness came as if from behind a cloud and shone on a nation wrapped in parkas and grief and suddenly it seemed OK, if just for a minute, to be happy again and that even Jackie might lift her black veil and smile at the sound.

In that "one, two, three, FAH!" we discovered a quality of being that would change us and remain with us the rest of our lives. We had discovered cool and its name, the Beatles. To fourth graders with buckteeth (who looked like Ernie Douglas from *My Three Sons*), cool was something entirely new, surprisingly.

Sean Connery was cool playing 007, yes; so was Spider-Man. They did cool things, had cool powers and gadgets. But that's just it—they had and did cool; the Beatles *were* cool. They were the embodiment of cool: cool given flesh, cool that drew breath, told jokes, created music, and made entire stadiums full of girls go all wobbly.

The way they walked out on the stage, the way they stood between sets on *The Ed Sullivan Show,* the cheek of their press conferences, their cigarettes at rakish angles. It was all so incredibly cool even Ernie Douglases like me were set to squealing in the sheer release of energy found in cool. We'd never seen anything like it. The subtle rebellion of their tongue-in-cheek, their conspiratorial air, the jujitsu responses to questions from reporters with short haircuts—it all fascinated us as much the music.

Q: "What do you call your hair style?"

A: "Arthur."

Q: "How did you find America?"

A: "Turn left at Greenland."

Until now, the most sophisticated comedy we'd seen was what we now remember as "Dad Humor"—Dean Martin in Vegas making shitty, thinly veiled jokes about big boobs, or Sid Caesar's seltzer in the pants. Beatle wit appealed to our intelligence. With the right turn of phrase and a deadpan delivery we could laugh up our sleeves at the adult world. The Beatles were, above all else, cool.

The Beatles' brand of coolness became our cosmology. Cool wasn't on a continuum; cool was quantum. You could be a little cool, kinda cool, or very cool. Each age bracket got you to a new level. In fact, discrete levels of coolness had been firmly delineated by the arbiter of cool, brother Jeff—in descending order it went: Studs, Aces, Princes, Sprinters, and Dolts.

Studs were Totally Cool. The Beatles were Studs; so was Steve McQueen. According to Jeff, a Stud was "never perturbed by anything, never asks for help, and the fact that women can't resist a Stud simply doesn't occur to him." Studs were so beyond cool they didn't even *know* they were Studs.

Aces, on the other hand, knew they were Aces. Aces were cool guys but not the gods Studs were. Lucas McCain in the opening credits of *The Rifleman*—and the cool way he looked into the camera while reloading—was an Ace. The Beach Boys were also Aces, but only when they sang their fast songs. Though Jeff didn't come out and say it, we little guys assumed Kip, Jeff, and their cool friend Chris Hallenbeck were all Aces.

A Prince, on the other hand, was a self-conscious Ace—"an Ace who smiled about it," according to Chris Hallenbeck. A Prince could conceivably do something as cool as an Ace, but then laughed and looked up for approval while doing it. Dick Van Dyke or Soupy Sales, they were Princes. So was our brother Chris, who was too young to be an Ace and too old to be the next one down the list, a Sprinter.

I was a Sprinter. Irritating little kids pretending to be Spider-Man, running around the Millstone, stealing cigarettes, and air-strumming the Pagans' guitars were Sprinters. Sprinters were just way too excited about everything. They were the wagging dog tails of an Ace's world, swinging wildly about and knocking stuff off the tables. Sprinters suffered from a syndrome known today as "Assumption of the First Person Plural," a condition that made us tag along behind the Aces asking, "So, where are we goin'? What are we doin'?"

Bringing up the rear were Dolts. The only example of a Dolt Jeff ever provided was Hoss Cartwright from *Bonanza*. (You didn't wanna be Hoss.)

Once we had seen the Beatles, being cool was all that mattered. The old icons were dead. JFK was gone. Elvis was in shitty Hawaiian movies. Even Paul Hornung, my halfback hero on the Green Bay Packers, had fallen from grace (something about gambling that I never quite understood, but he was dethroned nonetheless).

Copying the Beatles was all that mattered, and the easiest part to copy was the hairstyle. Dad didn't allow us to let our hair get as long as the Beatles'. But we occasionally managed to grow our bangs down to our eyes and that was all the length we needed to perform the coolest move in the book—the "Hair Flip." Brushing hair out of your eyes with your hands was for Sprinters. Cool guys simply *flicked* their head very quickly to the right—*WHIP*—preferably while saying something in a flat monotone that conveyed, "Everything that I have seen or heard since waking up at noon today has bored me."

A monotone delivery of the wise-guy line was key to pulling off cool. Some of this ironic remove we learned from the Beatles' first movie, *A Hard Day's Night*. Some we cribbed from old Laurel and Hardy movies.

Jeff perfected Laurel and Hardy's deadpan humor with his best friend, Chris Hallenbeck. Chris was the son of the Mayo Clinic's head of general surgery, the man recruited to remove LBJ's gall bladder (surgery made public in the *Life* magazine photo of the president showing his scar to startled reporters). Jeff and Hallenbeck would mimic the comics' famous deadpan as they visited destructive pranks on each other. Hallenbeck would walk up to Jeff, rip the pocket off his shirt and quietly hand it back to him. Jeff would look up at Hallenbeck, blink, and rip off *his* shirt pocket. Throughout the exchange there would be no knowing smiles, no twinkles in the eye—just cold retribution. Hallenbeck took one of Jeff's prized silver dollars, opened the window on the top floor of the Millstone, and threw his coin far down into the weeds near the forest. Jeff, channeling Stan Laurel, obediently watched the dollar's arc into oblivion. A pause. Without a word, he'd produce scissors and cut the laces to Hallenbeck's shoes. Hallenbeck would sigh and walk silently back to his home down the road from the Millstone, carrying his shoes.

Even we little ones were learning the sublime joys of schadenfreude. At the stone barbecue pit down in the large half acre of back yard we called the "Low Forty," we enjoyed watching each other's marshmallows catch fire and plop into the coals. To see your own treat browning to caramel perfection while your brother's bubbled, blackened, and slid hissing into the flames was deeply satisfying.

This cheerful disrespect for anybody that wasn't you, and anything that wasn't yours, applied to everybody—including our father. Jeff remembers sitting on the back porch with Kip on a hot day in the summer of '63, drinking iced tea. As they cooled their heels they could hear their hardworking father mowing the lawn in a distant part of the yard. The sleepy drone of the motor came to a metallic hacking end as Dad ran over one of his own workshop tools, carelessly abandoned there in the tall grass by one of his sons. At the report of this sound, Kip and Jeff began laughing into the straws of their iced tea, producing bubbles.

To hear your father run the lawn mower over one of his own tools was—in my family anyway—hilarious. Had we been standing right next to my father when it happened, it wouldn't have been as funny. But heard from a distance you could interpret an entire story in one hot-summer metal-on-metal sound—how one of the father's prized workbench tools was borrowed without permission, left to rust in the rain, concealed by growing grass, and then ruined by his own hand, even as he dulled the mower's blades. It was funny not just because we were all angry with Dad. It was more the graceful economy of its symbolism packed into one clang of finality. A sound of somebody "losing," of somebody being further behind than they were a minute ago, reduced in some way. It was classic victim comedy.

Watching the Beatles in *A Hard Day's Night* gave us the idea of making our own funny movies. They were all victim comedies and we called them the "Ridiculous Films." They were shot with an old 8 mm movie camera that Dad had given up on, and if they had a theme it was "Sprinters Getting Killed."

Their structure was classic.

We open on our protagonist, a fourth grader with buckteeth strolling along in front of the Millstone. In act 2, the antagonist is introduced with swift and economic storytelling—brother Jeff comes around the corner with a baseball bat and beats the shit out of me. (A pillow hidden in the victim's coat allows for the delivery of many cinematically robust and satisfying blows.)

The fourth grader collapses on the driveway.

Had the film ended here critics might have rightly argued that the work lacked finality; that the entire piece was ambiguous and left the audience asking, "What, ultimately, happened here?" But act 3 ties up the story lines in a tidy denouement. Thanks to a cleverly wardrobed body double, when the camera rolls again, we see Jeff driving Dad's car over the crumpled form of the Sprinter. Fade to black. (Cut, actually; there's no fading with a Brownie movie camera.)

Audience test scores were off the chart. Squeals of delight filled the living room when the little fifty-foot reel premiered on Dad's projector. "More blood," demanded the audience, and a sequel was released the following month (after we talked Mom into getting us a new roll of film).

What might now be called *Dead Sprinters II* built on the original's success and used the same opening: fourth grader stands in front of Millstone. But this time it is brother Dan who enters screen right, grabs the victim, and throws him into the house through the open door. The camera, still running, tilts seamlessly up to a third-story window where a stuffed body double suffers the indignities of defenestration and thuds on the pavement below.

Where's this going? a savvy audience might ask. Will the narrative clarify the victim's backstory? Who *is* he, really? What issues in his past led him to this development? Act 3, while answering none of these questions, does address the test audience's earlier call for "more blood." A crowd encircles the protagonist, now lying unconscious on the concrete. They're lining up to pay Dan a quarter. But for what, dammit, what?

It's the rental fee for the baseball bat, making its second appearance in the Ridiculous Films. As the curtain falls on act 3, the brothers pound the bejesus out of me.

"It's all so very easy to laugh at oneself. What we must learn to do is to laugh at others." So said *Saturday Night Live* writer Michael O'Donoghue, and this ability to look down on others was held in high regard by the six brothers.

Living directly to the south of us was a little boy, Jeffrey Hartman, five and a half years old. Jeffrey was not only a Sprinter, he was a mama's boy. Almost all his short visits to our yard ended within minutes of his arrival with the shriek of Mrs. Hartman calling him back home.

"Jeffreeeeeeeeeeee?!?"

It was the way Jeffrey's mother's high-pitched voice hung on the last syllable of his name that gave us the idea for the Jeffrey Game, which was all about lung capacity. Whoever could hold the last syllable of Jeffrey's name the longest, won. The fact that Mrs. Hartman, no less Jeffrey, could hear us over in our yard playing the Jeffrey Game never once crossed our minds.

"Jeffreeeeeeeeeeeeeeeeeeeeeeeeeeeeeeeeeeeeeeeeeeeeeeeeeeeeeeeeeeeeeeeeee eeeeeeeeeeeeeeeeeeeeeeeeeeeeeeeeeeeeeeeeeeeeeeeeeeeeeeeeeeeeeeeeeeeeeeee eeeeeeeeeeeeeeeeeeeeeeeeeeeeeeeeeeeeeeeeeeeeeeeeeeeeeeeeeeeeeeeeeeeeeeee eeeeeeeeeeeeee!"

The Beatles had set true north on our compass of coolness. And now anything that wasn't cool demanded our scorn: the way people dressed, the sound of their voices, their weight, it was all comic fodder.

One summer we focused our derision on the babysitter. She was a kindly overweight old lady named—and this is the part we loved—Mrs. Buttert. This irony sent us into paroxysms of Sprinter glee. There was "Butt" in her name. There was also "Butter," as in lard ass. It was a rich comic vein waiting for our genius to mine it. Eventually, all you had to do to make a brother laugh was to point at something flat. Flat meant "Mrs. Buttert sat on it." Flat frogs dead in the road were suddenly funny—"Mrs. Buttert's pet frog." The nickels we'd flattened on the railroad tracks were funny—"Change from

Mrs. Buttert's back pocket." Kids are cruel, we more than most, and if there's a Hell it's likely there's a reserved table for six there, with a helpful and instructive card waiting in the middle—SULLIVAN PARTY. In our defense, unlike the Jeffrey Game, we didn't make fun of Mrs. Buttert within earshot.

We did, however, go to great lengths to vex her. In metal shop at Central Junior High School, Chris discovered that thirty pieces of tin, cut to the size of a potato chip, would when dropped create a sound very much like glass shattering. We'd wait until Mrs. Buttert was settling into a comfortable chair and then, in a distant room, drop the thirty pieces of tin. Mrs. Buttert would come bustling into the room to find Chris quietly reading, the tin now concealed under his shirt. She would look about, raise an eyebrow, and retreat to her chair again and just as her ample rear married with cushion—CRASH!—the sound would happen again. Chris reported later that after five repetitions the subject seemed to accept the idea that shattering glass was, in the Sullivan house, simply ambience and began to ignore it. Harder to ignore was the night we locked Mrs. Buttert in her room so we could watch television.

"Lock" isn't actually correct. The Millstone's ancient doors all locked with an old-fashioned skeleton key, cold and about the length of a cigarette in your hand; and Mrs. Buttert kept the only key in her apron pocket. So to keep her from discovering we'd all sneaked out of bed to watch Laurel and Hardy, we rigged a series of ropes around her bedroom doorknob, looped it through the stair banisters, and tied it off with one of Kip's Boy Scout knots.

As the six of us watched TV and talked, we discovered her name sounded even funnier when you burped it. We practiced this in chorus, drinking green bottles of warm Coca-Cola pilfered from the midnight pantry to fuel our effervescence.

"Mrs. *Buuuuuuuuu*–tert."

On the houseboat in Winona, Minnesota, 1964.
From left: Collin, family friend Tim Desley, Chris, and Luke.

RAT HELICOPTERS

ℐℐ

If you were bad in a previous life, you came back as a bug in our yard.

Any anthill inhabited by the stinging red kind was subject to, forgive me, "The Red Anthill Solution." This usually involved a magnifying glass or peeing on the colony, and it brought more joy than pest control ought to bring. Fireflies, too, were sacrificed matter-of-factly to produce glow-in-the-dark war paint. We were kinder perhaps to larger animals, like Caesar our collie, but sooner or later every living thing at the Millstone was a Comic Victim. One game involved a cat and a tire swing.

One of us would hold our cat, Mr. Brown, in our lap and sit inside the tire's arc. A brother would then slowly rotate the tire, which soon knotted the rope like a balsa-wood airplane's rubber band, and then let go, allowing the tire and its occupants to spin into a propeller blur. When it came to a stop, Mr. Brown was placed on the ground and the drunken zigzag our poor cat made was, to us, the zenith of comedy.

One summer we realized our pets didn't wear clothes. They were, in fact, naked. Just watching the dog walk to his water dish became funny. Watching Mr. Brown walk away, his tail high and that one eye winking back at you, brought us boneless to the floor in laughter.

Another day, while feeding a carrot to our horse, Coppersmith, we noticed his lips didn't quite entirely shut. In their resting state, Coppersmith's lips formed a small circular hole which made the horse look like he was whistling. To bring this comic image to life, you stood in front of Coppersmith and looked at his lips while a brother stood behind you and whistled the theme song from *The Andy Griffith Show*. We spent hours doing this.

Another cruelty I blush admitting to was "rat helicopters." To make a rat helicopter, you held a bed pillow with hands at either end. You put your pet rat in the middle of the pillow and bent it inward, enclosing your ratanaut in its fold. Then, with a quick and hard outward yank the rat popped up about two feet in the air and, to stabilize its flight, the poor thing would rotate its tail round and round, completing the effect.

"Hey guys, look! Rat helicopters!" (I know, I know. But we were kids.)

Rats were our favorite pets. We liked how their tails gave girls the willies and we appreciated rats' underdog status. They were just, well, rats. We'd hold our rats, look 'em in the eye, and say in a James Cagney voice, "Why, you dirty rat. You killed my broth-ah."

Our first pair of rats (we called them "blats") was a gift from Dr. Zollman, presented after a tour of the Mayo Clinic's Institute Hills facility, just up the road from the Millstone. We figured we'd saved them from getting cancer and so they were accorded special status at the Millstone. But after the first batch of babies, and then a second, special status was revoked and Mom had us move the blats from the Rumpus Room to the garden shed in the back yard.

We emptied out the shed, threw away the small cages, and turned the entire structure into one huge blat fraternity house. Without cages the blats had run of the place, resulting in, of course, more blats. At its peak, the population of Blatopolis was forty-six. Lying on the shed floor and letting the city of rodents crawl over you was a delight we found visitors generally eschewed. We even fashioned a dinner bell for them. Pulling a string on the outside of the shed clanged together two Folger's coffee cans hanging inside, and if you waited a minute for the congregation to assemble, when you opened the door forty-six dirty rats would be lined up at the threshold to greet you, with a few scrubby souls hanging high on the interior of the door itself like hippies on the scaffolding at Woodstock.

With the green shed as the only available gene pool, mutations occurred, and we loved these deformed rats more than the others. One of the institute's great-grandblats was born with his head permanently tilted to about two o'clock, making him look as if he was always checking to see if that was his name they just called over the intercom. Our favorite was a poor little rat born without the use of his hind legs. He was a happy little guy and seemed to get along fine dragging himself around, though after a few months we noticed the fur had rubbed off his belly. Perversely, we called him "Jim Walker."

Jim, of course, was the rat we proudly displayed to surprised visitors at the Millstone—rushing into the room to show off Mr. Walker's scraggly-assed mutant rat belly to the ladies in Mom's bridge club.

Kip with Caesar, circa 1952.

CAUSE OF DEATH: UNKNOWN

◈

Death was introduced to me by a hamster.

The Millstone was home to many hamsters over the years—so many we had a nickname for the species. The word hamster, when spoken as if you had a stuffy nose, was "habster." We shortened it to "hab."

The hab I loved the most was Mama Hab. Mama lived in a small cage on my desk, which filled my bedroom with the comforting smell of cedar shavings. It was here she bore six babies that looked like pink kidney beans; and it was here I watched in horror as she ate them. I wasn't familiar with the species' natural tendency for infanticide when they feel unsafe, and so I was angry with Mama Hab for a while. After a successful litter, however, I came to forgive her and the little wheel in her cage spun regularly every night for a year or so until one morning I discovered her paws-up.

Using the funeral of JFK as a model, I immediately chose a room in the Millstone where my hamster could lie in state—the quiet of my mother's Tower Library seemed fitting for the rites. To fashion a coffin, I emptied a box of the large wooden kitchen matches and with a little toilet paper serving as bed and pillow, Mama Hab was respectfully displayed for viewing on the ornate desk in the middle of my mother's oval library.

Though Mom and all five brothers were invited to pay their respects, attendance was low. So I set the burial date back a week, extended the invitation to neighborhood kids, and waited for the lines to form.

With time running out and the crowds somewhat thinner than expected, my agenda shifted from crowd control to odor control. A liberal application of my Dad's Old Spice would have been the preferred mortuary science, but I was unable to locate the bottle and settled for spraying half a can of Right Guard antiperspirant onto my ex-hamster. It took about five days before my mother discovered my aboveground pet cemetery and told me to commit the critter to the elements. Mama Hab was finally buried in the pine grove near the garden with only myself in attendance.

Death came next for our most beloved pet, the family collie, Caesar. But this wasn't just death—it was murder.

Caesar was part of our family long before I was. He'd been with us since the family lived on the farm, when the oldest boys—Kip, Jeff, and Chris—were toddlers. He was a beautiful collie and to us looked prettier than Lassie (and she was on *television*). When we moved into the Millstone, Caesar inherited a dog's kingdom of four acres to find sticks and six boys to throw them. Then came the morning I found Caesar dying on the front lawn. It was long before his time and there were no apparent injuries, but there he lay. By the time the family had all gathered around his fallen regal form, he was gone.

Caesar was no hamster. He was our dog, our guard, our angel, the one you met coming home from school, waiting for you by the mailbox. His sudden death changed everything. JFK's assassination hadn't happened yet, nor had our parents separated; we'd never felt loss before. All of our little-boy lives had been about addition; new little brothers arriving, Grandpa and Monnie pulling into the driveway bearing Florida oranges, big homes being bought, Christmas following Christmas. And now something was taken. Loss was new to us.

It was just minutes after my father's graveside pronouncement "Cause of death: unknown" that the rumor began of Mrs. Hartman and her "orange dog food."

Mrs. Hartman, who lived over the fence to the south of us, had been known to complain about Caesar from time to time. Caesar would dig the occasional hole in her garden. She'd shoo him off and then mention the trespasses to Mom at every opportunity.

Our grief turned to anger and, needing an outlet, we chose her. It seems one of us (today nobody recalls exactly who) remembered seeing Mrs. Hartman "feed Caesar some orange dog food." Of course this was nonsense and Mom did her best to disabuse us of the notion, but the conspiracy theory took. Mrs. Hartman officially entered the family shit list and shot to number one. And though none of the boys ever confronted her with our suspicions, urinating through the fence into her garden became common practice and our passive aggressions continued for some time. Even six years later, whenever Kip and Jeff's rock-and-roll band, the Pagans, practiced on the porch at the Millstone, we would point the big amplifiers in the direction of Mrs. Hartman's house, just to rattle the old dog-killer's china cabinet.

The Pagans on the balcony of Myra's library.

THE PAGANS

of

The new "sound of music" is defined simply—play it as loud, long, and hard as you can. The Pagans, to put it mildly, follow this recipe—as does any other teen band. None of them apologize for it—in fact there is sort of a contest to see which group can play the loudest.

— *"Pagans Teen-Band Named After Dog,"*
Rochester Post-Bulletin, *October 17, 1964*

The sexual and political repression of the 1950s created its own worst nightmare—longhairs playing rock and roll that made the girls shake their boobies. It made the men with short haircuts and white short-sleeved shirts put down their slide rules and try to stop all the tomfoolery. But by 1964 guitars and amplifiers were being dragged into basements all over America, including the Millstone's.

For a Sprinter, this was the coolest thing that could possibly happen. Real rock and roll right in your own house, with cigarettes and everything. The Pagans were just five high school boys, but to us Sprinters they were living gods—and two of them were my big brothers, Kip on lead guitar and Jeff on bass.

Kip, like many firstborns, had an easy confidence that helped him succeed in most of the things he took on. Dark haired and Irish handsome like his father, Kip was an Eagle Scout, a state debate champion, a competitor for the state high school diving championship, leader of the Pagans, but more than anything he was the Big Brother. Sprinters who were seen using the Big Brother's bathroom *heard* about it, and if Kip's toothbrush was discovered wet to the touch, woe be unto any Sprinter with Crest on his breath. Kip should also have won the state championship for best girlfriend. Linda, his steady of several years, was a stunning '60s beauty who had a devoted following of Sprinters trailing her like dwarves behind Snow White.

The vice president of Cool, on the other hand, was brother Jeff. He was Bobby Kennedy to Kip's Jack; *The Man from U.N.C.L.E.*'s Illya Kuryakin to Kip's Napoleon Solo. Jeff dressed cool, walked cool, and slumped cool.

He had a bonelessness to his gait and a way of draping himself over chairs that said, "I care less than anybody in this room." Making Jeff laugh counted for something; Kip would laugh just to be nice. To add to his mystique, Jeff was an artist. He painted in oils and acrylics as well as pen and ink and had undeniable talent.

Kip remembers learning boogie-woogie piano by ear around sixth grade, playing along to Elvis or Jerry Lee Lewis. The band got its start when Kip was on the diving team at John Marshall High School. There he recruited friends for a one-time performance at a high school talent show: Jay Gleason on drums and Collin Gentling on piano. They enjoyed it enough to keep playing, and though the band's lineup changed a few times, they settled finally on a roster of Kip, Jeff, Jerry Huiting (sharing lead guitar with Kip), Jim Rushton (rhythm guitar), and Jay Gleason behind the drums.

Jeff's best friend, Chris Hallenbeck, was the Stu Sutcliffe of the Pagans. Chris was a decent keyboard player and could sing, but was with the band only briefly; he died in a car accident. In 1965, the Pagans' first drummer, Jay Gleason, would also die in a car.

In an article on the Pagans, the *Rochester Post-Bulletin* said the band's name was "unusual" and "might bother some people." Kip and Jeff liked its subversive, antireligious connotations but assured the reporters with short haircuts that Pagan was simply the name of Caesar's replacement, one of our new Irish wolfhounds—"a constant presence at their practices." (The fact that pagans were godless creatures, heathens without religion, also likely figured in the choice.)

Dad was a drunk by the time the Pagans formed, but not the bourbon-guzzling, elbow-bending, ethyl-to-urine system of his final days. Some part of him enjoyed the confidence it took his sons to get up there onstage and bang it out, and on one occasion he even paid them to play at a Mayo Clinic party hosted at the Millstone. He also put up with having band practices at the Millstone, this to the great delight of the sweaty group of Sprinters who attended every session. In between songs we'd try to bum cigarettes or slip behind the Ludwig drum set when Jay went to the bathroom.

"Hey look, Kip! I can do the drum roll from 'Wipe Out'!"

Everything the Pagans had, we Sprinters wanted. Their cigarettes, the cool VW van they used to haul their equipment, even Kip's and Jeff's girlfriends, Linda and Bonnie. With my father slowly checking out of family life, the Pagans became our male authority figures. A joke wasn't funny until it made Kip or Jeff laugh; clothes weren't cool unless they wore them first. When the local menswear shop M. C. Lawler's had the Pagans pose for an ad in the store's new blazers, I carried the newspaper ad around for a week as proof I knew somebody famous.

The first time the Pagans played in public tellingly set the tone for their short, lively career. In April of 1964 one of Jeff's friends, Steve Rossi, threw a party and invited the Pagans to be the entertainment. The Pagans played ten songs to an appreciative, slightly drunk audience. At 11:00 p.m., word filtered through the crowd that "the cops had the place surrounded," which in fact they had. Almost every kid at the party had something to lose and panic spread. There were student council leaders, sons and daughters of doctors, football team members and other athletes, including cheerleaders. Most of the crowd managed to scatter past the police. Caught in the net were Rossi (it was his place) and the Pagans (who couldn't abandon their equipment).

Rossi's statement to the Rochester sheriff's department is still in their files. His words are in that stilted "I Am Now Talking to the Police" cadence some people get in the presence of Johnny Heat. *("Officer, I had no previous knowledge that beverages of an alcoholic nature were in the trunkular space of my motorized vehicle.")* It's also evident he didn't rat out his friends:

> I would assume [Rossi stated] that a few of the kids brought beer but I couldn't identify who or how many. Kids started coming about 9, and the band started playing. I do know that beer was consumed in my apartment but am unable to identify the parties who did consume. I myself did not consume any beer. This is a true statement to the best of my knowledge.

But the next morning every athlete who'd been at the party was kicked off his team for a year, including Kip and Jay. It upset them because as juniors they'd both made the diving finals in the state meet; Jay placed fifth, Kip sixth. They were eager to do even better in their senior years. Strangely, there were no recriminations from Dad. Looking back, Kip thinks Dad was so checked out by then he simply didn't care. Though he was still on the high school debate team (Kip won first place at state the next year), without sports he now had more time to put into the band.

From Kip's 1964 diary

Great night!! Curtain opened and we smashed out "Good Golly Miss Molly." For the first time, everybody clowned. I tickled back of Steve's head with guitar, Jerry swiped Steve's mike, Jim made Jerry laugh on "Boys." Speakers excellent. Wait till we get new amp with 110 watts! At home last night, Mom broke down and cried when the little ones argued about TV. Tensions increasing around here.

Myra and Roger pose in front of the Millstone's fireplace
before going to a Mayo Clinic party.

"SPATS WITH THE WIFE"

৶৫

Roger confided in me only once. He would come to my house, only occasionally, to talk about his troubles. He claimed his problems stemmed from serious marital difficulties he was having. He defined them as a competition between him and Myra. Competition, mostly on intellectual matters. Your father told me he thought Myra "put him down."

I had to go out [to the Millstone] more than once. One incident happened on the front steps and I remember that very clearly. I was called to see if I could come talk to him, to settle him down. He was extremely angry and did a great deal of shouting. Just a lot of verbal abuse from Roger. He'd get out of control. His face would get red. He'd rant, rave. [Raving about?] About Myra. Conflict. A conflict between the two as to who was going to dominate the other. He felt dominated by her and said he "didn't want to be dominated."

—Interview with Dr. Mark Coventry,
my father's boss at the Mayo Clinic, 1992

Chris Raymer is a chemical dependency counselor at La Hacienda, a treatment center in Hunt, Texas. He says he's heard a thousand reasons for alcoholic drinking.

"My job is so hard."

"My boss is so mean."

"I have so many responsibilities."

"I need to relax."

For fun, we'll throw in "My wife tries to dominate me."

Chris says every "reason" is simply an excuse to drink. As an example he facetiously mimics one patient whose circular logic went, "One day, it's 'Yay! The Yankees won! Let's have a drink.' And the next it's, 'Shit! The Yankees lost. Let's have a drink.' There's *always* a reason. But the fact of the matter is alcoholics drink because they like the feeling."

After several years of heavy drinking, every cell in the alcoholic's body becomes addicted, and drinking moves from emotional medication to a cellular requirement for continued existence. What once gave a pleasant buzz is now required simply to get from below zero up to feeling normal. The intake of booze reaches a point where the alcoholic faces a double horror: a continued life *with* drinking (impossible) or facing life *without* drinking (also impossible).

If asked, the alcoholic will cheerfully point out the things that cause his drinking. In an early interview with his Mayo psychiatrist, my father said his drinking always increased after a "spat with my wife." Whether Roger was lying or actually believed this, he'd say with a straight face that he drank a quart of bourbon a day because his wife was angry. The idea that his wife was angry because he drank a quart of bourbon a day, well, it just didn't seem to come up.

Lots of stuff didn't come up when you were talking with Roger.

Regarding that "spat with my wife"? Roger probably didn't go into details, but had he done so the psychiatrist would've heard about the time Roger was shitfaced, sitting in the passenger seat of the car while his wife drove. Too drunk to be able to yell at her any longer, he took out his anger by shaking her as she tried to drive. Unable to steer safely because of this "spat," Myra stopped the car, got out, and hoped the change of venue might calm him down. Roger stumbled out of the car but couldn't walk steadily. As he weaved down the middle of the road, Myra saw another car approaching and had to push him off to the side of the road to save his life.

How Roger ever felt "dominated" mystifies my mother to this day. "Dominating? I was the wimpy wife who didn't protest this treatment," she remembers. "I was the doormat who let him get away with saying such nasty things to me and to you children."

By 1964, things at the Millstone had become even worse. In a poem my mother wrote years later is the line "I was raped more times than I can remember." That's the most she ever said about it—a line in a poem. She doesn't talk about those nights and none of us ask her to. One of them, however, I came close to seeing myself.

I was in fourth grade. We were on a weekend vacation at the Curtis Hotel in Minneapolis—Dad, Mom, Collin, and me. My little brother and I played in the pool most of the day as Mom, reading poolside, watched from behind her big white plastic sunglasses. Dad was off somewhere drinking. We had two rooms that night—one for Mom and Dad, one for us boys. After putting us to bed Mom deliberately fell asleep in our room. At midnight I heard my father lurch through the connecting door and, in a voice bubbly thick with bourbon and Winston cigarettes, growl, "Let's fuck."

I cannot remember exactly what happened next. How Mom got him out of our room, I don't know. Whatever she did, he soon left the rooms. Hours later, when Dad hadn't returned, Mom went out into the city to look for him. Collin was asleep and although she'd told me to sit tight, after an hour of waiting I too headed out into the rain looking for the place I'd heard her mention—*the Normandy something*. I remember going down in the elevator alone and going through the lobby alone and out the door and down a street until, wow, there it was—the Normandy Inn Bar—all big-city and outlined in yellow lightbulbs that splintered into wet stars through the raindrops on my black 1964 glasses and I pulled open the heavy oak door and walked in and smelled the smoke and saw the red carpeting and the hunched backs of lonely men and I could tell the bartender didn't much like seeing a wet fourth grader in his place at one in the morning but out he came from behind the bar to show me around and prove my parents were not there. And I left.

Back in the room there was only Collin, little and asleep, and I soon joined him. In the morning Mom and Dad came out of the other room and on the two-hour drive south to Rochester, nobody said anything.

They say summer colds are the worst.

Turns out, actually, it's summer Tornado Lightning Planet-Shattering Anger Rages from the Volcanic Thunder Bourbon God that are the worst.

You know—"spats."

The Millstone wasn't air-conditioned, but in high summer there was always plenty of ice for drinks and in the July heat Roger's binges began to last whole weekends. At first sign of one of these summer rages Mom began packing us into the Plymouth station wagon and we went to stay at a motel for the night. When these rages became a pattern, Mom started taking us to out-of-town places so neighbors (and Dad's colleagues) wouldn't wonder why we were poolside regulars at the Klinic-Vu Motel.

My little brother and I enjoyed those trips. Motels were high adventure—pools to play in, long balconies to race down, and candy machines in the lobby. Seeing the Volcanic Thunder Bourbon God start to crank up another summer rage was scary, but it also meant it was time to get your swimming suit off the line!

In mid-1964, Mom finally told her parents the truth about life in the Millstone. Blue Book letters that had once been about sailing ships and

Shakespeare were now about brutality and trauma and written on the stationery of motels. Even the continued existence of their letters was threatened that summer when Roger began raging whenever he found one of Mom's Blue Books lying about the Millstone.

"Is this another letter to Daddy packed full of chitchat about me? Like the one I found last week?!?"

Grandpa stops writing in Blue Books and starts typing
letters on 8½- x 11-inch paper: August 28, 1964
I believe I shall discontinue our usual Blue Books and return to the typed sheet, where I need not restrain self carefully in what is writ and which can be destroyed upon reading. With the hope that before too long, matters may improve and our traditional Blue Books can be resumed. Your mother and I are talking about the tragedy which has overtaken our daughter. I expressed a feeling that your parents were almost deserting you—here we sit in comfort and do nothing for you—but what can we do? Can we accomplish anything by coming up to Rochester? A "secret mission" unknown to the other party? Could I help in any way?

But RJL liked the Blue Books; they were easy for him to bind into hardcover volumes. In a subsequent phone call, he and his daughter agreed to go back to Blue Books but temporarily restrict all discussion of problems at the Millstone to the last pages; pages they could cut out after reading, thereby preserving the format so good for binding. Today the bound volumes of 1964 and 1965 have missing pages as well as passages that tell of their absence.

"What else is there to write about?" Myra queried. "Believe I'll turn to Page 7."

The summer of '64 was tough in its own way on Grandpa RJL. Age had finally nudged him into selling his home on Lake Winnemissett, where he and Monnie had lived since 1949. They made plans to move into a retirement home outside Jacksonville.

Grandpa's letters, 1964
Am just now packing my grandfather's tools and putting them in the second trunk to send to you who have space for such things. I suppose I am a sentimental cuss, but I just stood out by lakeside to see the yellow moving van with said possessions round the lake to

the south and on its way to you. In the van were some Longstreet treasures, headed 1,500 miles north to one who knows how to take care of them. Bless your heart. A part of me is on the way.

Memory: I Am "Suave Ghost"

I am nine years old and standing in full uniform in front of my big brother Chris. I am wrapped in a sheet. I am "Suave Ghost." Not only am I a ghostly spirit, I am suave.

Suave Ghost takes everything in stride, and no matter what happens he keeps a suave James Bond remove. Nothing can touch him. Who would have thought detachment could be a Marvel Comics superpower? No one. Except, maybe, Suave Ghost.

Say something mean to the quiet specter that stands before you. Go on, give it your best shot.

"You have huge buckteeth," says Chris, "and I can see the rims of your big black glasses under the sheet."

Hardly a fold of my sheet twitches; I am unruffled. Why? Because I am Suave Ghost. Say anything you want. Suave Ghost just stands there and thinks, "Is that all you got?"

Chris says, "Hey look, everybody. It's my bucktoothed little brother who looks exactly like Ernie Douglas from My Three Sons, *standing under a sheet."*

No answer. Just silence. What power! I sweep from the room, triumphant. God, how it must rankle my foes! Is there no chink in his armor? What iron must lurk 'neath his sheet to repel such barbs as these? They gnash their teeth and fall to the floor in front of the Untouchable One. (Ooh, that's good— "The Untouchable One." A secondary descriptor, like Batman's "The Dark Knight." Imagine it in the headlines: "Downtown Disturbance Fails to Vex Untouchable One.")

Retiring to his lair, Suave Ghost hides his costume by making his bed and as he does so, he thinks back to how it all began—The Early Days. Volume I. That day when the mild-mannered schoolboy first discovered he wasn't ticklish. Neither finger nor feather could coax a giggle from him, however light the touch. No matter where his brothers tickled him—under the feet, the arms—it was as if there were no feelings at all.

The Polaroid Dr. Lund took of my father the night of the Beaux Arts Ball.
Roger is second from left.

THE ALCOHOLIC'S GUIDE
TO RUINING EVENINGS

⚜

At the Millstone we had no father figure, and when a sane adult male drifted into our lives, we swarmed him like a lifeboat. There were two such men in our world—the Tonys.

One was Dr. Tony Bianco, himself an orthopedic surgeon at the clinic and head of his own large household of seven just down the road. The other man we looked up to—often literally—was our dentist, Dr. Tony Lund.

In Dr. Lund's waiting room I'd page through the *Children's Highlight* magazines, stare at the goldfish in his quiet aquarium, and actually look forward to being with this man who whistled cheerfully as he stuck needles in my head and ran drill bits over the nerve highway connected to the center of my brain. Dr. Lund was simply a likeable person.

My father thought so too, and if the insular Roger Sullivan could be said to have had a best friend, it was this talkative, gregarious, huggy man—Tony Lund. He and his wife, Mary, were soon going out for dinner with Roger and Myra, and on one of these outings they gathered for a ride down the Mississippi aboard the Lunds' houseboat, the *Sneaky Pete*. It was a small craft, not grand by any means; more like a floating motel room and moored in nearby Winona, Minnesota. Drifting down the river, the vista moved my father to say, "Tony, I'd love to own one of these things. It would add umpteen years to my life." That was 1964. Dad died in '66, so umpteen apparently equals two. Roger bought one anyway and our houseboat, the *Lethe,* was soon bobbing alongside the *Sneaky Pete*. We'd pile into the family station wagon on Friday afternoons for the hour trip east and by three o'clock the *Lethe* was in the water and Dad was behind the wheel half in the bag.

With enough booze, even a strip-mining executive can go all John Muir on you, and Dad was no different. After a few tumblers of liquid conversation, he'd wax beatific on the timeless beauty of the river and I'd get the

"Have you ever really *looked* at a sunset?" speech, delivered with that condescending earnestness of the florid drunk whose cerebellum is on autopilot.

Autopilot would've been a nice feature for the houseboat actually, considering the captain was seeing two rivers and trying to drive between them. At the end of one particular excursion my mother could tell Dad wasn't capable of pulling the boat safely into the dock.

"I walked around to the side of the boat where the housing hid me from Roger's view," recalls my mother, "and pantomimed our plight to Tony across the water on the *Sneaky Pete*."

When Tony understood what was happening, he gave the wheel to his wife and did a 007 leap from his deck to ours. Somehow he managed to get Dad away from the wheel to guide us in safely and did it without us kids knowing how close we came to appearing on the local news.

It was on the houseboat that Dad first accused Tony Lund of having an affair with my mother. Roger and Tony were relaxing on deck chairs watching Myra walk down the dock to retrieve a life vest when my father said, "Why don't you just get it over with and screw her?"

Tony was a children's dentist and this may have explained his hesitancy to rearrange Roger's teeth. It was his good nature, however, to respond with only a gentle, "What are you saying? Don't *do* this, Roger." When I call Tony Lund to learn more about this incident, I can almost hear him shaking his head as he remembers it. "I loved your dad. I really did, but this was, well, it was too much."

Both my mother and Tony are certain Roger's jealousy surfaced the year before at Rochester's annual Beaux Arts Ball. It was on this night that Tony, after waltzing with his wife, Mary, asked Myra for a dance.

"He was such a marvelous dancer," recalls Mom. "I could just shut my brain off and go."

Tony takes pains, needlessly, to assure me there was no affair. "But your mother could dance well and I remember what a great time we had at that first ball."

"Looking back," says Myra, "Roger must've just been consumed by insecurities. He had so little confidence he couldn't even let himself believe he had a loyal wife."

It was at the second Beaux Arts Ball in 1964 that my father pushed Tony too far. The evening started off with drinks at the Lunds' house with everybody dressed formally for the big do. Tony took a photo of my father, using his new Polaroid camera, and remembers, "Your dad, he'd had a snootful before we even left for the ball."

At the Kahler Hotel downtown, my parents and the Lunds were seated at a large table for eight and—as *The Alcoholic's Guide to Ruining Evenings* suggests—Dad started throwing the drinks back before the food arrived. One drink followed another while the table guests covertly locked eyes and formed conversational couplets on either side of Roger to avoid getting trapped with him. Set adrift at the table without a close audience, Roger mumbled things to the general vicinity and, if not for the tux and ballroom surroundings, could've been mistaken for a street drunk talking to his haircut.

There are different levels of difficulty achieved in alcoholic stunts; it's kind of like competitive diving. There are the smaller stunts: inappropriate jokes or, say, throwing up while waiting for the valet. But accusing your wife and best friend of having an affair—publicly—that's the triple gainer of evening ruiners and Dad threw one flawlessly. Roger's accusations were overheard by everyone at the table, including Tony.

"I didn't come back at him right away but waited for the appropriate time," Tony remembers. "When he got up to go to the bathroom I went in right behind him. I took his shirt in my fists and *lifted* him right off the floor, slamming him hard against the wall. I mean, I really slammed him, Luke."

Tony backpedals a little bit here, caught between the memory and the realization that he's recounting it to Roger's son. "You know, I'm generally a pretty easygoing fellow, but with something as bad as this . . . well, I just told him, 'Roger, don't you ever, *ever* say that again.' I turned around and walked out."

With a beep, the Polaroid image Tony took of my father that night arrives as promised in my e-mail. On my screen, the Internet downloads the picture from top to bottom like an upside-down theater curtain unveiling a scene from another era. The four men in tuxes have period haircuts and eyeglasses and it looks like the office Christmas party at Houston's Mission Control. The thick black eyeglasses, the high-and-tight buzz cuts, it's all very 1965. My eyes, of course, go to my father.

I lean into the screen to scrutinize his face and the closeness sparks a memory of kisses that don't count; affection triggered by chemicals and given through a veil of bourbon mist.

It is strange to discover a picture of my father outside the familiar images in the box of family photos; like it's a deleted scene from a movie I know well. Stranger still is the knowledge that he is drunk at the very moment the picture was taken. Here it is, the thing itself, captured on film like a Jim Beam Sasquatch a bare ninety minutes before a legendary stunt. This is what I've been looking for. This is Him. The thing I'd heard through the walls yelling at Mom. Shouldn't there be music swelling here, a flash of memory? *("That's the face, that's the face!")* But the cotton padding of years protect me. It is only a picture of a man. The memory is there; the emotion, locked inside amber.

The front yard of the Millstone, where we did horrible things
to each other with snowballs.

SNOWBALLS SOMEHOW
MADE IN HELL

Ten-year-old Kip gives a status report to Mom,
who is away visiting her parents in Florida, 1958
Lukee is not getting along with Christie. They're constantly arguing about who's going to have the big, brown chair in Dad's study.
Christie will cross his right leg over his left. This makes Christie's
knee get in Lukee's half and when that happens, Lukee rises up
and bops Christie on the head with a cardboard roll filled with the
rolled up newspaper. Then Christie rises up and makes a swing and
a miss. While he's off guard Lukee comes down with a good, solid
whack with his cardboard roll. This only maddens Christie and he
jumps up and connects with a right to the jaw.

Mom says the earliest sibling argument she can remember was watching toddlers Kip and Jeff ride trikes in a circle and fight about who was ahead of
whom, each loudly redefining the other's position on the circle.

Kip was born in 1947. With no brother to irritate him, correct him, or
attack him things were peaceful until 1949, when Jeff was born; after which
began a twenty-five-year-long series of arguments between brothers that
ended only when we all went away to college and had Nixon to be pissed
off at.

Every brother was assigned a nickname calibrated to irritate him. Chris
was "Rake." Jeff believed Chris's face was long and resembled the handle
of a rake. Strangely, the name Rake pissed Chris off even more than the
original appellation Jeff assigned him: "Mike Rosscopick." (Translation:
"Microscopic.")

The shape of brother Dan's head also presented rich comic possibilities to
Jeff. Dan, having a nearly circular head as a youth, was dubbed "Beach Ball."
Beach Ball was what you called Dan if you wanted to make him mad. But

most of the time his name was, mysteriously, "Learbs," for which no etymology exists.

Our littlest brother, Collin, was randomly named "Neil." This made him mad for reasons we never understood, but since it seemed to work we stuck with it. Even the oldest brother, Kip, was assigned a nickname: "Toe-Pay-Deh," the scrambled pronunciation of potato, a shape Jeff maintained precisely described the silhouette of Kip's head. Kip, in turn, noted that Jeff's ears made his head resemble a taxicab with the doors open and dubbed him "Tax." Jeff's friend, Chris Hallenbeck, appreciated the poetry of "Tax" but referred to Jeff as simply "Debbie."

As for me, Chris decided I was "Buggen," a name derived from "Flying Rug" (Sprinters *flew* through the house). It then became "Ruggen" and finally Buggen.

Referring to a big brother by his nickname resulted in "chesties." To give someone chesties you pinned him to the ground with your knees, holding his arms out of the way, and rapped the knuckle of your middle finger on his sternum for ten minutes. It didn't hurt at first but after five minutes of steady rapping it seemed prudent to call your brother by his given name.

Out in the front yard, we played games that hurt people.

In the winter, our front yard became a Currier and Ives print done by Quentin Tarantino. We created a vicious brand of snowball pressed to the density of croquet balls. Creating such ordnance took fifteen minutes of packing and squeezing after which we misted them with water and put them in the freezer for an icy sheen. If a snowball could somehow be made in Hell, this was it. Parking one of these babies between the shoulder blades of a retreating brother was a satisfying experience, and when one of us came in the house crying, within a half hour his parka was back on and he was out in the yard using his anger to squeeze a new snowball to the density of a diamond.

In the summer, we played a short, rule-free version of football called "Smear." The object wasn't getting touchdowns, making passes, or even winning. It was about smearing the guy who had the ball.

Five brothers lined up on one side of the yard and kicked off to a lone brother who—standing way down at the other end of the yard—appeared an inch high and extremely vulnerable. The single offensive player had one shot at getting a touchdown, but this never happened because all games of Smear ended 0-to-0 with somebody crying.

Smear wasn't about the guy who had the ball anyway. The ball itself didn't matter either; he could have been carrying a portable radio. In fact, even if he dropped the radio and tried to run into the house, the defense would pursue because Smear was about landing on a brother with great force. If there was any art or strategy to Smear it was in creating the dog pile that ended the game. Everybody (and his brother, in this case) piled on, sometimes leaping from six feet away until the ball carrier was pressed to groaning breathlessness at the bottom of the heap.

As we grew older, the stakes went up. In 1964, one of us received a BB gun as a birthday gift. (We'd all whetted our appetites for target shooting with Dad's .22-caliber rifle.) After a chorus of whining from the unarmed brothers, another three or four BB guns appeared on the grounds of the Millstone and the Great BB Gun Wars of '64 began. Sometimes there were teams, but allegiances were built on sand. A brother who felt safely part of a group one minute could suddenly become "it" and be peppered with BBs, which stung like wasps.

Somewhere in our sweaty little brains remained a small group of perhaps four or five brain cells that recognized the possible injuries from shooting BB guns at each other. So we called a truce while we designed eye protection. We fashioned masks by bisecting the round plastic tops of gallon jugs of ice cream and fastening the semicircle to our heads with string. But in order to see, we cut eyeholes. That these holes exposed the very thing we were trying to protect never entered our heads. Neither, fortunately, did any BBs.

The little brothers were content to conduct the Great BB Gun Wars in the horse pasture and Low Forty, but Jeff and Chris Hallenbeck took to staging their fights at an abandoned farmhouse. Jeff remembers dashing from window to window shooting at Hallenbeck as he tried to make it across the barnyard, up to the porch, and inside. Out in front, Hallenbeck fell to his knees and screamed, "Oh, God! My eye!" Jeff, white in the face, ran out to help the crouched figure, and at the sound of his footsteps, Hallenbeck brought up his rifle and made it rain copper.

Their Three Stooges *nyuk-nyuk-nyuk* abuse of each other continued long after a truce had been called. Returning home in the car, Jeff shot Chris point blank in the ribs. Later, when Hallenbeck and Jeff were experimenting with methods to take the sting out of the BBs, Jeff tried on a leather jacket, turned his back to Hallenbeck, and told him to shoot. Hallenbeck shot him in the calf.

The stakes were raised yet again when brother Chris discovered that a wooden kitchen match fit snugly down the barrel of a BB gun. The match flew a good fifty or sixty feet and on striking rock, popped like a cap and fell burning to the ground. Experimental launches at the back of a brother's head, though satisfying, never struck fire and the fad soon passed. It did, however, spark a new idea: if a person were to quietly borrow Jeff's bow and arrow and then perhaps tape a cherry bomb to that arrow, might it not make for a pleasant afternoon's diversion? Thus, the Gemini space program was honored in the Sullivan yard with multiple launches of the sleek, exploding rockets. The supply of cherry bombs usually ran out before the arrows, and the remaining arrows were recommissioned for a new game, "The Parabola of Death." In this game, you shot an arrow straight up into the Minnesota sky and then stood there blinking at your brothers—*Where will it land?*—playing chicken with ballistics, gravity, and skull trauma.

The eighty-foot fir trees along the east side of the yard were another source of ordnance. The cones that fell from them had none of the heft or distance of snowballs, and so combatants simply paced off a distance of ten feet and pelted each other. In one cone skirmish (with a local kid named Chris but whom we called "Fudd"), hostilities escalated until Fudd retreated across the road from the Millstone and hid in the sumac. He was out of range of our cones, so I switched artillery and lobbed a golf-ball-sized rock into the bushes.

Most childhood injuries are announced after five seconds of complete silence. So it was with Fudd, and about five seconds after my rock disappeared into the bushes, he began to wail loudly and when he came out he was holding in his hand exactly one half of his big front tooth. Fudd ran home, combatants scattered, and rice-paper-thin alibis were constructed.

I was fingered and though I do not remember my consequences, I recall having a solemn little discussion with an insurance agent where I was deposed on the events leading to Fudd's injury. I don't remember what I said, but looking back I wish I'd confessed, "Yeah? Well, a rock isn't the worst thing I ever whipped at somebody's head anyway. That would be the bowl of my own piss I threw in my brother Chris's face."

All boys fight, but by 1964 the unhappiness and anger that ran through the Millstone seemed to amplify our confrontations. As Dad got sicker and drunker, our fights, once flurries of anger, fanned into daylong rages.

Of the six of us, Chris and I were the most vicious adversaries. When he was thirteen and I nine, my age represented everything Chris had grown out of. He was a Prince. I was just a Sprinter.

Memory: I Am "Little Brother Man"

Little Brother Man's power to create rage in his victims is legendary. Today he uses the popular Copy Cat power.

Chris screams, "Stop saying what I'm saying!"

"Stop saying what I'm saying!" echoes Little Brother Man, now holding a finger one maddening half inch away from Chris's ear.

Chris screams, "Stop touching me!"

"I'm not 'touching' you."

"It doesn't matter! Just stop it!"

"It doesn't matter! Just stop it!"

Little Brother Man did not list force fields among his powers and was pummeled regularly. Once you'd been beaten up and were crying, it was the victor's turn.

"Oh, so you're crrrryyyyyyyying now?" taunts Chris. "Are you gonna go running in your diapers to Mommy?"

As much as you wanted to go to Mommy, honor forbade it. You had to just stand there in the sun and bawl. You tried to move away to recover in private, but a clever adversary would pursue. Just looking at you as you cried would consecrate the victory, bring the rage anew, and through your tears you'd yell, *"Why dontcha come closer so you can get a better look, huh?! YOU WANT A CAMERA?!"*

One of these exchanges led to the Bowl-of-Piss-in-the-Face Incident. Chris had enraged me with some horrible comment I no longer remember and I retreated to brood revenge. Some evil sister to the Muse of Creativity visited and whispered, *"Hey, why not get one of those small metal cereal bowls, you know, the ones up in the cabinet over the sink? Why not get one of those, piss in it, and throw it in his face? . . . I'm just sayin'."*

That this act seemed reasonable to me and that I carried it out is testimony to the level of anger that boiled in the Millstone by the summer of '64.

The same muse must have visited Chris a few weeks later because that summer he came up with the idea of "Poison Ivy Squirt Guns"—a horrid little invention that should be spoken of only in the classic mad-scientist cackle (*"It's aliiiiiiive!"*). To prepare Poison Ivy Squirt Gun solution, Chris donned his mother's dishwashing gloves (*"Playtex living gloves, so thin you can pick up a dime!"*) and went into the hills behind the Millstone. There he harvested a bucket full of the shiny three-leaf plants and brought them back to his mad-scientist laboratory. Perverting a page from his Gilbert Chemistry Set, he poured rubbing alcohol into the bucket and boiled the whole mess down to a solution he hoped would be the essence of poison ivy venom. This he poured into the hole on the stock of a water pistol. The exact formula of Chris's weapon and its effects on citizens has been lost to history, and considering the lessons of Los Alamos, perhaps that is for the best.

The anger that burned in every room of the Millstone in the summer of '64 was also evident in the black turn our humor took. The Ridiculous Films developed special effects that made deaths gorier. It was in '64 that my best friend, John Maynard, and I created the "Horror Club." At school, members of the Horror Club tried to outdo each other drawing the grossest possible torture chambers and dungeons. *("Here's the conveyor belt where you get chopped up and here's where the chunks drop into the vat of boiling goat urine and rat guts.")* Hours and hours of this grim stuff.

Grim, too, were the things we did to our GI Joe doll. Poor old Joe would represent some person who had offended us and for that he had to die. We found a hangin' tree to string 'im up and carefully measured the drop, cutting the string the exact length to stop Joe's ten-foot fall one gory inch above ground. When Joe wasn't "doin' the Air Dance," he'd find himself spread eagle on a dartboard. Today, old Joe is in pieces somewhere in the landfill outside Rochester. But considering the risks taken in our other games, how we, his tormentors, survived is the mystery. Especially after we learned how to light our hands on fire.

We'd discovered that the lighter fluid for Dad's Zippo made an excellent sort of sidewalk pyrotechnic. Spray a line along the walkway, set a match to it, and you had just the kind of movie fuse that whooshed down the mineshaft toward the villain's dynamite. When some fluid spilled on my hands and poofed to flame along with the fuse, the blue fire surrounded my hand and burned briefly on its own fumes before becoming painful. One-sixteenth of a second after learning how to set my hand on fire I learned it could be put out by slamming my hand under an armpit. So armed with this new knowledge, I approached poor old Mrs. Buttert with my hand on fire just to see the look on her face and was amazed to see how fast somebody that overweight could move.

With the Zippo fluid now hidden from us, we turned our scientific energies to other projects. We decided the big tree stump near the garden had to go. Heading into the garden shed for the ax, we came out with a shovel and a gallon of gas. We dug a moat around the stump, filled it with gasoline, and the job foreman struck a match.

"Wait," cried the job safety manager. "Let's water down the area around the gasoline."

As we prudently doused the area with the garden hose and congratulated ourselves on our caution, we didn't notice that the gas simply spread out over the top of the water and now covered the entire garden. This oversight was soon brought to our attention. The whoooosh-explosion could be heard from inside the house, and when Mrs. Buttert looked out the window she saw the four of us through a wall of flame a story high, our images bending like summer taffy in its heat.

Whatever Mrs. Hartman and Jeffreeeeeeeeeeee thought of the huge plume of smoke next door is lost to history. Lost also were four pairs of eyebrows and any memory of how we walked over the lake of flame and escaped the Great Garden Explosion of 1964.

A smaller explosion took place in the basement that summer. I'd determined that the batteries to our toys needed to be recharged. All that was needed was for some enterprising young scientist with buckteeth to figure out a way to pour electricity back into the batteries.

Thesis: If one were to snip off the cord of that old lamp in the basement, strip some insulation to expose the wires, plug it in, and then touch the two live wires to either end of a battery, should not the empty battery simply "fill up"?

Results of experiment: When the battery exploded, the seam of its silver casing was facing away from me and so it was the wall above Dad's workbench that was spattered with hot battery acid, not me. Had the battery's seam been facing other way, this book might well have been titled *The Horrid Face with Buckteeth*.

After a long day of torturing GI Joes, defoliating the garden, and playing with crackling workshop electricity, nothing quite hit the spot like a good cigarette. By 1964, I was in fourth grade and smoking regularly. With two friends, I formed the "LBJ Club" (for Luke, Bill, and John, as well as a tip of the hat to the country's new president). We'd steal our parents' cigarettes and gather behind garages, in culverts, or in barns to smoke.

The act of smoking, of putting flame to dried weeds and taking the toxic gases into my pink fourth grader's lungs, was unnatural, and the first inhalations produced wet coughs forceful enough to resemble regurgitation. Of all the insane things we did at the Millstone, this one came closest to killing us.

The summer barbecue, abandoned to winter.

LEAVING THE MILLSTONE

My father's Mayo Clinic psychiatric record, November 17, 1964
The patient Dr. C. R. Sullivan consulted me on this date regarding marital problems. . . . It would appear that he never drinks during the day but in the evenings when tensions rise, his drinking complicates the total situation.

By the fall of '64, Roger's drunkenness reached a level that even Mom, thick of skin from years of abuse, could no longer bear. The night's booze had begun to linger on Dad's breath when he arrived at work the next morning. His boss, Dr. Mark Coventry, weighed in expressing concern, and now with pressure from two sides, Roger grudgingly agreed to see a Mayo psychiatrist. "But he is very slippery about any promise to stay with him," warned Mom in a letter to Florida.

Two problems made this effort futile. Alcoholics are fabulous and convincing liars. And psychiatrists are not chemical dependency counselors.

Roger lied to his psychiatrist, minimized the amount he drank, and attributed the few thimblefuls he did drink to having a hysterical wife. His psychiatrist believed the lies Roger told him and so his conclusion was essentially written backward. Where the psychiatrist wrote:

But in the evenings when tensions rise, his drinking complicates the total situation.

His logic flow should have been:

But his drinking in the evenings makes tensions rise and the total situation is not complicated . . . dude's an alkie.

There are no records of any subsequent visits Dad made to the psychiatrist and it's likely he broke the promise almost immediately. Given the treatment model of the times, it hardly mattered.

On Thanksgiving Day, 1964, just nine days after the psychiatrist made those notes, Roger's drinking "complicated the situation" again; he went on a bender and we had to leave the Millstone, this time abandoning the holiday turkey on the kitchen counter. The seven of us had our Thanksgiving dinner in the restaurant of the Howard Johnson's hotel downtown and managed to have a good time of it. "It was classic us," remembers Chris. "We didn't know whether to weep or burst out laughing. So we laughed."

The HoJo dining room was empty except for one large, nearly identical family sitting on the other side of the room. No father sat at their table either and we assumed they also were alcohol refugees, sharing what Chris describes as "a sort of generic grief in our culture, but still calling it their family's own." There were stolen looks and the occasional eye lock while we muddled through another broken evening telling jokes, making fun of Dad, and jabbing at our own emotional itinerancy. We relished the dysfunction of it. Being different was cool.

The next day, we crept back into the Millstone and it was quiet. Mr. Hyde was gone and upstairs asleep on the bed in his clothes lay the doctor.

Mom, December 4, 1964
The weekend faces me again, like a nightmare ogre. Only the thought of Monday morning—like a carrot dangling ahead of the poor donkey—sustains me through Saturday and Sunday. Every year the pretense of gay holiday festivities is harder to assume. My poor poor helpless children . . .

The word "divorce" had been said as early as 1958.

"After Collin was born I took him to Florida to see his grandparents," Mom remembers. "Of course, that trip sparked another one of those horrible rages. Even selling the tickets didn't buy peace and he of course purchased them again and forced me to go."

Sitting in an Adirondack chair on the shore of Florida's Lake Winnimesset, she wrote Roger a letter. "It was a long letter. I suggested I would agree to a divorce if that would make him happy," Mom recalled. But upon returning to Rochester, Roger never even mentioned the letter, and looking back now, Mom knew a divorce wasn't ever in the cards. It wasn't written policy, but no Mayo Clinic doctor could expect to retain his job with something as unseemly as a divorce on his résumé.

But by late 1964, Mom finally had had enough. A divorce wasn't going to happen. The psychiatrists hadn't helped. Family friends weren't able to help. Warnings from Dad's boss didn't help. And even though it was school season and midwinter with Christmas just around the corner, Mom realized it was time to leave Roger and move her six boys out of the Millstone. The woman who'd been shamed out of taking music lessons, who'd hidden her five-dollar books while her husband spent hundreds on booze, and who'd stood in a wind tunnel of verbal abuse, finally dug in her heels and said something she regrets to this day.

Myra, 2005
My decision to leave was made in an instant. It came on a night of another ceaseless, tormenting, inescapable, long-into-the-night harangue. I had confined it to the kitchen as I often did. It was more of the same, just hours and hours of his quiet drilling voice, his vicious invective, a poisonous stream of accusations one after another. Along with half-closing my eyes, my only other defense was silence; any attempt at an answer would only inflame him.

I was standing at the sink having all this ugliness dumped on me and when he put down his reloaded glass to go for ice, I swatted it into the sink. This was the first and only violent gesture I ever made. And then in that moment I whispered through clenched teeth, "I hate you so much I could kill you."

I might just as well have shot him. The color left his face and he leaned against the counter and slowly sank to the floor. He looked as if he he'd finally gotten what he'd been waiting for. The horror to me was not so much that I could have said such a thing, but that I could have meant it. I knew right then I had to leave.

Mom in a letter to her parents, December 7, 1964
The first decision is whether anything is to be gained by waiting another day to move out of this house. The prognosis is poor—even under the best of treatment, should he succeed in overcoming it, there are years of psychiatric care to go through—and my children haven't that much time—nor have I. My love for him is dead—and probably irretrievable.

So what does it profit any of us to remain in our present situation? Nothing that I can see, only more damage done to the boys. My decision therefore is to leave this house as soon as possible, enroll at Winona State College and when I am qualified to teach fifth/sixth grade, move to another part of the country. That requires I have the courage to give up this house (which despite all I do dearly love), give up the life of ease I have come to enjoy, face the necessity of going to work, and hope that I have made the best decision for the future well-being of my boys. I hope I have what it takes.

Mom, December 14, 1964
[The letter bears our new address: 2551 13th Ave. N.W.]
Dear Momma and Poppa: So it is done. We moved out of the Millstone on Friday the 11th—from the house where Collin was born, where Luke has lived since he was a month old; in truth, the only home any of them but Kip and Jeff remember. But ever since our first few years there, it has not been a happy home. Perhaps my most serious mistake was in having stayed there so long.

The decision to move out was made a week ago yesterday. While his manner and attitude toward me was not markedly different, his treatment of Kip and Jeff was degenerating rapidly. Every morning they left home in a fury—and arrived back to find him lying in wait for them in the evening. He did not wait for an excuse—but launched out at them with insults the moment they walked in.

Monday night I told him that one of us had to move out. He refused to do it—in the face of every argument I could offer. Wednesday I rented the house and began the necessary payments for utilities. Thursday I arranged with Allied to move us out on Friday.

I wish I could say the boys are happy here—but they are not. They have only their clothes and one or two possessions with them, so there is a feeling of being adrift. And the move itself has been traumatic. They have been fretful and argumentative for two days—it is hard to keep them content even for a few moments at a time. But I hope this will pass.

Each of the six of us reacted differently to the new house. Much of the time it felt fun, like we were on one of our motel retreats. At least we were out of the battleground of the Millstone and our military readiness stood down to DefCon 3. But when the novelty wore off and we looked out at the postage stamp of winter that was our back yard, we realized we weren't vacationers but exiles. We continued to fight as much as ever, but a new camaraderie developed, too. We didn't have our big back yard with the wolfhounds pounding through the snow, we didn't have our regular neighbors, our usual paths through the woods to our friends and our forts. It was just us now.

It might have been this feeling that led me to sit down in my room with Mom's antique quill pen and inkpot to scribe—in "olde tyme" calligraphy—this screed.

DECLARATION OF A NEW HOME

When in the course of human events it becomes nessary to have a family split up, it does not mean we die down in work, chores, and duties. It means we should even work harder and longer. We must work and make this house as strong as it has never been before. It does not mean we argue among ourselves and say this person does your chore or the other guy takes it. It does not mean we be assigned to do all work, but each one do a little bit more and make this house a little bit better!! And if one does not believe this he is not one of this family!!

—Luke Sullivan

I briefly considered charring the edges of this seminal document to give it an authentic precolonial feel but opted instead for a long John Hancockian flourish at the end of my signature. I tacked my Magna Carta to our front door and was sure Mom's reaction would be a sort of Vince Lombardi attaboy fist pump. I was surprised when she came through the door with tears in her eyes. I remember her hugging me in the little living room. I remember feeling the house, for all its deprivations, was safe.

Mom had pulled it off. When the emergency flares hadn't worked, she'd gotten the women and children into the lifeboats and lowered us to safety. But on the very day we left the Millstone, Grandpa became ill. Within a week her brother, Jimmy, would be calling to say, "Perhaps it's time you come to him, Myra."

Christmas, 1963: Mom with one of her cute holiday creations.
Her composure doesn't quite conceal the strain.

"WE'VE ALWAYS LIVED IN THIS CASTLE"

ℐℛ

Mom, December 16, 1964

My good brother Jimmy just phoned to tell me about your illness, Papa. As I told Jimmy, if only I had delayed the move out of the Millstone by two short days I could have found a housekeeper and come to you in Florida. But to leave the boys out here in this little house at this time is out of the question. They are already so very upset by this move that I cannot leave them even for a few days. I hope you will not think me callous—it is a hard choice to make—but I hope you can accept my judgment that I must stay here.

Mom, December 17

Still I have had no word on Poppa's condition. I have just sent a wire hoping it will find you at the hospital. I am concerned for both of you and feel so very far out of contact. I trust you'll call when you receive the wire.

In the mean time, our lives here continue along such as they are. This morning the temperature was 14° below zero. Naturally our cars sitting unprotected on the street would not start. It was 9:00 before the truck arrived to put us in motion. So the boys were all late to school.

You should have seen us in this little house—all in our boots, mittens, caps, coats, ready to run when our cars were started: Kip standing before the stove clock delivering his citizenship speech, Danny & Jeff practicing guitars, Christie showing Collin magic tricks, the dog & the cat caught up in the excitement and chasing one another around the Christmas tree. And I, clomping about in my big boots, trying to get some housework done. Kip shouted out over the hub-bub [referring to the Shirley Jackson book about a house full of crazy people] "We've always lived in this castle!"

People continue to call—to offer their help and sympathy— but truly there is nothing anyone can do. Two have invited us for Christmas Day dinner, but of course that is a day I would not go anywhere.

By Christmas Day, Myra would in fact travel fifteen hundred miles. Just as we were settling in for as normal a holiday as we could muster, her brother, Jimmy, called to say a stroke had landed RJL in the hospital; he could not speak or move, his vital signs were not good, and no matter what her circumstances were in Rochester, Jimmy said, it was time to come.

The next train to Florida left at noon and Myra had just one hour for emotional triage. Since none of us lay dying, the choice seemed clear and so on the way out the door to the train station, she handed the reins to Kip and Jeff with orders to "make Christmas happen" for the little ones. But within a day Kip and Jeff decided to strike the tents and move the family back to the Millstone for the week. They packed it all up: the Christmas tree, the pets, and the bags of unwrapped presents Mom had hidden in the basement. We moved back into the drunk's castle for a Christmas not one of us remembers. There's blank spot in our collective recall. We have photos of Christmas '63; films of Christmas '65; but of '64, nothing but a single image.

Where our father was on that Christmas morning none of us can recall; we know only he wasn't with us. There was no tree either. (Dad had "sent away" the tree Kip had brought from the little house, lashed to the roof of the Plymouth. "She" had picked it out.) What we *do* remember of Christmas morning, 1964, is the six of us gathered in our parents' empty bedroom standing in our pajamas around a pile of bags full of unwrapped gifts. As we pawed our way through the pile guessing at what was whose, nobody looked up from our business to ask, "Isn't this weird?" None of us wondered if the neighbors' kids weren't also pawing through bags of unwrapped gifts in their parents' empty bedroom. This is just the way it was at the Millstone. If there was trauma it was limited to seven-year-old Collin, whose belief in Santa Claus was surprised that morning the way Sonny Corleone was surprised at the tollbooth in *The Godfather*.

. . .

As we sit in the study of my mother's little Minneapolis house discussing Christmas of 1964, it's clear her decision to leave for Florida still troubles her.

"You couldn't do everything, Mom," I tell her. She shakes her head, says, "But still."

She holds one of the books bound years ago by her father. Burned into the spine in silver-colored ink is RJL's script identifying the year: 1964. The volume is thicker than previous years, the letters more numerous now; she no longer cared what Roger thought of her letter writing. The letters here begin to take on a gallop, one after another, reeling out the story: her unraveling marriage, her collapsing husband, her disintegrating life, and of course her Christmas trip to Florida.

Grandpa had finally recovered and when he was released from the hospital on Christmas Day, Myra took the train back to Rochester.

Mom, now back in Rochester, December 29, 1964
I unpacked, took a bath, cleaned up the little house, and even took a nap. I could not go get the little ones at the Millstone because the two big boys (asleep in the basement) still had the car loaded from a Pagans' engagement the night before. It was nearly noon when Kip and Jeff came upstairs and my little ones had been calling from the Millstone every 15 minutes to ask when they could "come home." When Kip and Jeff left, it was 10° below. At the Millstone, they loaded the car to the roof with mattresses and blankets and Christmas gifts and dirty clothes, one cat and my 6 boys.

You know with what joy I greeted them all again. We had a peculiar supper, being without an ice-box here, but we were all so happy no one noticed.

Grandpa [transcribed as is]
dear chn here goes foran expriment—typing wyth my right frtrfingrt and i bet i make so mzny mistakes that yt will bw herder to read than my usul spastic scrawrl. . . . appetite reamins ok. and if your t-v carrisx the same cultursl ads as does ours, you will understand me when i say that carters littlr liver pills or ex-lax produce desirable results. your mother sez i am showing more skill in the use of my walker. but i declare to you that progfrtess seems a bit slow. i cannot use my right hand at all, but enuff of this tripe.

Mom's letters to her parents, December 30, 1964

Tomorrow is New Year's Eve. The Pagans are on stage somewhere, so I will see the last of 1964 with my four little ones. And glad I am to see the last of '64—the most miserable year of my life. But "things are looking up"—so I am welcoming '65.

Tonight Danny has a friend to spend the night with him. And Kip brought his Linda home about 8:30. We all watched the "Danny Kaye Show" and then sat in the living room eating candy and talking—in the middle of which Collin got out of bed (hearing Linda, whom he loves), Christie took a bath, Danny & his friend were playing guitars, the dishwasher spurted water all over the kitchen floor and the bathroom doorknob mysteriously locked itself (the punch-in-the-middle variety), requiring the concerted and individual efforts of all of us with a tiny screwdriver to open it again. ("We've always lived in this castle!") But dear heaven, it was fun and relaxed and fearless and happy!

The Millstone in winter.

HAUNTED HOUSE

❧

It is midwinter—January 1965—and the sun is setting.

The driveway gate to the Millstone is open and the two Irish wolfhounds have run away.

Snowfall has gathered unplowed for a month and almost entirely blocks the driveway. Chris, thirteen, is sitting on the stone gateposts at the end of the driveway, looking at the house he used to live in. A scarf covers his mouth. Of the six boys, he is the one who looks most like his father: aquiline nose and intelligent eyes that have a dark and haunted look—like the windows in the house at the end of the driveway.

No one knows Chris is here. He'd simply walked out of the little house in Elton Hills, trekked the six miles over back roads through Rochester, and arrived in his old neighborhood as darkness fell. He wants to look at the Millstone for a while, but the ten degrees below drives him in.

He's pretty sure his father is not here or the sporty little British MG would be parked out front. The front door is unlocked and he enters. His feet crunch on something. In the dim light it's hard to tell if the dried puke is from one of the wolfhounds or his father.

There is trash everywhere, with no overturned garbage can nearby to explain it. This trash has been dropped right where it is—aluminum trays of Swanson TV dinners, empty bottles of mixer, a china cup with coffee dried to a lacquer. Across the room in the dog bowl, Chris sees the wolfhounds have been fed Cheerios. The empty cereal box, too, has simply been tossed to the floor. It is a mess that looks *angry,* a home vandalized by its owner.

Chris walks through the kitchen to the pantry and clicks on the light. The red-and-white cans of soup on the middle shelf are gone, moved to the Elton Hills house along with almost everything else. But there's a can of corned beef hash he could heat, and abandoned out on the porch Chris finds a frozen can of Coca-Cola with its newfangled pull-ring top. He takes his dinner to the living room, builds a fire, and after opening the cans, sets them near the flames.

As they warm, he watches his shadow dance across a strange living room. There's a reading lamp but no chair to read in. Where the sofa was are four square imprints in the carpeting; its absence gives the matching coffee table an unmoored look.

The corned beef hash is passable, but the Coke is without fizz and he sets it down. He goes up to his old room and lies on the plywood frame where his mattress used to be. As the coals settle in the fireplace downstairs, he falls asleep under his coat. His father never comes home that night.

While our parents were separated, all six of us took trips back to the Millstone; sometimes together, sometimes alone. We'd walk around the place like it was a crime scene, and even with winter sunshine pouring white through the windows, the feeling in every empty room was "something bad happened here."

We'd visit during the day, running over from school during lunch period so we wouldn't risk meeting Dad. To see what, we weren't sure; to dig through our disassembled rooms perhaps; a bit of childhood archaeology. There is a sadness to the detritus of a separated household. Each particular thing, even in its correct place, has a discarded look. Everyday objects like a pen in a drawer, or a pair of ice skates in the entryway, feel abandoned. This spatula on the kitchen floor, is it Dad's spatula now? Mom's? Ours?

We were angry at Dad for betraying and exiling us, so we came for mischief as much as curiosity. During one of these lunchtime visits, Chris and I went through the house and tilted every framed picture on the walls a few degrees to the left. We hoped Dad would return home, mix a stiff one, and seeing the ever-so-slightly canted pictures wonder, "Ye gads, has at last the drink turned on me?" We poured out bottles of Old Grand-Dad, went though his *Playboy* magazines, and picked through the rooms of any brother who wasn't with us. After lunch, we'd return to school where Mom would take us back to the tiny house in Elton Hills.

Had we not been born into a home like the Millstone, it's likely we'd have been happy in the Elton Hills house. It was an honorable dwelling. It's still there on Thirteenth Avenue and has likely been nest to several generations of happy children. But as refugees from the Millstone we felt the crunch of space, the loss of privacy.

On the first floor at Elton Hills, Mom had one of the two bedrooms and Collin and I shared the other. The unfinished basement was one large room and the older four each claimed a corner as his own, with the backs of dressers and footboards of beds indicating where one room ended and another began.

That Roger could sleep at night while exiling his wife and six children to a tiny house is testimony to the miracles of fine charcoal mellowing in the sugar-maple barrels of Kentucky distilleries. But now, with nobody to argue with when he came to, he began driving out to the Elton Hills house to pick fights. And the phone calls began. Hundreds of phone calls.

Entries from Kip's diary, February and March 1965
Dad called six times. Mom doesn't know what's next.... Dad over here. One more try at reconciliation. Mom and Dad can't even talk. He just bitched about the car situation and money.... Dad called for seventh time at 10 at night, "just to talk." Poor lonely bastard.... Dad has been bitching about Mom's reading. How it "hurt the family." Christ.

Mom, January 22, 1965
I will not go back to Roger yet. I have had enough experience with these periods of abjection to know that they are short-lived. I cannot live with him until some very fundamental changes are made in him. I simply cannot step back into that chaotic, violent, senseless life.

Mom, February 5
At no moment since December 11th have I had even a flicker of regret over leaving or a beam of hope I could live with him again. I am no longer (except spasmodically) angry or disgusted or outraged— my foremost emotion toward him is tiredness. I'm tired of trying to deal with him, tired of hearing the same stuff over and over again, tired of shaking off the clinging, whining, consuming dependence. Tired *tired tired*!!! And I wish I could decide what to do. If I were dealing with just a sorry marital situation, I would get a divorce and be done with it. But I am tangled with a psychiatric problem and such decisive action might threaten my economic security and the futures of my boys. There are so many decisions to make.

Mom, February 10

I have got to force this situation. He called yesterday to say he was done "jumping through hoops," that it was "high time I quit having my way" and that he was getting a divorce and keeping the house. Like it or not, I am going to force him to sell that house so that I can buy a house with the minimum amount of space for these boys to live in.

Mom, March 15

Thursday morning at 10:30 I have an appointment with the lawyers to hear them explain why they think ¼ of Roger's salary is adequate for seven people to live on.... When I consider how breathlessly busy I am hour by hour every day, I wonder how I can handle a steady job—a problem I may not have to face very soon since I am having no luck at all finding work. If I had ability to write short-hand it'd be much easier to find stenography work. I have brought home my shorthand text and will review it until such time as I can get a course started.

From Grandpa's letters, April 16

Do not give up. A way will open.

If divorce law seems unfair today, in the 1960s it was worse. Somehow an Olmsted County judge was able to keep a straight face when he awarded my mother just one quarter of Roger's salary—one-fourth of the money to house, feed, and clothe seven-eighths of the family. Unable to find a stenography job, Myra temped for the U.S. Census Bureau and then one day came home to discover that the Elton Hills house was being sold. She had to move the family again.

"I simply could not find a place for the seven of us at any figure I could afford," she remembers. "There seemed to be nothing left to do except to crawl, humiliated, back to the Millstone."

From Grandpa's letters

Your wire of last evening was troubling, indeed. Perhaps the return to the 'Stone has the advantage of a three-month playground for the boys. Otherwise, one fears the effect on you.

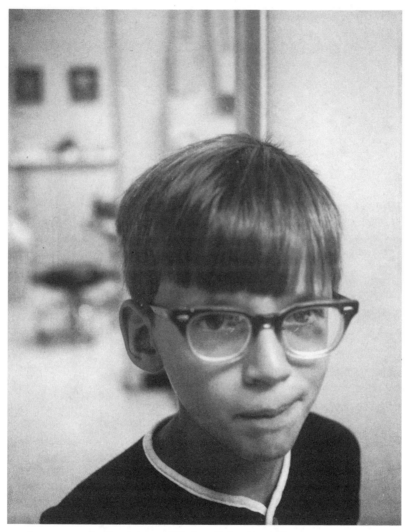

August 25, 1965: Coming out of Dr. Lund's dentistry office with half my face numb.

CEILING TILES OVER A
PSYCHIATRIST'S COUCH

ꙮ

I cried two times that spring. The first was when I heard that Stan Laurel of our Laurel and Hardy films had died.

The snows were melting in Elton Hills, running off the great hill where the convent still frowns over the small houses of north Rochester. I'd come indoors from snow-damming the cold waters as they came in freshets down the edges of Thirteenth Avenue and was warming up in my bedroom when Jeff leaned in and told me Stan Laurel was dead.

Something happy and good was taken from my world in that minute. Let fathers be assholes, I thought, let families suffer; but the empty space where this gentle clown had been, who had babysat the six of us on a hundred popcorn Saturday nights, could not be filled. Minnesota Aprils are all gray and mud and now with an uncertain summer months away it may as well have been November.

Perhaps it was the chill in my soul that spring that led me to steal some colorful packs of spring flower seeds from the local grocery store. Perhaps I was showing rebellion. Or perhaps I was just a larcenous fifth grader with sticky fingers. Whatever the reason, there I was, bookended by two store clerks back in the manager's office, in tears and calling my mother to come bust me out of the joint.

Mom, who had given up any hope of mapping the demons in Dad's psyche, wasn't about to let one of her sons grow any new ones of his own. And so the week we moved back into the Millstone she took me to the Mayo Clinic, and I had my first look at the ceiling tiles over a psychiatrist's couch.

From notes of Mayo Clinic psychiatrists
Drs. Delano and Morse, May 11, 1965
INTERVIEW WITH MOTHER: Mrs. Sullivan states the main complaint is that Luke has been taking things from his brothers

and denying it for the past year. He was caught stealing flower seeds from a store and finally broke down and cried about it, one of the few times he has cried and told her he didn't know why he'd done it—though one reason he gave was they were to be a birthday gift for his father.

Mother emphasized she and her husband also have seen and are seeing psychiatrists. When I asked if she had any idea about why Luke was doing this stealing, she said she knew little about psychiatry but thought perhaps he might be searching for security, going on to state he is involved in a very unpleasant family situation and has been for most of his life. When I asked her to elaborate on this, she said, of course I was getting only her viewpoint on the problem and she was sure she was partly to blame but also that her husband was probably paranoid and there has been a severe marital problem for the last seven or eight years. She described this as severe emotional violence at home, which included drunkenness and fighting.

Chiefly verbal attacks, she says, with no physical violence although the husband may go on with his foul language and verbal lashing for up to six or seven hours at a time. He says ugly, obscene, and untrue things about her and in the past two or three years has said these things in front of the children. Things such as: she was really no woman at all, she has no normal sexual urges, that she "couldn't earn 25 cents by spreading her legs," that she is abnormally attached to her father, that she is stupid, and reads the wrong books, that she keeps the household in a chaotic state, that she cannot manage money, etc. In December of 1964, "he drove me out" and this was chiefly due to his rantings about her lack of sexual interest. This abuse was occurring in front of the two older boys, and she finally, after threatening to leave, did walk out.

This drunkenness has interfered at times with his work and he has been unable to report for work on occasion. He apparently has been encouraged very strongly by his Section Chief to get psychiatric help, otherwise his job is in danger. She began seeing [adult psychiatrist] Dr. Steinhilber about a year ago and has continued to do so. She candidly admits she is now a very "stony" and cold person and is sure . . . she is a "different person now than ten years ago." She is more determined now but before she would always do what was the best thing for her husband. He has told her since their marriage that she wasn't good enough for him and she said she believed him for the first part of their marriage. She believed for some time it was all her fault and withdrew from her friends and became depressed. At the present, she has no sexual urge at all for Roger and this is one of their problem areas. She says she has gone from one extreme to the other and is very determined now to do things she wants to do whether her husband wishes it or not.

A break in the psychiatric records, then my session begins:

Luke is a ten-year-old fifth grader, rather short, horn-rimmed glasses, big teeth, and quite a deep voice for a boy his age.

When I asked him if he knew why he was here today, he said yes, and after some hesitation said he had been taking things. The only reason he gave for stealing was that they were "things I don't have."

He was quite guarded in telling me about other things he had taken. He mentioned taking stamps from his brother's collection at one time but then said it "wasn't really his fault." He then mentioned taking ten cents from another brother—"But that was two years ago." Throughout this part of the interview, he was continually looking around the room surveying things.

About his dad, he said, "He is a doctor who works on West-6 at the Clinic and I think he is 43 years old and sure gets enough bills. I suppose he told you about his drinking? He is nice and he gives me a good job and allowance, and a room. He has a room with Mom. He likes to go on trips and goes out with Jeff with their rifles to shoot at targets."

While he was sketching a picture, he asked me if I knew his dad, to which I said I hadn't been able to talk with him yet. I asked if he would like to be a doctor when he grew up and he said "I would like the money" but he didn't think he would like to "look inside of guys."

RECOMMENDATION: His parents clearly have severe marital strife. They are attempting to resolve some of this with psychiatric help. Suggest watchful waiting in that Luke shows little in the way of disturbing signs besides the stealing.

Memory: I Am "Quiet Man"

Every night my little brother puts on a Beatles record and sings himself to sleep, rocking back and forth on his bed in a trance. Dad won't let Mom put us to bed anymore so the rocking is my little brother's lullaby to himself. But the singing, that's his fantasy. He is singing himself to a better place; he's probably onstage at The Ed Sullivan Show. *But in my fantasy, down here on the carpeting of my little brother's dark bedroom, I am "Quiet Man."*

Quiet Man's superpower is ninja stealth. For the last fifteen minutes I have been slowly crawling through the dark toward my goal: to hide directly under Collin's bed. He will never know Quiet Man is in the room with him.

Quiet Man knows precisely what he is doing. He times each carpet-burning inch forward to a lilt of John-and-Paul harmony, rubs his itchy nose at Ringo's cymbal crash. No one is more silent than Quiet Man. He could move under a librarian's nose and make it all the way to the card catalog and never show up on her radar.

Chicks dig Quiet Man.

When you get right down to it, though, Quiet Man's supersilence is sort of a Woolworth's five-and-dime superpower. He can't really do anything once he's arrived wherever he's sneaking to. He just sort of lies there under the bed or behind the couch. It has another drawback: nobody ever says, "Look, down on the carpeting! It's Quiet Man!" Best he ever gets is, "I think I just heard something."

Collin hates it when Quiet Man invades his privacy like this. If I crawl over a crinkly candy wrapper and reveal myself, he sits up in the dark and screams down at the floor.

"Get out of my room!"

Quiet Man also uses denial; he doesn't answer, doesn't move. Like the Devil, his greatest trick is to convince you he doesn't exist.

"I know you're down there! Get out!"

But John and Paul pick up a new beat. "'CAUSE I DON'T CARE TOO MUCH FOR MONEY. MONEY CAN'T BUY ME LOVE." It's too infectious a song for Collin to let pass. He doesn't want to get out of bed, feel his way across the room, and set the phonograph needle back at the beginning of the song. So he warns the darkness, "You better not be there!" and resumes his singing and rocking back and forth.

"I MAY NOT HAVE A LOT TO GIVE, BUT WHAT I GOT I'LL GIVE TO YOU."

Quiet Man has finally made it under the bed. The springs of Collin's mattress now creak rhythmically, inches from my face. There is a kind of cocoon safety to hiding under your little brother's bed at night. Nobody knows where you are. And you know your little brother is safe, too.

The Millstone gates at night.

THINGS THAT WERE
SCARIER THAN DAD

⁂

We used to play an incredibly scary version of hide-and-seek called "Beaster." It was the last organized game any of us remember playing with Dad before he went over the edge.

It was always played at night. To begin a game of Beaster the six brothers would scatter through the four floors of the Millstone and extinguish every light. Wherever you were when the last light went out, the game began.

My father, armed with a rolled-up newspaper, was now waiting for you somewhere on one of the four floors of the huge house. His job was to whack you with the newspaper. Your job was to not make a high wailing girlie scream when his form loomed out of the darkness and the whacking began.

So you crept through the Millstone looking for a hiding place. The Minnesota winter banished any thought of escaping the game by going outside. There were thirty rooms to hide in, but most were too scary to be in all alone. After a half hour of hiding in a distant hallway closet, part of you wanted to give up and run screaming and public through the house and just get it over with. Eventually, though, you tiptoed past the dead end of the music room to the relative safety of the living room.

It was in the living room where my last game of Beaster ended.

I'd made it to the red chairs near the fireplace and tucked myself into a small triangle of space behind the back of the chair and the corner of the room. It was a good place to hide but offered no escape if you were discovered. On the far side of the living room was the stereo amplifier (or the "hi-fi," as we called it then). From where I hid in the corner I could see its little orange on-light, the only illumination in the room and a sort of lighthouse, a reminder that the room was the way I remembered it in sunshine.

As I looked at this light I listened, trying to hear Dad's footsteps overhead; listening for the discovery of one of my brothers and the high girlie scream that would surely follow. I fixated on the little orange light and waited; listened.

That's when I saw something begin to move *between* my hiding place and the hi-fi. The little orange light, my connection to the world, went out—was blocked out—and I began to scream like a teeny little girl.

At work, office employees get free coffee. Bone doctors—they get free skeletons.

"Roger is now lecturing down at the boys' school on an appropriate Halloween subject, the skeleton," wrote my mother in October 1959. "He brought it from his office and it now stands in lonely dignity in the Music Parlor, lending a rare atmosphere of horror to the gleefully told ghost stories Kip and Jeff concoct."

This skeleton was the real thing. It wasn't made out of plastic; it was made out of a person. To preserve it for medical study, the bones had been dipped in shellac and they all bore tiny ink markings, as if the worms that had picked them clean left notes, like food critics.

During the day, we little ones had nervous fun with the skeleton, making it wave its hand at the passing dog (or perform some worse indignity). But at night, the skeleton exacted revenge simply by standing there in the moonlight, dangling from its support pole in all its clickety marionette horror.

What made the skeleton especially frightening wasn't so much its toothy gravestone grin or the twin dark crypts of the eyes. It was the idea that it was once a living person, a man, with a name.

"It used to be . . . a reeeeallll guy," Jeff told us, leaning in for effect. "It's Kevinnnnnnn . . ."

One of our favorite ghost stories was W. W. Jacobs's "The Monkey's Paw." But the ghost story Kip and Jeff told that night at the foot of the skeleton (the feet rather) used the great size of the surrounding Millstone and its thirty rooms to good effect.

"It happened one night in a house just like this one," Jeff would say with a gesture to the rooms looming around us. He probably cribbed the plot from a *Twilight Zone* (none of us remembers now), but he expertly adapted the story to happen in our own house and to a man who could've been our father: *". . . a famous photographer, who once lived all alone in a big house."*

And this photographer, he had a darkroom downstairs in the basement, just like Dad has here. So, one night he's down in the darkroom developing pictures and he's got the radio on listening to music when the announcer comes on: "We interrupt this program to bring you a news bulletin. A convicted murderer has just escaped from the local mental hospital."

This wasn't just any murderer. No, this was "Ol' One-Eye," a psycho with a birth defect that left a huge black hole where his left eye should've been . . . kinda like Kevin's eyehole right here. Aaaanyway, the thing is, after Ol' One-Eye murdered his victims, he GOUGED OUT their left eye and ATE IT, always hoping that it would help him grow a new eye.

Well, since the famous photographer guy is all alone in the big old house, the news is too scary, so he just turns the radio off. But now in the silence, somewhere overhead, he hears a footstep. Just one footstep. Someone's in the house with him.

He realizes that to call for help, he's gonna have to make his way up to the kitchen where the phone hangs on the wall. As he starts creeping out of the darkroom he hears the footsteps overhead again. But this time the steps seem to be coming from farther away, the sound quieter. The guy thinks, God, please let him be leaving the house.

He finally makes it up the stairs to the phone and just before he dials, he stops to listen. There's no sound anymore and he notices the front door is standing wide open. He quickly dials the police department and next thing you know the whole driveway is just full of cop cars with lights flashing and police are everywhere with guns drawn. They go through the entire house . . . but find nothing.

Later, out on the front steps as the squad packs up to leave, the photographer walks up to the lieutenant and apologizes for the false alarm. The lieutenant guy, he just brushes it off, says no big deal, and then the photographer goes, "Hey, as a favor, what say I take a professional portrait of you and the squad? You know, to put up back at the precinct?"

The cop says sure, why not, and soon the whole squad is lined up on the front steps of the old house, posing with hands on gun belts. He takes a few pictures but they're no good because none of the cops is smiling.

"Come on, you guys, smile."

The cops finally all light up and he gets his picture. "I'll develop it and bring it downtown first thing tomorrow, okay?" He waves. "Thanks again, everybody."

The cops all drive away and the guy goes back inside. This time he locks the door.

Back down in the darkroom, he starts developing the pictures. He exposes the best negative, the one with all the smiles, and drops the photographic paper into the tray of developing chemicals. He watches the image slowly form.

Yep, there's the lieutenant, standing in front with a big smile. And there are all the cops lined up by the front door. They're all smiling too. Perfect. He got the shot.

And that's when he notices it.

Up high in the dark, just beyond the lights of all the cop cars, looking down from the attic window is a white face. It has only one eye. The worst part is, the face is looking right at the camera. And it too is smiling.

At the Millstone, the food chain went like this: big brothers scared the bejesus out of little brothers and never the other way around.

Our father had set the bar quite high for scaring the family. So to truly horrify a little brother, you had to do something so frightful you could make his little bottom slam shut hard enough to snap a pencil.

At the top of the food chain was our oldest brother, Kip. He was an Eagle Scout. And given his proficiency at scaring the bejesus out of me, he must have had a merit badge somewhere, one embroidered with the icon of a fifth grader and Jesus bursting out of his chest.

Kip's best early work was a minimalist piece, thrown together really, a forerunner of Christo, come to think of it. He draped himself in one of Mom's dark tablecloths and stood outside in the night wind in the middle of the yard, motionless. He'd arranged for his coconspirator, Jeff, to casually mention to me, "Go out and get Kip 'cause *Bonanza's* almost on." A quick sprint around the Millstone brought me screeching to a cartoon halt in front of the dark ghost. That it didn't move, rattle Marley's chains, or say even "Boo" made the specter all the more horrifying. It just stood there. I did not.

Chris was the next to win a merit badge in scaring the bejesus out of a little brother.

It was a cloudless night in September 1963. Mom and Dad were hosting a Mayo Clinic party and Chris and I were outside. The Millstone was lit like a ship on dark water, and from an open window on the deck came Erroll Garner on piano and the sound of grown-ups laughing at grown-up things.

Eavesdropping, then losing interest, we wandered away from the house and decided to climb the crab apple tree at the far end of the driveway. Reaching the top we settled on branches to view the stars.

Chris began to talk quietly. Just some thoughtful big-brotherish musings about the heavens—how far away stars were, how unchanging the constellations. Then his talk drifted to some "recent scientific exploration." For instance, this new thing scientists were studying. "Have you heard about the Horrid Light?" asked Chris.

"The Horrid what?"

"Nah, never mind."

"No, tell me about this . . . this Horrid Light thing. Actually, I think I did hear about it."

I shifted on my branch.

"Well, apparently . . ."

And it was the way he lilted the word "apparently" that did the trick. "Apparently" meant "Personally, I'm not sure about this, but scientists in white lab coats said it and who are we to question men with short haircuts?"

"Apparently" meant there were very likely remaining horrors out there, beyond drunken fathers yelling in the night; horrors undiscovered, even uncategorized. New nightmares to pile on top of all the other fully documented menaces to life and happiness at the Millstone.

"Apparently," he went on, "there is a single star up there that once every, I don't know, million years or so sends out a disintegrating ray that just *fries* you."

"Disin . . . a what?"

"Well, and again, I'm only summing up what I've heard, but apparently, it's like a bolt of lightning that's . . . sort of straight, like a ray, that comes down from this one star. The good thing, though, is that it only happens about once every million years."

The trick to achieving pencil-snapping horror in a fifth grader was to raise the threat level, lower it ever so slightly . . . and then strike without mercy. The timing must be perfect; his was.

Seconds after assuring me that people were turned into bacon only once every million years, he said, *"Oh, Jesus, that's the star! Right there! I see the Horrid Light! It's coming!"* He leapt out of his perch, dropped the story and a half onto the soft lawn below, and ran into the warmth of the safe and distant house—leaving me alone, stuck high in a tree like an hors d'oeuvre on a toothpick served up to an interstellar horror traveling toward me at 186,000 miles per second.

I jumped.

Falling, I felt a prickle between my shoulder blades where I was certain the Horrid Light would strike. The Horrid Light would then travel through my body, exiting my anus to start a fire on the grass below where my body would land with whatever thump my sixty-five pounds might make.

Falling, I realized I would die in the air and not have even the final dignity of being able to brace my feet on the ground for death's impact and perhaps allow myself to collapse with some sort of plan. I would be simultaneously dead and in motion, with no say in the position they'd discover my body.

I landed, lived, and while trying to outrun the speed of light realized Chris had pulled one over on me.

Once back in the presence of the adults' party and unable to retaliate, I consoled myself by giving Chris an especially radioactive version of the hairy eyeball. It hardly mattered. He'd heard me snap the pencil and it was game, set, match.

Chris probably got the idea for the Horrid Light while watching *The Twilight Zone* with Rod Serling. The television show appealed to our dark little souls and we watched it every week. In fact, watching it with my brothers was a sine qua non; it was too scary to watch alone. (My preferred viewing option would have been in Grand Central Station at high noon surrounded by concentric circles of exorcists and army guys.)

But one night I watched it all by myself.

Mom and Dad were out for the night and my brothers were scattered throughout the Millstone, doing homework, playing records—they were around somewhere but not with me. I was down in the basement fallout shelter with the black-and-white TV.

And Rod Serling.

It was the famous episode "Nightmare at 20,000 Feet" in which passenger William Shatner sees a horrible gremlin out on the wing of his passenger jet. I made it most of the way through the episode but in the third act, when the thing appeared directly outside Shatner's window, I cracked and ran out of the basement room with a low moan.

The scariest part was having to turn my *back* on the TV, to make for the door that led upstairs. As any fifth grader knows, that's when it gets you. It was common knowledge that the retreating, unprotected backs of fifth graders in flight were the Devil's dartboard. The Devil must've missed because I made it upstairs to the kitchen. But before I could even catch my breath I realized I had to go back down. I'd left the TV turned on and would get in trouble with Dad if he discovered it. And so back down into the fallout shelter I crept, armed this time with big brother Kip's hockey stick. I had a plan.

I came back around the corner into the room where the TV was now broadcasting a commercial for Kent cigarettes and their Micronite filters. The commercial, I knew, was only temporary. At any moment it might end and the horrible image of the thing on the wing would be back and with it, of course, the Devil's hands reaching out of the screen for me—for a little bonbon, a sweet something before bed.

My plan was to use Kip's hockey stick to push in the TV's off-button, giving me a full five-step head start on whatever it was that was going to come shrieking out of the screen. Creeping toward the TV, I held the stick out in front of me, closer,

closer,

until the tip

touched the off-button

and I pushed it in.

—click—

When you turned off one of the old black-and-white TVs, the picture slowly collapsed into a white dot. A dot that lingered on the screen as the tubes inside ticked and cooled. It was the dot itself I found terrifying. I looked at this horrible white window into Hell and realized I had just angered the thing on the wing and even Rod Serling was probably pissed. I was looking at the white period at the end of my life. That little dot in the middle of the TV screen was the scariest thing I'd seen that night. Snap went the pencil and up the stairs I fled into the arms of my Sweet, Sweet Jesus.

The Millstone was an old house. And there was no place in it that was not scary. The basement fallout shelter had the evil white dot and Rod Serling. Then there was the attic. It was in the attic that brother Jeff earned his merit badge.

Even the word "attic" scared us three youngest boys. We'd sit up in bed at night and experiment with the word's power, whispering it into the dark just to feel our flesh crawl.

"Aaaaattic."

I think there's a law somewhere that says attics must be lit by fifteen-watt bulbs exclusively. Their wan light was just enough to let you think you could see, while leaving shadows black enough to obscure even the whitest fangs. Fifteen-watt bulbs were like evil lighthouses falsely placed to direct ships onto rocks.

Illuminating the Millstone's attic was an especially dim bulb we were all certain must have been a rare fourteen-watter. It dangled on an ancient cloth-covered wire descending from the high dark of the attic's wigwam ceiling. I stood one night under this light with my brother Jeff. I'd agreed to come only because I was with a big brother, one armed with a flashlight.

But the big draw was what Jeff confided he'd found there. He'd discovered the one artifact fifth-grade archaeologists seek above all others: the Holy Grail of pith-helmet-wearin' kids with buckteeth—a mummified dead animal that still had guts in it.

"It musta crawled in here this summer," intoned Jeff, his shadow leaping ahead of him into the far corner. "It died and it's still way down there."

Only the Millstone could have a "way down there" in the attic.

Behind the chimney in the attic, where it finished its four-story climb through the house, was a deep hole in the floor that dropped ten or fifteen feet down into perfect darkness. Whether it was a contractor's mismeasurement that had created this column of dead air down the spine of the Millstone or simply a crenellation in the complicated plans of the old house, there it was. And we called it the Hole.

When you looked down the Hole, you were chin to chin with the Abyss. Jeff shone his flashlight beam down its gut and the Hole ate it. The Hole took the dim light of the flashlight and shushed it like you would a baby in church. Shamed it. There was only blackness.

Jeff said, "There it is. I can *just* see it."

"Just see what?"

"There."

My eyes were adjusting and now I could see that the flashlight fell on the top rung of what seemed to be a ladder leading down into the Hole.

"Mmmm. That ladder won't hold me," observed Jeff. "I'm *way* too heavy," said the 110-pound-soaking-wet eleventh grader. "But you . . . you're perfect."

Nothing felt better to fifth graders than being informed you were somehow special. Your hunger for compliments of any kind allowed older brothers to use you in all kinds of ways. They could make you run down four flights of stairs to grab them a Coke and run all the way back up just by saying. "You're the fastest runner here, no question about it." Compliments were like the crack of the race starter's gun—*Pow!*—and you were off, doing what only you were uniquely qualified to do.

Now that I was being told my lithe, aerodynamic physique was the final key to the discovery of the Holy Grail, my foot was on the ladder. I began my descent into the Hole. The well-established inverse-square law of light states that the brightness of light is inversely proportional to the square of the distance from its source. This maxim would seem also to explain the proportion to which the buttocks of fifth-graders squinch ever tighter as they move farther away from the lights of civilization, be they lonely campfires, distant porch lights, or flashlights held by big brothers as you descended into the Hole.

As I felt my shanks tighten, I would test the umbilical cord between Jeff and me, throwing falsely conversational questions back up the ladder.

"So . . . what kind of animal you think? A squirrel?"

Down the Hole came Jeff's terse "Probably."

"Oh. A squirrel, you say? . . . Makes sense."

"Yep." More distant now.

Neil Armstrong had not set foot on the moon yet, but the similarity of my P.F. Flyer touching the gravel surface of the Hole's bottom is noted here. Simply to have made it down the ladder, grail or no grail, was an event I thought worthy of a cover story in *Jesus Christ, You Did WHAT??* magazine.

"I'm here. I see gravel. Just gravel."

"Try over there," said Jeff, directing his light to the area where he'd placed the gizzard, liver, and neck bone of a chicken Mom was preparing for dinner that night.

"WOW! It's here!" I said. "It's really here!"

"No kidding?" said Jeff. "Lemme see, lemme see."

I directed his attention to the small mess in the corner.

"Wait a minute," said Jeff. *"That's no squirrel. Those are pieces of a human being! There's a dead guy down there!"*

He snapped off the flashlight, strode back through the attic, and before closing the door, extinguished the fourteen-watt bulb, leaving me in an interstellar blackness of such velvet even a visit from the Horrid Light would have been welcome.

Dreadful things lurked on the grounds of the Millstone.

Fathers who raged for entire three-day weekends were certainly dreadful. And though the horrible things he said made you grow up fast, in the end you were still just eleven years old and what you really worried about was whether your friends thought you were cool or not. Or being seen naked, by girls. You worried about things that had sharp teeth, like the Dobermans owned by the Plunketts or the water moccasin in Grandpa's pond down in Florida.

Closer to home was the giant snapping turtle Sam Martin allegedly had in the abandoned fountain pond behind his house. Some doubted its existence, but none doubted the fact that a snapping turtle's jaws could fold a silver dollar like a warm pancake. This finding, published exclusively in *The Encyclopedia of Big Brothers,* was accepted fact.

The only item of debate was what kind of food snapping turtles most liked to crunch between their fabled jaws. The agreement around the jungle gym was, of course, penises. Snapping turtles almost certainly grew fat on the penises of fifth graders who disturbed the turtle's sleep by taking short cuts past Sam Martin's abandoned fountain pond.

Why my penis should occupy the apex of the snapping turtle's food pyramid was never discussed. Nor was the curious chain of events that would have to take place in order for this obscure part of the food chain to go its natural course. It was just the horrible *possibility* of such an encounter, the snipping sound, the image of the creature and its captured prize disappearing under green water. It was so horrible it had to be true.

And so the footpath past Sam Martin's pond sported two separate paths. One, closer to the pond, was where boys safe in groups swaggered by scoffing at the whole idea of snapping turtles. The other, farther out, was where little boys walking alone swerved wide to give the penivore its due respect.

Up the road, in the opposite direction of the Martins, was the Mayo Clinic's Animal Research Institute, referred to simply as "the institute." The squat buildings swarmed around a huge water tower that fed the complex, and it all had that government-issue sort of architecture one suspects is on the grounds of "Area 51." Occasionally the head physician there, Dr. Zollman, gave us tours through all the labs, past the wide, clean cages of little animals. It made us sad to think the rats and guinea pigs were being given cancer, and we always felt a little guilty after a tour. In fact, it was here at the institute where I contracted cancer too, or thought so anyway.

I'd gone up to the institute on a Sunday to poke around in the piles of medical waste just behind the high water tower. I was looking for syringes—the kind with detachable needles. Earlier in the week my brother Chris had amazed me with a new syringe–weapon he'd purloined from the institute's junk pile. He'd poked the needle of a salvaged syringe into a candle, clogging it. Then, with a hard thumb on the plunger, you had a blow dart straight out of *The Man from U.N.C.L.E.* I succeeded in finding a few syringes, pocketed them, and on my way off the grounds thought I'd take a peek into the institute's windows, maybe get a look at animals with cancer.

The first windows I tried were paned with fogged glass, so I went farther down to the end of the building to an odd-looking window with slats. I pulled myself up and at the moment I had my face in position, the exhaust fan inside turned on, the slats blew open, and I received what I was certain was a faceful of hot cancer.

This was surely air so rank with infection the doctors inside thought it best to rush it out of the animal cancer ward through the nearest pipe and just pray it dissipated in the Minnesota winds. And now I had placed my face directly in front of a propeller blowing the carcinogens from a laboratory of tumors, served up hot and fresh like malignant food from a charnel house diner. I had looked in the asshole of the famed Mayo Clinic, inhaled its cancerous fart, and had at best only a few days left.

Rushing home, I consulted my father's medical journals to see how I might suffer my final days. Dad's journals were normally a form of great entertainment—mutation and injury, amputation and necropsy, all the things that delight fifth-grade boys. Now it was less a journal and more a travel brochure of a place I was going.

The most-thumbed page in Dad's entire medical library featured a photo of a man suffering from elephantiasis of the scrotum; the poor soul had privates so public he had to cart them about in a wheelbarrow. "At least he'll *live,*" I thought, flipping past Wheelbarrow Man, to my section—tumors of the face.

There was my future: page after page of immense suppurating wounds that would soon be erupting under my thick black eyeglasses. In shock I went running upstairs, journal in hand, to confess my crime to an elder brother.

Big brothers, however, have no interest in scaring the bejesus out of you if it's not a job they contracted themselves. Jeff quickly laughed off my concern, told me not to worry about it, and kept the journal to thumb through later.

Scaring yourself was the greatest achievement: the Eagle Scout of the bejesus-scaring merit badge system.

High up in the Millstone, through a door off Kip and Jeff's fourth-floor bedroom, was the rooftop balcony, a tar-floored twelve-foot by twelve-foot area where we regularly courted death.

During tornado warnings, when the Hartmans were likely down in their basement listening to the radio, my five brothers and I would race to this highest point of the Millstone to greet the great twisting beast. We'd commandeered the large umbrella that shaded the table by the pool, and as the rain sprinkled and lightning flashed over the valley, there we were on its highest point holding a large metal pole. We never spotted a tornado, but we did co-opt the storm weather and its strange green-yellow atmosphere as a stage for another assault on the peacefulness of Bamber Valley. We lugged the amplifiers from Kip and Jeff's rock-and-roll band up to the balcony and boomed our voices out over the neighborhood.

"CITIZENS OF ROCHESTER! THIS IS GOD!

"YOU HAVE ANGERED US—ME—I MEAN ME . . . BY BEING . . . BY BEING JUST SO NOT COOL. FEEL MY WRATH!"

During better weather the balcony was base camp for great climbing treks across the roof of the Millstone, where we'd ascend the red slate tiles to the peak of the house and then higher still to stand on the top of the chimney, an additional eight feet above the red clay roof of our world.

Getting back down from whatever part of the roof our adventures took us often meant descending the south face of the Millstone. We'd usually head for the safety of the balcony off Mom's Tower Library, but that meant coming down the steep pitch over our parents' bedroom and then dangling by hand from the rain gutters. From there it was fifteen feet of hand-over-hand dangling until the tips of your sneakers found purchase on the library's balcony railing. Dan remembers hanging from this gutter when Dad pulled into the driveway and caught him there. ("Just ten feet," Dan remembers, "from completing the trek. Ten goddamn feet.")

Another balcony stunt that entered family lore was the day Jeff stood on the railing of the fourth-story balcony backward—like a diver—the balls of his feet on the edge of the railing, his back to a forty-five-foot drop onto a stone patio, which a little math ($V^2 = 64 \times S$) reveals would've had him moving at about thirty-seven miles per hour when he hit.[1]

To make the game more interesting, Jeff would jump off backward, fall a couple of feet, and arrest his descent by catching the railing with his upper

---

1. Equation for calculating velocity of falling Sullivan brothers provided by Jeff Sullivan, a capable mathematician (as well as an Ace).

arms. (That all six of us survived to adulthood is a statistical anomaly that should astound both my mother and insurance actuaries.)

Scariest of all was climbing the fifteen-story water tower, the one up the road at Mayo's Animal Research Institute—fifteen monstrous stories, where the estimated impact velocity for a fifth-grader falling headfirst would be sixty-seven miles per hour. Chris was the first of us to make the ascent, proudly laying his hand on the warm glass dome that covered the blinking red light at the tower's very apex. But the scariest part wasn't going up, Chris later reported; it was coming down.

"Descending from the top of the water tower meant inching backward out over the *lip* of its conical hat," Chris recalled, "with your feet reaching blindly around for that top rung of the ladder. I remember my foot waving about in the high air, while my attention was focused on a single square inch of chipped paint two inches in front of my face."

Only three of us ever summited the water tower, and why my brothers Chris, Jeff, and Dan ever did a thing so dangerous remains a mystery.

Perhaps it simply felt safer up there.

You can hear both sides of the Pagans' 45rpm at thirtyroomstohidein.com, or buy them on iTunes.

BABA YAGA

JP

The Pagans of Rochester, a teen-age band composed of five John Marshall High School students, have cut a 45 rpm record for Kaybank Studios in Minneapolis. The record is "Baba Yaga," with "Stop Shakin' Your Head" on the flip side, and is due for release in local stores late in April. Both songs were written by Kip Sullivan.

—*"Pagans Cut Disc for Kaybank Studios,"*
Rochester Post-Bulletin

I'm with the band."

That's what you say when you're a roadie or a groupie going past the ropes.

"I'm with the band" is the essence of borrowed cool. If there had been a 1965 bouncer who stood between the Pagans and me, my patter might have been different.

"Yes, I know I look like Ernie Douglas from My Three Sons *but let me through.*

"Why, yes, I do happen to be a Sprinter, but perhaps you haven't heard me perform the opening drum roll from 'Wipe Out'? So if you'll just let me . . .

"Oh yeah? Well, if you're so cool, tell me, have you ever borrowed cigarettes from Kip or Jeff Sullivan? Huh? Bet you never sat in the band's VW bus and pretended to drive it either, have you, Mr. Big Shot? Noooo? Well, there you go then."

To fifth graders with buckteeth there was no difference between being cool and standing next to someone who was actually cool. Borrowed cool was legal tender.

This is why choosing which Beatle you were was important. Once you declared your fealty to John you immediately derived his characteristics. Choosing John, I was suddenly witty (though it bothered me that Dick Bianco, who'd chosen Paul, was suddenly cute). Still, you made decisions and lived with them.

Having two brothers in Rochester's coolest band put you in elite company. Being able to point to my brothers in an ad for the local menswear shop was impressive. But when the Pagans went to the Twin Cities to make their own record, the Assumption of the First Person Plural made "us" famous and I became cool enough probably to need my own agent.

It was over Easter weekend in 1965 the Pagans got into their black VW bus and drove the two hours to Minneapolis to record two songs for release on a 45 rpm. The A-side was a song Kip wrote about a witch from an old Russian folktale, Baba Yaga, who flew out of the mountains in her big black mortar, brewed thunderstorms, and spread fear.

> She shrieked at the clouds
> as they rumbled toward her,
> laughed at the winds
> and pounded on her mortar,
> Baba Yaga.

In *The Flip Side: An Illustrated History of Southern Minnesota Rock & Roll Music from 1955–1970,* Jim Oldsberg wrote, "The guitar work in the song is fantastic and Kip's vocals are as dominant as ever, but the sound quality of the record left a lot to be desired."

Though they had only four tracks to work with, the Pagans cut the wax on two songs that were solid mid-'60s rock and roll. Side B was *Stop Shakin' Your Head,* a more traditional Baby-I'm-not-comin'-back number. The Pagans pressed five hundred copies and began distributing them all over Rochester.

When copies of the record arrived back home, it was as if I had been inducted into the Rock and Roll Hall of Fame, anointed with glory everlasting. To actually hold the black plastic disc in your hands, to see the songwriter's name printed thereon—Kip Sullivan—you were officially with the band, my friend. You were in.

As for the guys who were actually cool enough to make the record, well, I imagined the Pagans enjoyed it in their own way too. In *The Flip Side,* Kip remembers, "It was such a rush to hear yourself on a record that you produced coming over the car radio on the way to high school."

Kip's diary, April 27, 1965
I was at practice over at Rushton's when [brother] Chris came down, said Mom wanted to see me. I went out, looked in car window and there were three packs of records! Grabbed two, ran inside, and the whole band jumped up and down yelling.... "Baba Yaga" on WDGY up in the Twin Cities! Jeff heard it. The D.J. said, "Here's new sound from Rochester." I was downtown and found out Dayton's sold a bunch more. A WIN DAY! SHIT, I WISH I WASN'T GOING TO COLLEGE. WOULDN'T IT BE COOL IF THAT RECORD GOES BIG?

Kip, now living back in the Millstone, May 12
It's almost 11pm and Dad is still bitching about the bills from "the goddamn Bach Music Store." God, what frustration. I just went upstairs to take a shower and he came up and pulled on me. I said "Get your hands off me," and he hit me in stomach. Not too hard but it sure as hell surprised me. Mom came up with hell fire coming out of her eyes and Jeff joined the argument. They're still at it. I imagine I'll be up late tonight. Practice was good. Wrote new song. Oh, God, I think he's coming upstairs to our room again. Jesus, I hate that bastard.

Mom's letters to Grandpa, May 14
Kip is in the hospital with unexplained belly pains.

Memory: I Am the Fifth Beatle

I am in fifth grade. I am standing just outside the door of Bamber Valley Elementary School as kids run out into the spring air for recess. I am standing in a pose that is exactly—and I mean exactly—the same pose John Lennon strikes on the back of the Beatles VI album.

I am holding a rolled-up piece of paper just like Lennon did. My chin is up at the same roguish angle and I am looking off at the same spot in the distance. Precisely three-quarters of my weight is on my right foot, making my right hip—like John's—jut ever so slightly. Mathematically there is no difference between the two of us. Aside from the fact that I look like Ernie Douglas and my sole musical accomplishment is mimicking the drum-roll opening to "Wipe Out," the similarity is unsettling. Wait till Debbie Laney gets a load of this.

Debbie, my winsome classmate of five grades, should be coming down the hall presently. When she sees how well I've nailed this pose she will finally know what I've suspected for some time now: that I am so very like the Beatles in word, thought, and deed I may well be the fifth member of the world's greatest rock-and-roll band.

Scientifically, it is feasible. The possibility of my being the fifth Beatle does not challenge any established physical laws of the universe. Gravity remains unseated; the sky remains blue, the sun still rises and sets. My fantasy asks only an open-mindedness to the possibility that, but for some backroom Liverpool screwup—perhaps a dropped bit of paper or missed phone call—I was meant to share a microphone with Paul McCartney and belt out "Kansas City," the opening track on the A side.

Paul's the cute one. John's the witty one. I am "the fifth-grade one." Again, I claim only feasibility. And consider, too, that it took only a last-minute personnel shift by the producer to push the original drummer, Pete Best, out. Is it not possible that by similar whimsy I have been pushed in? And where the hell is Pete Best, by the way? Not standin' here with me lookin' way cool and waitin' for Debbie Laney, that much I can tell you.

I'm just sayin', it's feasible.

The .22 caliber rifle that Roger pointed in the other direction.
And the sunglasses he knocked off.

HIDING IN THE BATHROOM
FROM BULLETS

By the summer of '65, we found ourselves back in the Millstone playing Beaster for real. Now we crept through the house at high noon wondering when Dad's anger would lurch from a corner. It could come for any of a hundred reasons now: for roughhousing, for being a child, for existing.

Nothing had changed as a result of the three-month separation. When Dad came home from work, the hinges of the liquor cabinet creaked the same as before and by dinnertime he'd be hovering behind Mom making his accusations *("You've never liked sex, have you, Myra?")* and she would listen in silence. Her anger, however, would show in her quick physical movements: she'd slam a drawer shut, or set a pot down on the stove harder than she had to. Dad seized the opportunity to coin a term he used the rest of the summer, a degrading, childish insult. He called our mother a "Slam-Banger."

"OH, THERE SHE GOES AGAIN, BOYS. MAMA'S A SLAM-BANGER, SHE IS."

Roger's attacks now began as soon as he got home; everyone had to listen. But the main show in the center ring—the late-night abuse down in the living room—continued. There were the same tired themes (money, sex, books, the letters to Grandpa), the same vitriol, the same ice rattling in endless drinks. But alone with her downstairs at night, his tantrums took new measures.

"One night he grew so angry he picked up a chair and held it over his head like he was going to kill me with it," she told me. "I just looked at him, thinking, 'You are a tyrant, but you are also a coward. You will threaten, but you will not do it.'"

The abuse she found most painful was the horrible things he said about her to her children. Many nights, after he was too drunk to continue an energetic attack, he would crawl into my bed, or my little brother Collin's bed, wake us up, and begin telling us horrible things about our mother. All of them untrue, of course, but for eight- and eleven-year-old boys the poison and filth he substituted for bedtime stories were scary nevertheless. We didn't know it at the time but Mom was always there, standing out in the hall by our bedroom door, torn between roaring in and defending herself or just letting the serpent bleed its venom until it passed out on the bed.

"I decided it was better to remain silent than to create a fight in front of you children in the middle of the night," says Mom, remembering the loneliness of that hallway. "I always trusted that, even if you boys grew up thinking you had a horrible mother, one day you'd figure out the truth for yourselves."

In the summer of '65, the six of us went into bunker mentality. We hid. Hiding was easy because drunk dads were like zombies in horror movies—they looked ugly and could kill you, but because of the way they lurched about, even fifth graders could outmaneuver them. The older brothers could go stay with friends, but we little ones had to find hidey-holes in the Millstone where Dad didn't go. "Only the smartest of mice would hide in the cat's ear," goes the saying and perhaps hiding in Roger's liquor cabinet would have been brilliant, but I chose the cool and the dark of the fallout shelter. I moved my bedroom down to the basement and bunked in the safety of that concrete metaphor.

That was the summer I discovered the distant land of Marvel comic books and spent hours down in the fallout shelter drawing my own superhero comic book about "Dr. Fear," an angry wounded soul who saved the world. Upstairs the adult world continued to need saving. Vietnam was just getting started, the Freedom Marches moved from Selma to Montgomery, and the Watts ghetto was boiling to an August riot. Even Grandpa's life was unsettled; he'd begun to have second thoughts about having moved into a retirement center. (He didn't like the medical care.)

At the Millstone, we fought back in what ways we could: pouring the odd bottle down the drain; making fun of Dad behind his back; and when he screamed at us, defiantly not crying. That June, Kip and Jeff tried something ambitious. They hid their new cassette tape recorder in the kitchen on a night when Dad was gearing up for another rage. Like tornado chasers they left their recording equipment in just the right spot and captured an F5 on tape. Kip referred to the recordings as the "Rage Tapes" and made good use of them, taking them directly to Dad's Mayo Clinic psychiatrist, Dr. Martin, and pushing PLAY. Later in his diary, Kip wrote hopefully: "He said the tapes 'give a different picture.' Said it helped."

Whatever Dad was telling the psychiatrist about "spats with the wife" was finally being countered with grim evidence. Still, another two months would pass before the psychiatrist would recommend hospitalization. Mom continued to seek counsel from her own psychiatrist, Dr. Steinhilber, who knew full well what these "spats" were, and, ultimately, he warned her she might be in danger: "Be on the lookout for extreme violence," came the advice.

Mom continued the battle on another front as well. "Mom says she has to talk to Dr. Coventry cuz Dad not in shape," wrote Kip. "Goes to work after lunch with booze on his breath."

Of course, when Roger returned home after being questioned by Dr. Coventry, it only got worse. He threatened Mom with the .22-caliber rifle, bringing it down from its high shelf in the entryway closet, out of its canvas bag, and waving it back and forth in her face. Although she never thought he'd pull the trigger ("He was gutless, a paper tiger"), it scared her. Some nights she locked herself in the bathroom to sleep in the tub, where she felt safe. A dogleg in the bathroom's design put the tub around a corner, out of a bullet's straight trajectory.

She sought assistance where she could, and the most helpful person of all was our good neighbor, Dr. Tony Bianco. Tony remembers getting several panicked phone calls from Myra, the one in particular when she mentioned guns. He drove the half mile from his house and parked his station wagon across the front of our driveway, blocking it so Dad couldn't grab his keys and go roaring off in the MG. The best Tony could do was divert Roger long enough for Mom to pack us up and leave for a motel. Eventually, he also did our family the service of removing the rifle from the Millstone.

But the stiletto remained Roger's weapon of choice; his tongue was a surgical blade. One day, near the very end, he made a withering comment about Jeff's flying lessons. (As preparation for a possible pilot's career, Jeff was taking flight lessons in a Beechcraft.) In an almost casual assassination on the front step Roger told his son, "The airlines aren't interested in pipsqueaks who fly those little putt-putts."

"Dad got me with his stiletto as well," Chris told me. "Remember when we were on the houseboat with Dad, Kip, and his girlfriend, Linda? I was around a corner changing into my swimming suit, a little anxious about Linda possibly coming around the corner. Dad heard me worrying about this and his public response was, 'You don't have anything she'd be interested in.'"

As I sift through these stories from brothers and try to piece together a picture of my father I wonder why a world-class Mayo Clinic surgeon would go out of his way to humiliate two teenage boys, much less his sons. I realize my difficulty in understanding Roger is that, by 1965, rationality may no longer apply. Maybe I won't be able to *think* my way through to where he was, that I'll have to consider alcohol was simply pickling his brain. Dad could stand in the kitchen with a bourbon-and-ice glowing right there in the sun and deny it was booze. Look you right in the eye: "I'm not drinking." But perhaps it was simply denial—a break with truth, not reality.

Still, there seems no rational explanation for a phone call Roger made to Myra's parents that summer. He'd called RJL before to tell him what a worthless wife his daughter was, but now he reported she was "throwing tantrums" and had "scratched my face so badly I had to go to the hospital." Grandpa, of course, knew this was delusional, but the violence of its bloody imagery made him worry for his daughter's safety. He telephoned back just to hear Myra's voice. Had RJL heard the "Ax Story," however, he would have sent the Florida National Guard to the Millstone.

It took years for my mother to tell us the Ax Story; she peeled back the layers of my father's outrages as she thought we could handle them. The details of this particular attack she kept to herself well into the 1980s.

On a day when we were all in school, Roger drank to insensibility, began his assembly-line verbal assaults on Mom's character, and as his anger grew she retreated to the master bedroom. She'd discovered that by placing Collin's toy wagon flush against her side of the door, it could not be opened more than an inch. Roger pounded on the door growling nobody's gonna keep him out of his own goddamned bedroom. Behind the door she remained silent, dripping no blood into the water to feed his frenzy.

"WELL, THEN, I'LL JUST GO OUT TO THE TOOL SHED AND GET THE AX AND SMASH THIS GODDAMNED DOOR IN! WHAT DO YOU THINK OF THAT?"

There was no dialing 911 in those days. But on hearing this threat, Mom placed the first and only call she ever made for official help—to the volunteer fire warden of Bamber Valley. She barely knew this man, having met him once at a school function. But he was a man, he had a uniform and a siren.

"When I got him on the phone and told him what was happening, all this man said was, 'There's nothing I can do for you' and hung up. No mention of calling anyone else, no empathy, just a report of impotence and the dial tone," she remembers. But she knew Dad heard her making the call, and she believes it's all that kept him from breaking down the door that day. Such were the times—no alcoholics, only "party boys." No spousal abuse, only "spats with the wife."

When we thought things couldn't get worse, the bottom dropped out, and then the bottom of the bottom dropped out—we fell deeper into the heat of the summer of '65.

Kip's diary, June 7, 1965
Came home to find Mom just haggard. Says it was one of worst rages so far (that he was hitting her with a fly swatter, throwing laundry around). We might take off to hotel again if he goes nuts again. This could be a week-long rage. This could be it. He could go crazy.

By the summer of 1965, little Collin, so long at the edges of the storm, now found himself caught in the gale with the rest of us. He'd inherited all the lessons we'd learned: freezing, hiding, surrendering. Only eight years old at the time, his memories of the summer of '65 are like mine—flash frames from a violent film roaring through a broken projector. Sometimes not even an image but a sound, like the jingle of coins in a pocket.

"I remember being mad at Dad," Collin says, "and I leaned over the railing and yelled downstairs, 'I hate your guts!' All I remember next was the sound of him running up the stairs after me, change and keys jingling in his pockets. I don't remember what came next. Only that I was scared and running to my room. And behind me the sound of change jingling in his pockets."

Collin and I seem to dissolve into each other's memories of that summer. He remembers part of one incident, I the other.

"I was out on the screen porch," Collin says, "when Dad started in on Mom. I knew there were some neighborhood kids on bikes out by our driveway and they could hear all of this going on at our house. I got up to leave but Dad told me to *stay where I was.* So I sat. He was raging at her about something and Mom said she was going to scream. I thought, 'I don't want everybody to hear this.'"

He headed outside.

The baton of memory passes to me and I'm standing out by the station wagon in the driveway; all its doors are open for another medevac to a motel and the fight spills out of the Millstone as Dad follows Mom and Collin, who are heading for the car. Dad's demanding the car keys in her purse and Mom says through clenched teeth, chin down, eyes looking up, "Roger, if you touch my purse, I will *scream*." I look again to check if my friends by our front gate have moved on. They have. Good, they won't see what's happening to my family. *Unless*... they turn their bikes around and ride past our gate again. Dad moves for Mom's purse with that bourbon-zombie lurch and my mother screams and I look to the gate and my friends have in fact turned around... they're gliding right past our driveway, threading the needle at the exact screaming second, and they all see my disintegrating family and the blood rushes to my ears, which burn in embarrassment, and I dive into the back seat of the station wagon to hide. I feel the hot vinyl of the car seat against my face and the sense of Mom's weight settling in the car as she gets in to drive away but suddenly she's out of the car again and there's the sound of a scuffle and another scream.

My mother remembers: "He pulled me out of the driver's seat and when I resisted he socked me in the face, knocking off those big white sunglasses I had at the time. They went flying into the grass. I reached down to get them and as I rose back up I said, 'You *animal!*'"

Collin's memory differs slightly: "I think he hit her and she fell down into the grass. The only thing I remember after that is the hurt and rage in Mom's eyes as she rose to meet him."

Neither Collin nor I remember how it ends. It just ends. There is no final scene, just that scream, that image of Mom getting back up to face Dad, the fury in her eyes—and then the last sudden foot of film is through the projector, going round and round, hitting the empty upper reel, *whap, whap, whap, whap.*

Luke playing superhero on top of the Millstone.

HIDING IN THE
TOWER LIBRARY

❧

Open this door, goddammit!"
 BOOM! The oak door rattles. My father is outside the door. He is drunk and pounding with a flat hand. In his other hand is either a drink or the rifle. From inside we think we can hear that ice-in-glass clink, but we can't be sure.

It is July 1965. A half hour ago I'd been alone down in the fallout shelter reading one of my superhero comic books. The basement is cool and quiet in the summer and a good place to hide year-round. Dad had begun drinking at noon and by three was raging, saying horrible things calibrated to hurt my mother and by saying them in front of us, hurt her more deeply.

"Couldn't earn twenty-five cents by spreading her legs! ... Open this door, goddammit!"

BOOM!

Around four thirty his raging became demonic. The older four brothers, whose witness sometimes buffered my father's anger, had gone downtown to see a movie. When he mentioned the gun a second time, Mom gathered Collin and me, and we retreated to the locked safety of the tower library.

Behind us now are the French doors that open onto a small balcony. Square in front of us is the oak door and it's standing up well to his blows. But its solidity only makes his rage burn hotter, until we can almost feel it radiating through the keyhole.

"Won't let me in to see my own GODDAMN KIDS!"

BOOM!

Silence.

We sense him leave but when he comes back a minute later we can hear he's brought the whole sloshing bottle and our retreat has become a siege. Mom puts her arms around the two of us.

BOOM!

The blows on the outside of the door are much harder now. We huddle in closer to Mama. Some nights the look in her eyes is reassuring. ("We'll be fine. He'll be asleep soon.") But this time feels different. The hour seems here for our father to carry out the threats he's made so many times but always scuttled when the alcohol took him down for the night.

BOOM!

Memory: I Am the Incredible Hulk

BOOM!

All this noise is starting to make me mad; not a good thing because when I get mad I get green, I get huge, and I become a mass of muscle and rage and righteousness horrifying to behold, but—I should point out—with deep sad eyes that, were Debbie Laney from my class only to glance into them, she'd throw her arms around me and say, "Oh, you tortured complex creature, I must have you!"

BOOM!

"WON'T LET ME IN!" rages the man outside.

My body begins to change. Mama looks at me with eyes that plead, "Please don't do it, my tortured, complex son. Don't unleash your unholy power!" I hate Mama havin' to see this ugly bit of business, but the whole thing is really out of my hands. I raise my fists and—

BOOM!

The door explodes like balsa out into the hallway. Lurching through the smoke in the doorway looms the outline of a giant killing-rage-justice machine, its lime green rhinoceros bulk filling the small hallway. The monster glares down at the little doctor-man still holding the rifle and his beaker of amber liquid.

The monster's first roar is loud and the doctor's eyeglasses and beaker both shatter in a defeated tinkle of crystal. Without elixir now and powerless, Slurring Doctor-Man stands blinking before Judgment. As he tries to bring the rifle around, two watermelon fists lift over his spiteful head and . . .

BOOM!

Mom cradles my face in her hands. "Honey, do you think you can make the climb down from the balcony? And maybe go get help at the Martins' next door?"

This was a climb I'd made many times before, pretending to be Spider-

Man pursuing Marvel foes like Electro or Mysterio. Climbing down the side of the house isn't scary. Scary is the heat coming through the keyhole.

I go over the wrought-iron railing and put my left foot out to the rehearsed spot, the stone jutting from the wall over the first-floor window. One last look into Mom's eyes, a look into my little brother's—their eyes say *hurry back hurry back*—and I'm climbing down the side of the Millstone. Above me, the pounding continues. Two more handholds, one toehold, and I'm down.

When my feet hit ground I'm running through the July heat down our driveway, past the stone gateposts, out onto the road leading to the Martins' house.

I will get help. I will be a superhero. I will tell my big brothers the whole story when they get home. How I climbed down from the library balcony, how I brought back help and everything was OK.

I'm at the Martins'. I ring the doorbell. I'm panting. I will tell them and they'll do something. It's taking them a long time to come to the door. But they're here; I know it. Their car is in the driveway.

Wipe the sweat out of the eyes, ring again.

Please be here, please be here.

There's a fumbling inside at the lock. *Yes!*

Mrs. Martin opens the door and she too is terribly drunk, slurring her words, unable to understand me, unable to do anything for me even if she could. The world reels a little bit and the lesson tattoos itself inside: there are no sane adults in power anywhere in the land.

Memory: I Am "Lonely Guy"

The coolest kids in the neighborhood have circled their bikes in the quiet sun of the Saturday playgrounds at Bamber Valley School. This is the Elite—the coolest of the cool kids—and handsome nine-year-old Steve Carter is there in its center. From here it looks like every word he's saying is funny; the beautiful Debbie Laney and Jennie Sudor laugh uncontrollably.

It's noon and the kids' August shadows fall directly on the warm gravel around their feet. But twenty feet away, just outside the playground, the weather is cold, rainy, and gray. Because it's <u>always</u> cold, rainy, and gray around . . . "Lonely Guy."

Where Lonely Guy walks there is perpetual November drizzle. The wind blows sad newspapers down the empty street and somewhere far off a dog barks.

Lonely Guy stays at the edges of things. He doesn't join, but he wants you to <u>know</u> he's not joining and so he orbits around the action just out of range. If Lonely Guy were to join the group, oh, the smart things he might say. Debbie and Jennie would at last see the flash of true wit, see the sunflare glint on the knife edge of the perfectly placed word.

(Jennie giggles: "That was so funny and true, Lonely Guy. Would you mind if I jotted that down?")

But he doesn't go into the playground. He could. If he wanted to. But Lonely Guy has a lot on his mind lately and turns to walk away.

If Lonely Guy has a superpower, it happens here: when girls look at him, they see him walking in s l o w   m o t i o n, or they should anyway, because in the movies walking in slow motion is very cool. Everything looks better in slow motion—especially Lonely Guy. If Debbie and Jennie would only glance over, they'd see the graceful poetry of his forward motion; not the clip-clip-clip cadence of ordinary pedestrians but the slow pistons of his contemplative and determined stride.

As he moves out of sight around the corner, he imagines Debbie sees him from the corner of her eye, and in the last second she calls from summer through fall to him, "Stop! Come back. Forever." But he's too far down the street now, into late November. He can't hear her.

But that's okay. The credits have begun to roll past and the music comes up: it's the Beatles singing "This Boy." And Lonely Guy walks in slow motion into the cold November dusk.

The Pagans pose in jackets for a local menswear store in Rochester.
From left: Jim Rushton, Jeff Sullivan, Kip Sullivan (sporting a black eye
from a "rumble"), Steve Rossi, and Jerry Huiting.

PAGAN RITES

⁂

The main juvenile officer in the Rochester Police Department was a man with the perfectly cast name of Dutch Link.

Dutch was the guy who sent the hoods upstate to the juvie in Red Wing. He also had say over which bands were allowed to play in the police-sponsored mixers at the armory. Dutch became acquainted with the Pagans in both capacities.

The armory was the best steady gig in town, and all the bands wanted to play there. But Dutch was no desk cop and knew all about the Pagans' occasional drinking during performances. Kip remembers Dutch "calling us in a lot, but he never really busted on us. He was a pretty good guy."

Dutch's warnings were avuncular. Jeff remembers a big arm being thrown over his shoulder and a lesson in moral arithmetic: "Now Jeff, it's like this. There's nothin' wrong with a motorcycle, right? And there's nothin' wrong with a motorcycle *jacket,* see? But when you put the two of 'em *together* . . . people might get the wrong idea and sort of, well, react poorly, if you take my meanin'."

In Jim Oldsberg's *The Flip Side: An Illustrated History of Southern Minnesota Rock & Roll Music from 1955–1970,* Dutch filled in the rest of the equation in a speech to all five band members: "There's nothing wrong with calling yourselves the 'Pagans' and there's nothing wrong with young men having a good time. But when you do what you boys *do,* well, people get the wrong idea."

The Pagans *liked* giving people the wrong idea. They liked hearing the story passed around about how a Mayo doctor paid the band forty dollars to play at a party and how, after hours of loud, boozy rock and roll, paid them another forty dollars to stop. The Pagans had created a lasting reputation. So much so that when the organizers of John Marshall High School's twentieth reunion invited the Pagans to play one last nostalgic gig in 1985, the planners included a caveat: "You guys had a reputation as being rowdy drinkers back then. You're not going to do that for this, are you?"

As far as Kip and Jeff were concerned, Roger drank to exist; the Pagans drank to have fun and make trouble. But the fun came to a head on August 7, 1965, at the Olmsted County Fair.

The men-with-short-haircuts had arranged another Battle of the Bands for the big fair, and the night began with a six o'clock radio interview of the Pagans on Rochester's KROC. Kip noted in his diary that the band was in fine Beatle form: "All of us talking at once, giving wise answers." The Pagans had sailed through the prelims in the afternoon and had several hours to kill before finals at eight. Kip's diary continues: "Went out on empty road by Plunkett's, boozed. God, did it ever hit me."

By the time the Pagans assembled back at the county fair, everyone realized there was no way Kip would be able to perform. They poured him back into the VW bus and drove out to the Zumbro River. They stripped off his clothes and pushed him into the cold water.

Jeff, interviewed in The Flip Side, *1991*
I can still see Kip's naked white body tumbling through brambles and down the muddy slopes into about a foot and a half of water. Kip had a riot, standing there throwing water into the air, naked with his sunglasses still on. We finally got him out of the water and dressed. Behind the stage tent, we started pumping boiling coffee into him to the point where we actually burned his mouth.

It finally came our turn to take the stage in front of a crowd of around 500. Kip still couldn't even stand up, so we found a [tall] stool backstage for him and brought it out front. We started our set doing all of the songs that Jerry and Steve sang lead on, until it came to the point where Kip had to sing. [It was] quite a sight to see, Kip sitting there on his stool behind the mike, sunglasses on, wet hair hanging in his eyes, in a clinging wet shirt. I don't recall exactly which song it was [Rossi says it was "Dizzy Miss Lizzy"] but Kip had just completed singing the same verse twice in a row, completely screwing up the words.

As it came time for Jerry's lead, Kip leaned back on his stool and the whole thing went over—Kip, the stool, and the amplifier behind him. It's hard to describe what live amplifiers with reverb springs sound like when they're falling off of bandstands. On his way down, Kip's head hit Steve's boom, making the boom swing around in two big circles and Steve had to duck behind his drums as it crossed over him. There were amplifiers crashing all around and in the middle of all this chaos, there was Kip lying amidst a tangle of wires and amps with his guitar half on, looking very confused. The audience went absolutely berserk. People were jumping up and down and screaming for more.

Phone calls about the incident made their way to the Millstone, and Roger's response was to ground his oldest son "until college" and lay into Myra for being such a poor mother. His drinking increased and then, the same weekend the Beatles played Shea Stadium in New York City and the riots burned in Watts, life in Rochester hit a new low.

Kip's diary, August 15, 1965
Tomorrow is my birthday. Oh yay. [Sad face drawn in the diary.] It's a long story. After the band practiced, we went to the liquor store where Rossi managed to buy three 6-packs of Grain Belt. Jim and I went to drink with Eddie P. Had to be in by 10:00 so the band just came back to my house to drink. I announced our arrival home to dad, then we walked way down to the back yard and drank and talked. 10 minutes later dad came down with flashlight. "What's going on, boys?"

He sat down beside me. I held up my beer and asked if he wanted a swig. He started bitching, "You boys get on home. Get going." He said to me, "Get in the house." I go, "Have to finish my beer." He swung at my beer and knocked it away, yelling, "Get in the house!" I said, "You wanna polish it off?" He says, "Wise guy." [I say] "You're a nosey old bastard." "What'd you call me?" "A nosey old bastard." He swung, said I was a "spoiled shit." I backed down the hill.

He ran down, swung at me again with the big flashlight, I ducked, and put one in his paunch. As he went down, he pulled me on top. I just put my head in his chest and wailed about five blows in his face; I only got my ears boxed. We separated.

He said, "Get in the house!" but I just walked back up to driveway. I heard "Get in the house!" again but I headed for the front gate where Eddie's car was parked. Mom came out and asked, "Is he drunk again?" I just got in [the] car, took off, finished the beer, went to Eddie's, watched TV and slept.

The next morning Dad came to the breakfast table with bruises on his face and there was no looking away. When the elevator doors opened on the sixth floor of the Mayo Clinic, everyone could see the doctor needed to be in a hospital, not work in one.

Myra on the front deck of the houseboat on the Mississippi River.

EYE OF THE HURRICANE

∞

Notes from Dad's psychiatrist, Dr. Martin, July 26, 1965
Psychotherapy has continued, however little progress has been made. The focus has tended to remain on the marital conflict and we have made little progress in terms of therapy. The situation has reached the point that he can no longer really function effectively in his work and arrangements have been made for a referral to the Institute of Living in Hartford, Connecticut.

Most chemical dependency counselors will tell you alcoholics do not voluntarily submit to accepting help—they simply run out of options. Old-timers in AA often say the door to their meeting rooms ought to be just one foot high. "Like those dog doors," one member told me, "because that's how most of us came to our first meeting—crawling on our hands and knees, completely humbled."

Whatever made our father finally decide to accept help in August we'll never know. Perhaps he woke up that next morning, saw his black eye in the mirror, and knew he wouldn't be able to explain it at work. By then, it was no secret his boss, Dr. Coventry, was losing his patience.

"People were talking to me about smelling alcohol on his breath during working hours," Coventry told me during our interview in Rochester. "He finally admitted he had a serious problem. But by that time it had gone beyond me to the board of governors and they recommended he go to the Institute of Living in Hartford. Roger could not go on the way he was."

With the news of Dad's impending hospitalization, we felt the eye of the hurricane move over the Millstone. In the sudden quiet we shared what little information we had; even Kip was unsure, recording in his diary, "Dad in sorrowful mood. Told me he planned to fly to Philadelphia Institute Of Living (or is it Hartford?) at 4:00 this afternoon. Can't quite believe it. No one seems to know how long he'll be gone. Estimates run from 2 months to 2 years."

Like the weekend runs we'd taken in our motel hideaways, this too happened fast, but now it was Dad leaving the Millstone, not us. There he was standing in the hallway holding a suitcase and suddenly we were being called to come tell him goodbye. Jeff was going to drive him to the airport and remembers waiting for Dad out in the car in driveway.

"The top of the MG was down. Dad got into the passenger seat and as he closed the door Mom appeared out of nowhere and gave him a very affectionate but reserved series of strokes on his head. She said something like 'Good luck.' Dad didn't look up. He muttered something I recall along the lines of '*You* don't care.' He looked like he was going to cry. He didn't. But on the way back from the airport, I did."

The next week, the first of many hopeful letters from Florida arrived in the mail.

Grandpa's letters, August 21, 1965
Dear Daughter: These pages I suppose you will prefer to tear out and dispose of, inasmuch as these Blue Books are bound into volumes for purposes of family history. But I can hardly write without some comment on the great significance of what happened yesterday. I judge that your strength (which I marvel at) must have been taxed almost to the limit.

Today all we do is think of you and pray for your deliverance from a tragic situation—you and the boys. What seemed so auspicious and happy in 1944 has become a sad business indeed. We turn over in our minds this development and wonder why and how. At the same time, we deplore our helplessness. There is nothing we can do. Our one and only daughter is in deep trouble and her parents cannot help her.

I am not sure whether this Steinhilber is your attorney, or friend or the psychiatrist but I shudder at the necessity of his advice to be alert for violence. I telephoned your friend Tony Bianco about that (when you first revealed the situation) and he assured me that the gun was not available to CRS. [When Grandpa was mad at Roger, he referred to him by initials.] Of course, he could buy another. I cannot escape the fervent hope that none of you will ever see him again. It does worry me that he might leave Hartford and suddenly appear at the 'Stone. It is my judgment you should change the locks on all doors. Your mother agrees with me on this.

We believe the crisis has passed and your success is a good one. But I confess to continued disquietude. I do hope that CRS's absence is long-continued and that this will bring some surcease to you, battered and bruised as you must be. How dear you are to our hearts.

May God bless you and your boys.

The Millstone.

NO HELP FROM GOD

ↄↄ

For decades alcoholism was considered a lack of willpower at best, a moral failing at worst. It wasn't until 1956 that it was even classified a disease by the American Medical Association, and even then treatments for addiction were medieval: electroshock therapy, insulin shock, heavy sedation.

That this was in fact the kind of treatment my father was about to receive in Hartford is no dishonor to the doctors there; it was simply the best medical thinking of the time. Western medicine loves to cure stuff, but alcoholism can't be cured, only arrested. No matter how many needles doctors stuck in their drunks, or how many Rorschach inkblots they showed them, on dismissal most of their patients gave them a cheerful thumbs-up and walked out of the hospital and into a bar across the street.

As the doctors scratched their heads over their patients' continued drinking, strange meetings were being called to order in basements of churches everywhere. Gathering to sit in the uncomfortable folding chairs were some serious Grade A Losers—booze hounds, smack heads, pill gobblers, men, women, a Noah's ark of dysfunction—everyone swilling horrible church basement coffee and smoking way too much. Hardly any of them had ever spent a Sunday sitting upstairs in the regular church. God had never offered much to this crowd; religion, next to nothing.

"Religion is for people who want to avoid Hell," one AA old-timer told me. "Spirituality is for people who have already been there."

Sitting happily in the folding chairs of Alcoholics Anonymous, people who had completely rejected the church or had simply never believed in God were discovering a new form of spirituality. Like the good Christians upstairs, they too were lowering their heads and praying—but to whom or to what, it didn't matter. "As long as it's something bigger than you," they were told.

Down here in the basements of AA, it didn't matter what your higher power was. It could be the power of group, the Twelve Steps poster on the wall, good ol' God, or the divine luminous being at the center of your personal Buddha. Fine with them if you thought the Bible was bullshit or if your ass hadn't warmed a church pew in decades. What mattered down here was humility and surrender. What mattered down here was admitting that you, by yourself, were completely unable to beat your addiction. What mattered was developing a willingness—that's all, just a *willingness*—to believe that something outside your excellent self might be able to save you from the insanity of your excellent self. And absolutely any higher power would do.

One veteran, sober for thirty-five years, recalls arguing about "all this higher power crap" with his first AA sponsor, a man named Bennie.

"I told Bennie, told 'im, I don't believe in God.

And Bennie says, 'That's fine, I *do,* so you just go ahead and pray to Bennie's God. That's right. Just put your hands together like so and say, 'Dear Bennie's God, I seem to need some help gettin' my sorry ass out of this deep pile of shit I've put myself in.'"

"I know, I *know,*" the old-timer says, shrugging. "But ... Bennie was right."

These people didn't care about religion. It was all about getting out of yourself, about a willingness to believe that *something* out there could restore you to sanity. In fact, whenever the word God was used in AA they went out of their way to clarify this higher power was *"God as we understood him."* They even underlined this phrase in all their literature.

Unfortunately, Roger Sullivan had never heard of Bennie's God. God— as Roger understood him—was *Irene's* God and He was fucking scary.

Irene's God thundered down at all the skinny boys whacking off in the bathrooms of Daytona Beach and roared, "ONANISTS, GO YE TO HELL!" People who didn't pray to Irene's God went to Hell. People who missed Sunday services went to Hell. People who had heretical thoughts, or who were horny or opinionated or drank, were all sent to Hell by Irene's God.

Further separating Roger from any consideration of spiritual help was the disease itself. Doctors do not expect patients to lie to them about their ailments, but that's what Roger did once he arrived in Hartford; it's what all alcoholics do—*"I'm fine."* How strange it would be to hear a patient protest, *"Shut up. I don't have lupus. .... You have lupus."* Yet an alcoholic will look up from his pool of vomit, from his slashed wrists, from his smoking wreck of a car and say, *"I'm fine. Leave me the fuck alone."* Little wonder AA calls the disease "cunning."

It is chilling, in fact, the similarity between alcoholism and good ol' fashioned demonic possession, the kind seen in *The Exorcist*. Like the devil, an alcoholic just wants to hide in his room, curse God, puke on visitors, and die. Attempts to cast out either alcoholism or the devil get the same response: both demon and disease will deny they exist. And when exposed, both will try to make deals to survive, or threaten suicide, or lash out, or play dead. Alcoholism is well described as a sickness of the soul because it is in the soul that the alcoholic's problem lies.

In the soul of every alcoholic, of every addict, there is an emptiness. Years before he ever takes his first drink he feels this void, this sense of incompleteness and melancholy, and it tells him, "You are different. You'll never fit in. And you'll never be truly happy." One day that first swig of vodka comes along, or that first hit of meth, and as the feeling swarms up through his body it fills that empty place with light and warmth. He feels the missing piece in the puzzle of his life click perfectly into place and thinks, "I'm *home*." The experience is seared into his memory and not merely as the first time he feels high but the first time he feels human. "This must be how *normal* people feel," thinks the grateful addict, and so begins the long and fatal attraction.

Seen in this light, booze isn't the problem. To an alcoholic, it's the solution. Seen in this light, alcohol is a coping mechanism, the symptom of a deeper spiritual problem.

Unfortunately, none of this spiritual instruction was to be part of Roger's treatment. During the four months of his stay in Hartford, he was given pills and tests and lots of care by well-meaning professionals, but not once did anyone tell him it was his mortal soul that was in need of care.

Roger and his firstborn, Kip, circa 1948.

CASE #34233

ↄↄ

On my desk, dropped carelessly by the office mail-room boy, is a manila envelope that may contain some answers to my father's death. Inside are his psychiatric records that I'd ordered months ago from the Institute of Living in Hartford; fifty single-spaced pages of his private conversations with psychiatrists; Rorschach interpretations, IQ tests, and other measurements of Western medicine that had been dutifully recorded and stored away in a file cabinet through four decades of Connecticut winters.

I open the envelope as if it were an undisturbed crypt.

From the Hartford psychiatrist's notes
on my father, August 31, 1965
It is almost impossible for the patient to date the onset of his illness. The patient was brought up in a home in which there was no drinking permitted.

On completion of his [medical] residency, he was drinking only on occasion until one year after he became a staff member, when he was using alcohol to "get rid of my emotions." The frequency at that time was less than once per month. As he recalls it, the drinking was always increased after a "spat with my wife."

The intake of alcohol increased continually until the patient began seeing a psychiatrist about a year and a half ago. The patient was able to reduce the drinking, until Christmas of 1964 when his wife and family moved out of the house into another home.

Daydream: I Am "the Bullshit Police"

We've rappelled down the side of Building C at the Hartford Institute of Living and are hanging outside the window of the room where Roger is in session with his psychiatrist.

We're waiting for a "Code BS-10F"—SWAT lingo for Bullshit to the Tenth Fucking Degree. At 1300 hours, the conversation inside the room hands us a BS-10F on a silver platter.

"Well, I didn't drink much, um, until Christmas of '64 but then my wife and family moved out of the house, you see, and so that's when I began to drink and . . ."

"All agents, move in!"

The sounds of a breaking window. Of boots crunching over broken glass. Of the psychiatrist's Waterman pen clicking shut. Through the voice-speakers on our hazmat suits we warn the psychiatrist, "Sir, please step away from your notepad."

The psychiatrist's eyes say something to the effect of "Well, I never," but he obeys.

"Sir, are you aware you just came in full contact with Bullshit to the Tenth Fucking Degree? This part right here." My gloved finger taps a passage on his notepad:

The patient was able to reduce the drinking, until Christmas of 1964 when his wife and family moved out of the house . . .

"Do you have any idea how dangerous this kind of bullshit is?" I ask. "He's makin' it sound as if he began drinking after *his wife and family left." I gesture at Roger, who rolls his eyes (busted, goddammit), and I turn back to the shrink.*

"He's telling it backward. The family left because *of his drinking."*

I give the other guys the sign to "bag and tag" the notepad, and in seconds it's sealed in an airtight orange zipper case and on its way downtown for analysis.

Psychiatrist's notes, August 31, 1965
[After his wife and family moved out] his drinking increased to two or three Manhattans before supper, three or four scotches after supper, and a morning drink of gin and coffee. During this time, he would wake up at 3 or 4 in the morning feeling quite anxious. Dur-

ing the evening and sometimes at night he would have crying spells. This continued until April, 1965, when his wife and family moved back into the house. At this time, the patient said that as his drinking decreased, his wife "started throwing tantrums."

During the period preceding admission, the patient became more and more unhappy with himself and found it necessary to "get plastered and call up my chief." He would go to the home of his senior surgeon and talk about his difficulty with his wife at these times. During one of these visits, he indicated that his hands had begun to shake during surgery. He says he has not been assaultive but has struck his wife on two or three occasions in an effort "to get her to control herself."

Psychiatrist's notes, September 14, 1965
PERSONALITY BEFORE ILLNESS: The patient traced a history of being an only child who never felt close to his parents and indeed felt pushed by them into academic aspirations.... He recalls his mother saying, "Oh, you are so nervous" and going to church services and prayer meetings where it was difficult for him to "sit still."

The patient smokes three packs of cigarettes a day at this time and describes strong anxiety feelings, which include "a feeling that I'd like to die and a trembling of my hands." He has denied any suicidal tendencies but has stated that when he's had too much to drink he's talked about himself being better off if he were not alive....

INTERPRETATION OF TEST FINDINGS: Underlying the patient's unreliable defensiveness is the absence of a concept of self. He is analogous to a building with elaborate decorative features but without a foundation....

While he is presently able to regain control when lapses in reality testing occur, the inner turmoil and the increasing external threat he experiences are at such a boiling point that the potential for a psychotic reaction appears very great.

I put the psychiatric records down.

"The potential for a psychotic reaction appears very great."

It's the sort of thing you like to hear about somebody you're already mad at. I remember hating my high school study-hall teacher, and there were times when I would've given my letter jacket for a peek into his horrible little psychiatric folder. With such a file in hand, I'd get up on my desk and read aloud to the whole class the smoking gun. "Excuse me, people? Everybody? Mr. Vellue's psychiatrist says his 'potential for a psychotic reaction is,' and I quote, 'very great.'" Having made a Citizen's Diagnosis, I accept the applause of a grateful classroom and call the men in white uniforms to come cart the crazy bastard away.

Now, after forty years of wondering if my father was insane, here it is in black and white. Is this relief? Perhaps it's what victims of crimes feel when they hear the bad guy's been caught. There's no closure really; I'm simply reminded of the crime.

I used to look at criminals in the newspaper and study their pictures. I thought perhaps if I could somehow learn the telltale wrinkle of brow or glint of knife edge in the eye I might glean what marked a man as a murderer. *(So, this is a murderer's face.)* But it was always just a picture of a man. It feels the same way today. This phrase "psychotic reaction" brings me no closer to understanding my father. I look at his picture and see just a man.

SUMMARY: In view of his difficulties in his role as a husband and father, as evidenced by his need to be indecisive and clinging at times, and obstructive and irritable at others, it is apparent that the patient's diagnosis is most likely passive–aggressive personality, passive dependent type. Because of the use of alcohol as a primary defense against his inability to handle these stresses, he must be further classified as having the diagnosis of addiction, alcoholism. Additionally, one must consider the possibility of an organic brain syndrome considering the evidence of physical manifestations of the alcohol, as well as some apparent deterioration of judgment.

His frantic use of defenses seems to be a search for some kind of stability. His interpersonal contacts are affected by his own impaired sense of self, so that he cannot view people without projecting his own negative feelings about himself into the situation. While he appears to be maintaining a borderline adjustment at present, his precarious defenses and rapidly mounting inner tension suggest very strong potential for a psychotic mode of adjustment.

Psychiatrist's notes, September 28, 1965

Dr. Sullivan has been utilizing his town pass and denies any drinking on the occasions he has been off the hospital grounds, but admits that this is primarily because he's concerned that Institute employees might be observing him. He is still waiting to hear if his wife will be coming to visit him and is quite hopeful that she will come. However, he worries it will be "the same old story" in her ways of dealing with him.

The Pagans in '65. From left: Jeff Sullivan, Jim Rushton, the new drummer
Steve Rossi, Kip Sullivan, and Jerry Huiting.

SUICIDE

⁊℗

Mom's letters, August 21, 1965
Jeff has had his Beatles ticket for many weeks—locked away in a drawer and he checks it every day or two to see it is still there. I have not yet had the chance to talk to him about it but I know he'll think of it as an experience of a lifetime.

In August 1965, the Beatles' song "Help!" was number one on the charts and occasionally you could hear one of the Pagans playing it on the piano in the Millstone's music room. From their concert at Shea Stadium, the Beatles moved through America, arriving at the Met Stadium in Bloomington, Minnesota, on August 21. There, to the grinding envy of the other brothers, Jeff saw the Beatles live in concert.

Back at home, we gathered on the floor of Dad's study to watch the concert on television. It was a happy night in a house that was enjoying an uninterrupted string of them. Dad's sudden absence created only a temporary hole, one quickly filled by the busy lives of the family he had retreated from years ago. If asked, we might have said how much we missed our father and how eagerly we anticipated his return. Privately, we were elated; guilty about the feeling, but elated.

Kip was winding down life in Rochester as he prepared for a September trip to California to begin studies at Pomona College. He filled out the college financial forms and where it asked for "adjusted family income" he remembers asking Mom, "Shouldn't it read 'maladjusted family income'?" A week before the Pagans' final concert, Kip gave Jay Gleason—his friend, diving pal, and one-time Pagans drummer—a phone call. Because Kip was leaving soon for college, he was planning to invite Jay back into the band as lead singer.

Kip's diary, August 31, 1965

Jay committed suicide!! We were just getting ready for Collin's birthday cake. I called Jay's house, his step-mom asked who it was, I said, "It's Kip. Is Jay there?" Sad voice on the line says, "Kip, haven't you heard?" She cried. Jay put a vacuum cleaner hose from his car exhaust into the front window of his car. Our band is ended. It's over.

At the time, the idea of suicide—of actual suicide—was not part of our world. Maybe it existed on the cartoons and maybe we'd all heard about how Japanese soldiers did that hara-kiri thing. But real suicide? It was too big for Sprinters to think about. When we did try to think about it, what hypnotized us wasn't the existential finality of the act, or the loneliness and depression required to do such a thing. We mostly wondered about the unreported gory details of the final death scene—the gooey dead guy stuff. *("There was an actual dead guy? In a car?)* We pictured the lonely sedan way off on the side of Mayowood Road, the hose running from exhaust pipe to window. We wondered if the engine was still running; if the windows were streaked with soot. Was he wearing his diving team letter jacket?

Even when we *did* consider the act itself, we wondered only at its pain. But the actual idea, the very notion of killing oneself? It simply never occurred to us as a way out; even to us who crouched behind locked doors as armed fathers raged outside; to us who ran down hallways from shrieking bourbon dragons, the idea of exiting the dark maze through death never seemed like an option.

After the funeral was over and the shock had passed, the Pagans got back up to speed for their very last performance on September 10 in nearby Spring Valley. After the final song, Kip was to get in a car and drive to California. The concert was poignant for both the Pagans and my mother. She drove the four little ones to Spring Valley for the great good-bye.

This was her first child to leave home, but by then Kip was more than a son. He was her battle companion, her witness, a guardian who'd more than once kept Dad from hurting her or one of us. On those medevac–motel nights, Kip often stayed behind at the Millstone playing rear guard to our retreat. Now, with Dad's recovery more wish than certainty, she knew Kip's departure would make the Millstone feel lonelier than ever.

From Jim Oldsberg's The Flip Side: An Illustrated History
of Southern Minnesota Rock & Roll Music
The last recollections of the Pagans Kip can remember happened in
summer of 1965. "I can recall singing 'Kansas City/ Hey, Hey, Hey'
off of a flat bed trailer truck in Spring Valley. It was after 11 o'clock
at night and this was the last song we were gonna do. I was pouring
my whole heart and soul into the song; doing it the way the Beatles
did it—'Bye, bye. Bye, bye.' After we finished that song, I literally
grabbed my guitar and amp and jumped into Chuck Rushton's car
and headed for California."

Grandpa's letters, September 10, 1965
I know that you are lonesome tonight. Your #1 boy is on the way to
California. You have found him a real help in the recent years. Our
thoughts are with you. And eagerly you await the first letter home
from him. We also know that soon you travel to Hartford. This is,
of course, a very important trip and we await with anxiety what
will issue.

Christmas Eve for six boys. Monnie made all the stockings.

ONE LAST GOOD CHRISTMAS

Mom, in a long letter to her parents, November 6, 1965
I have just returned from Hartford very much encouraged and—
this you will find hard to believe but will have to accept as a fact—in
love with my husband! This whole thing is so mysterious to me—
the working of the mind and the heart—that I realize you cannot
be expected to understand any of it—nor do I.

From the moment of arrival in Hartford, I could see this was
a new man! He looks in splendid health—thinner, tan, his face
free from the harassed lines and frantic eyes. He may be greyer but
he looks younger. But the most miraculous part is the personality
change! He is kind, considerate, eager to understand me, tender
and loving. I spent the entire week with him—from Thursday noon
to Thursday noon—and never a hard word, never a criticism, nothing but gentleness! I know this is hard for you to believe—it is for
me, too.

But when my train pulled out of Hartford, I felt an anguish
of separation such as I haven't known since the Navy days. Except
for Monday and Tuesday when we were in Mystic Seaport and
two nights when we saw a play and a movie, we did nothing but
talk! It was as exciting as a courtship—it was like getting to know
a new person. Of course, there are many things I see in him that
are troublesome—he is very unsure of himself, uncertain how to
do ordinary things like make a telephone call, and he is extremely
nervous about being with people, and his memory is very faulty.
But Dr. Spence says these things will gradually improve. He thought
that it might be possible for Roger to make a Christmas visit home,
but warned that everything depends upon how he feels as that time
draws near.

He warned also that there are good and bad times in this process—and spoke of Roger as having been "very sick." So I am trying not to be too enthusiastic about the results of my week in Hartford.

Notes from the Hartford psychiatric record, October 29, 1965
The patient reported the visit went extremely well. He found that he was able to discuss many difficulties with his wife that they had been unable to deal with in the past.

It is evident both from the patient and his wife that the time spent together was the first time in their recent married life they were able to communicate with each other. The therapist has pointed out to both of them that the brevity of their contact was different from day-to-day existence at home. However, both the patient and his wife have agreed to another visit in the Hartford area and are also planning for the patient to go home for Christmas vacation to spend some time with the children.

A letter from Kip on one coast to Dad
on the other, November 10, 1965
Dear Dad: When I got letters from both you and Mom saying you both had a good time, I could've jumped for joy. You mentioned some of the changes in the family you've sensed already. Man, just think what a difference this will mean for all of us. God, that sounds good!

Dad, written while at Hartford, to Kip
in California, November 15, 1965
Dear Kipper: Monday morning has rolled around again—another week gone by and am delighted to report that I am feeling better and better. Do wish there were some way of speeding up this process of emotional regrouping. It is impossible to describe to anyone who hasn't been through this business how painful and actually exhausting it is. Am convinced, however, that the months spent now will mean so much more happiness in the future.

I've already, of course, seen the difference in your mom's response in the short time that she was here. Can also hear it in the kids' voices at home. Called yesterday and Collin and Luke were bubbling over on the phone. Even that experienced man-about-town, Jeff, sounded great. Mama's change since her return home after our visit has made itself felt in the kids doing better school work, staying on the ball more, etc. Needless to say you are in my thoughts so much of the time and can hardly wait to see you. Looks as if we'll both be getting home for Christmas about the same time and probably both leaving about the same time. I'll have to return here for a few weeks after my visit. Take care. —Dad

Mom, to her parents, December 6, 1965
I'm safely home again from a second visit to Hartford and it was just as loving as the first one. I still find it hard to believe that after such a nightmare we can now so thoroughly enjoy one another. We count off the days now till the Christmas visit. Roger and Kip will both arrive on December 17th—what a joyous Christmas this is going to be for all of us! We did little else except talk talk talk. We have so many years to catch up on.

Kip's diary, December 20, 1965
I talked all day with Dad. Oh, has he changed. He can be talked with!! It's unbelievable.

Jeff, 2006
When Mom visited Dad that second time, they bought new wedding rings. I've never seen Mom as happy as she was that winter. When she returned home she redecorated the master bedroom. She did, however, mention that while they were together in downtown Hartford, a car engine backfired nearby, a noise like a gunshot, and Mom described Dad's intense panic reaction at being startled.

Mom, 2006
This ring I have on now is the one we bought in Hartford together. We were walking downtown somewhere and in front of a jewelry store we looked at each other and agreed, "Well, the first part of our marriage hasn't been so great. Let's start over." That Christmas of 1965, he was loving, interested, and connected. Just like he was years before.

The last happy family film was taken on Christmas Eve, 1965.

Mom is in the kitchen wearing a red dress and her hair high in a bee-hive. Dad is next to her and together they're preparing the evening's feast. Mom does the pot stirring and finger licking but leaves the big job for Dad, who puts on the oven mitts and pulls the twenty-five-pound turkey from the oven. He places it on the new rollaway dishwasher (with its modern hose connection to the kitchen sink's spigot). The Mayo Clinic doctor has a poultry knife in one hand, a large fork in the other, and when he tries to transfer the turkey from pot to platter, the turkey comes in half, butchered a second time. Watching this film as I have many times, there's some sorrow in seeing the Mayo doctor fail to pull off the holiday photo op with surgical precision.

The other surviving artifact from Christmas '65 is an audio recording of our living room on Christmas morning. Dad recorded the festivities using, as it turned out, the same recorder Kip and Jeff had hidden to capture the "Rage Tapes" that spring. The tape is remarkable only in its banality. Tolstoy wrote, "Happy families are all alike; every unhappy family is unhappy in its own way." As I listen to this pointless and precious chitchat, the observation is confirmed again. Christmas carols play on the hi-fi in the background; the wrapping paper with its high-end crackling sometimes obscures the conversation, but snippets of the quotidian back-and-forth come through:

> *My father's voice on the Christmas '65 tape*
> "Jeff, that aftershave you just opened? That 'Double-O-Seven' stuff really grabs Mama. [Mom laughs.] . . . And I like this other shirt even better, with the zipper collar. Who's this from? Thanks, Chris. The perfect size. How did you know? . . . Well, if it's all right with you folks, I'm going to open this 'record-shaped' present. I sure hope it's that recording of Julie Andrews, *The Sound of Music.*"

Dad starts to unwrap the last gift and little Collin teases him; says the gift he's opening is a "just a fat slice of moldy old cheese."

Dad chuckles, "Is that all? Well, you just wait till *next* Christmas."

There will be no next Christmas, but the tape plays on and in the background Julie Andrews begins to sing. *("The hills are alive with the sound of music.")* I can hear myself announce the unwrapping of my new Kodak In-stamatic camera, which will take the last pictures of my father. The cheerful prattle continues and the Ghost of Christmas Future points at the tombstone, but for now, here on this tape of a man's last Christmas, I listen to my father and it seems no matter what has come before ("I'LL GO GET THE AX AND BASH THIS DOOR IN!") on this Christmas Day, on this thin brown tape, I hear Roger Sullivan is a good father, loving to his wife, kind to his six sons, and grateful that his whole life with all its blessings has been pulled from the edge of the abyss and, in an act of inexplicable grace, handed back to him.

The last page of the psychiatrist's notes, January 11, 1966
Dr. Sullivan returned to the hospital from his visit. The patient found he was able to deal with almost all situations with relative ease. Dr. Sullivan does not feel that he will have any difficulties returning home, except in relations with his wife. Final diagnosis: Passive–aggressive personality, alcoholism.

Condition on discharge: Recovered.

Chris's diary, January 10, 1966
Boy, life is going to be good when Dad gets home.

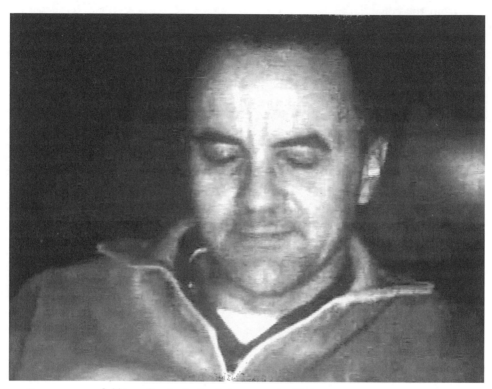

Roger reacts to flubbing a line in the family home movie, Christmas 1965.

TINY DETAILS IN
FAMILY PICTURES

ઝ

I can vividly remember after the Hartford episode, Roger and I were standing in my office at the Mayo Clinic. It was a beautiful day, we were looking
out the window and he said he was doing fine, felt great, and was very opti-
mistic. He said he was really off alcohol, now and forever.

—*Dr. Mark Coventry, my father's boss at Mayo Clinic*

Dad's sudden return to the Millstone was a car crash in backward motion. The metal popped smooth, the pieces of glass flew out of our hair
and assembled into a window, the grill of the Mack truck that hit us backed
away—and there was Dad again, sitting in the kitchen, smiling.

He simply showed up back at the Millstone. He never apologized to
any of us, showed no contrition, made no amends, just walked in the front
door—a drunk driver striding through the hospital ward where his victims
lay, waving and smiling in at everyone through the eye slits of their head
bandages. (*"Say . . . about that ax thing? Waaaaay outta line, I kid you not."*)
In 1965, the needs of the alcoholic's victims weren't part of the typical
treatment plan. Once the addict had dried out and filled in his discharge
forms, it was "Bye-bye, don't be a stranger" and a cab to the airport. Modern
treatment for alcoholism now addresses the needs of the family along with
those of the alcoholic. If only someone had come to us and said, "What happened to you was wrong. Let's talk about it. Here's why it happened. Here's
what alcoholism does to families, here's what it does to trust, here's what you
can do to rebuild." This didn't happen. When Dad returned in January 1966,
we simply picked up where we'd left off, hard-splicing the family film from
the "fistfight scene" to "Hi, honey, I'm home." There was no reconciliation.
All the crimes went under the rug, along with the injuries.

Denial of the injuries was denial of the car wreck, and since most of the
past eight years had been a car wreck, all the emotions of those years were
denied too. Family life was again refracted through that 1950s prism of

cheerful dishonesty. The billboard grins were back in place and everything was just hunky-fucking-dory.

But behind the grin, even we four little ones could tell Dad hadn't healed; he'd simply stopped bleeding. Where one might have hoped for a joyful rebuilding there was only a depressed sort of resignation. Remembering Christmas '65, Myra says, "There was a level of defeatism in Roger then. He wasn't the same vigorous person he'd once been. Something was missing."

Part of it was a sense of "victim" he carried with him, apparent even in a card game of Hearts he played with his sons that spring. Chris remembers ribbing him when Dad drew the queen of spades in a bad hand. "Dad took it personally. His reaction was disturbing. He just quietly put his cards down and walked away."

"Something was missing," said my mom. I've gone through the family photographs many times, looking for this missing something, and today I wonder if I've found it on one-quarter inch of film in a family movie— the one made on Christmas Eve, '65. In two frames of this 8 mm film, my father's self-pity and resignation show plainly: two frames in an emotional Zapruder film that capture him in an unguarded moment.

Dad is facing the camera speaking into the microphone of the cassette recorder. (He's making a sound track he hoped to marry to the 8 mm film at playback.) Though this audiotape has since been lost, by lipreading I'm able to make out one word, "holidays," and guess that he's making an introduction to the night's filming. But he flubs it. His introductory remarks have some small stumble of tongue and his shoulders slump, the muscles in his face sink, and just before the camera is turned off his eyes roll wearily to the left and then close in defeat. I see a weight descend on him. Perhaps I'm too unforgiving here. It's just a guy flubbing a take. So what? He's pissed, big deal.

But I roll the tape back over the play head and it is *there:* a heavy-lidded roll of eyes, an irritation much deeper than this stubbed toe of a moment merits, a look one might see in a teenager who has just been asked to move the refrigerator and barbells up to the attic. Rolling the film (now transferred to video) back and forth over the play head, it's plain the world is too much with him. Even if I am reading more than I should into this quarter inch of forty-year-old film,[1] the psychiatric records show that Roger's tenu-

---

1. This bit of family film can be viewed along with other family memorabilia at thirtyroomstohidein.com.

ous hold on sobriety was not founded on honesty or insight or strength of spirit—only abstinence. The treatment he received, though it was the best available at the time, was clinical, not spiritual. That he was diagnosed as passive–aggressive was probably correct. That his sense of self was not strong also seems true. But neither diagnosis helped him become whole or happy.

Daydream: I Save Dad

I am one of the drunks taking part in a group session in a modern rehab center. There are twelve steps written on a wall poster, five alcoholics in folding chairs, and a counselor. And in my fantasy, sitting with me in this twenty-first-century facility, is my father. He's getting a taste of modern chemical dependency treatment, the kind that could have saved him. There are no Rorschach inkblots in the room today.

The counselor is leading the discussion and you can tell he didn't learn this stuff from a book. He's a recovered cocaine addict devoted now to helping others beat their addictions. In this small room of chairs and drunks he has heard every story there is.

"Roger, during family week we had Myra in here with the group. We all heard her read a list of injuries your drinking has caused her and the boys. I was pretty shocked to hear some of that stuff. Like: 'Roger threatened me with a gun.' Interesting that you didn't bring that up during your intake week."

Another group member choruses: "Yeah, or that part about the ax? Jesus Christ."

Dad says, "Well, she's always dominating me, telling me what—"

The counselor leans over, interrupts. "Is that how you solve problems in your house, Roger? A glass of bourbon and an ax?"

"Well, of course not!" My father's anger flashes. ("Who does this ten-dollar-an-hour orderly think he's talking to? I'm a doctor from the Mayo fucking Clinic. Goddamn guy's probably got a bachelor's degree in psychology and he's telling me?")

"None of us here buy your bullshit, Roger. Sorry, but the 'She's dominating me' stuff doesn't sell here. We met Myra during Family Week, Roger; little five-foot-somethin' bit of a thing, sat right where you are now. Not quite the shrieking harpy we heard about from Roger during his first two weeks here, is she, guys?"

"She seemed scared of you," says another patient through the steam of his coffee. "And no shit, with you hittin' her and wavin' a gun around."

"I hit her just that one time, for Christ's sake!"

"Mmmm," says the counselor. "When you first arrived, you said you'd never hit her. Which is it?"

"What does hitting have to do with anything? Just tell me why I drink and I'll fix it! Look at my MMPI scores about my mother and you'll—"

"Roger, nobody here gives a shit about your mother or about why you drink; we already know why. You drink because you're an alcoholic and—"

"I haven't had a drop since—"

"Since the night you slugged your son, we know. Twenty-one days so far, congrats. But Roger, you aren't gonna get sober or happy until you get honest with us. This isn't about your wife, uh, 'dominating' you or whatever, or about your mother or any of that stuff."

"You have no idea of the pressures I face!" Roger erupts. "Have you ever— one goddamn time—ever had to tell a little girl where her leg went when she woke up?!"

"No," the counselor says, barreling on, "but I once had to tell a little girl, 'Your Daddy was decapitated by an alcoholic who hit him with his car.' An alcoholic kinda like you, Roger."

"THAT'S UNFAIR!"

"And then I somehow managed to get through the rest of that horrible day without getting drunk and threatening my wife with an ax."

"TOTALLY UNFAIR!"

"That's precisely your problem, Roger. You want the world to be fair and it isn't. The world isn't fair. Okay? This just in: some of us have shitty parents. Some of us get fibrosarcomas. Little girls lose their legs. We all get rotten rolls of the dice and you know what? Most people pick themselves up and just sorta move on. Most people when they get a flat tire, they call the Triple A. You get a flat tire and you call the goddamn suicide hotline because your flat tire is so much worse than everybody else's flat tire, because you are Dr. Sullivan from the Mayo Clinic and when things don't go Dr. Sullivan's way, well, that just gives you the perfect excuse to go medicate your feelings with a quart of bourbon and threaten your wife with a chair or a gun or an ax, doesn't it? Doesn't it, you big crybaby?"

Roger looks into the counselor's eyes; then up at the ceiling; down at his hands.

Boxes of Kleenex are usually set in the center of these group circles. If Roger could have opened that door just a half an inch, if he could have leaned forward and reached for a tissue, he might be alive today.

Dad came home armed with only a piece of paper: his diagnoses (passive–aggressive personality with a side of alcoholism). That, and the half-finished wallet he'd made in a crafts class where he practiced sewing until the shakes passed and he could pronounce himself fit for surgery.

Perhaps he did go through some kind of emotional scrubdown and humbling self-inventory that modern rehab centers require, but the record does not show it. Whatever insights he'd had were purely intellectual, not spiritual. He wasn't sober. He'd simply stopped drinking and had achieved this in a closed hospital environment. He had no clue how to face the slings and arrows of the real world, and when he stepped back into it, the first arrow went deep.

Mom, February 2, 1966
Roger left home this morning for St. Petersburg. Dr. Haslett called from Florida last night to say Roger's mother was in a coma and not expected to live through the night. I have not yet heard from Rog so I do not know if he found her still living when he arrived this afternoon. Poor man—this is a very difficult time for him, trying to re-establish himself at the Clinic and in his work—this could have come at a worse time (while he was in Hartford) but only just barely.

Luke on the last trip with his father to St. Petersburg.

The last photograph taken of my father, St. Petersburg,
February 1966.

GOODNIGHT, IRENE

Chris's diary, February 3, 1966
Things around here are like a soap opera. Dad just gets back from an insane asylum cured from drinking. First day of work, his mother dies. Oldest son far away in California college. Jeff smokes, does bad in school. Luke is a klepto and a smoker.

The weather records for Rochester, Minnesota, say January 29, 1966, broke a record when it reached thirty degrees below zero. It couldn't have been much warmer five days later, the day my father started back at the Clinic and got the call about his mother.

On the flight to his mother's deathbed in St. Petersburg my father wrote a letter to his oldest son, Kip. Somehow, during what had to be a stressful week of coming back home and returning to work, my father was able to come out of whatever dark waters held him and—in a voice that was calm, wise, and loving—write the letter reprinted here. Of all the artifacts in the family museum—the ancient photographs, the two frames in the Christmas film, the audiotape—it is a letter, on paper, that shows most clearly the man my father was. Kip still keeps this letter in his desk.

Dad's letter to Kip, February 2, 1966
Dear Kipper—Pardon dinky stationery. Am 5 miles above Illinois in the bright shiny sky—heading south to St. Petersburg on a sad trip. My mother is very sick & am doubtful that she will be alive by the time I get there. Got a call last night from her MD that she was in the hospital on oxygen, chest pain, difficulty breathing, high fever, coma & a "gallop rhythm" to her heart beat—all of which adds up to little hope for life.

Part of the sadness will be closing & leaving the house, disposing of her personal things and the few things that may remain of my father's. Grief—over a near one's death—is a mixture of sad feelings I think. Partly for ourselves—because we miss the familiar being & the good things that that person's life has meant to us—but perhaps we grieve more because life is good and beautiful and that person can no longer share it, feel it, love it & live it.

On the other hand—when one is almost 80, as she is, with little strength to do even necessary things—let alone exciting things— when pain is a constant concern—then death may be very welcome. Isn't it interesting to speculate, too, as to whether death is really an end or a beginning. Are the views of the dying [just] hallucinations or really vistas of another reality that we the living do not under- stand? My romantic old man in his last hours said he saw a land of flowers and long mountains & happily said he was going on a long trip—he loved seeing things that he had never seen before. How do we know that we aren't in heaven now? (Relax, I'm not off my rocker.)

I know there have been so many times in my own life when there was such happiness that "heaven" couldn't be any better—seeing the happiness on the faces of a child or its parents after a tough life-saving operation, feeling love in your mother's arms, drifting down the sunlit Mississippi River on a warm day (there really are "a thousand years of music" in those hills), feeling your triumph and happiness on my shoulders after a hockey game—"feeling" the beauty in Tchaikovsky's violin concertos—etc. etc. Maybe all this is heaven—at any rate, who needs more?

In spite of the sadness of my present mission there will be some happiness. I'm renting a car and I have my swim suit and I'm going back to a place I know—where the sand is white, the sun is hot, the palm trees whisper and the Gulf of Mexico is green and clear. Your mother and I went swimming there 30 years ago. I might even dig up a fishing pole.

Kip, take time to live your days well—remember the happiness and the good in each one of them and make them good. If you do, then all the rest of your days and hours will not only be good but they'll get better as time goes by—even the troubled ones.

My only regret is that until the last few months I never took time to really think about my feelings. Be good to yourself, and if you are, then you'll be gentle with others—perhaps they aren't as wise and strong as you—and they'll love you for it.

All my love, Dad.

Kip had stored this letter away and uncovered it—a year after Dad's death—while packing to return home from his sophomore year in college. Rereading it brought on his first racking cry over the loss. When Kip brought the letter home, we passed it around the circle and after finishing it each of us looked up at the others, wishing more than anything we'd known the author.

Roger's mother was alive when he got there, but barely conscious. After a week she seemed to stabilize and Roger felt he could return to Rochester and did so. But on February 14 he got the phone call. And when he went back for his mother's funeral he took me along.

Why he chose his fifth son for this trip no one knows, including my mother. I didn't know Irene very well; I'd sat in her bony, lifeless lap perhaps twice, quietly traded the "Grandma Rock" jokes with my brothers, yet somehow I was now the chosen grandchild to see her off to her maker. Dad and I spent the week together in St. Petersburg, and to remember the occasion, I packed what would be the first of my personal diaries. I also packed my favorite Christmas gift, the Kodak Instamatic camera.

In the very last series of pictures of my father, we are on the beach together. First, Dad has the Instamatic and it's pictures of me feeding popcorn to gulls. Now I have the camera and Dad is on a beach chair, pool in the background. He's smoking a cigarette and reading a paperback. Even with the magnifying glass I can't read the book's title. In the next shot it's me who's sitting and I can see Dad has set the book on his beach chair so he can take my picture. In this photo I can read the title: *The Koka Shastra*, an ancient Indian text of erotica and sexual positions.

Looking at a small grainy image of a paperback left on a beach chair forty years ago, I see that my parents were trying to reconnect, to rejuvenate their love life. When Dad returned from Hartford, Mom had surprised him with a completely new bedroom: new bed, new dressers, new side tables. A sweet gesture: *"We can love each other again. Here is our bedroom. Here is where we can be husband and wife again.*" I was eleven when she refurbished the master bedroom at the Millstone and at the time thought simply, "Cool furniture, Mom."

Returning now to the very last picture taken of my father I see he looks pensive, sitting in a chair on a dock in Florida; pensive, not troubled really, just inward, distant. When I look at him I wonder what he is thinking. In his final photograph he's looking right into the camera, not a pose a man takes when he's hiding something and perhaps he wasn't hiding. Maybe he thought he was going to make it. Or perhaps it was an honest look into the lens, a "Hey, everybody, this ain't gonna work but I'm enjoying this last lap around the track." Maybe he was thinking, "I'm rid of the old witch." I study the picture under a magnifying glass searching for some clue. When I get too close it's just black-and-white shapes on shiny paper; too far back and it's just a picture of a man.

Two weeks after that final picture on the beach, Dad updated his last will and testament and made some minor changes, still leaving everything to Myra and his six boys. Perhaps it was his mother's death that made my father consider his own mortality. Or perhaps he was already dipping his toe in the river Styx. Given what the police would find on the dresser of the motel room where he died, the latter seems more likely.

Winter outside the Millstone's front entryway window.

WHITEOUT/BLACKOUT

✋

Mom says she knew Dad began drinking again soon after he returned from his mother's funeral in Florida.

There was now only one bottle of booze in the Millstone: gin, kept on hand for visitors and Clinic gatherings. Mom and Dad had agreed it would be okay to keep one bottle around the house as long as Mom was in charge of it and it was kept in a locked cabinet in the dining room. One March evening Myra had company, and when she went to the cabinet, she saw the lock had been compromised. It was broken but didn't look broken; a skilled hand had jimmied it. And the level in the gin bottle was lower than it ought to have been.

Then two weeks later Dad's cover was blown completely. A visitor remarked to Mom that the gin and tonic she'd just prepared for him from the cabinet bottle contained no alcohol whatsoever. Standing there in front of a visitor who could also put two and two together, Mom realized Dad had drunk the entire bottle and refilled it with water. Dad had not just jumped off the wagon. He'd thrown a Greg Louganis reverse two and a half with a triple twist.

Mom later said that after the switching-water-for-gin trick, she began looking through the house for hidden bottles and, finding no stash inside, looked in the back of Dad's MG. There, like a body in the trunk, was Old Grand-Dad. Reappearing at the Millstone along with Old Grand-Dad were old behaviors.

Chris's diary, March 9, 1966
Dan and I went to a movie tonight and Dad picked us up after. On the way home Dad kept telling us that he was hen-pecked. "Mom made me get Pagan. Mom made me put up the gate on the driveway to keep the dog in. Mom loves her books. Mom loves little pets.

Mom is a child." God that's irritating. I don't notice much change from his ways in the days of yore. Damn it.

The final storm at the Millstone began with a blizzard.

My father was scheduled to attend a children's clinic in Fairmont, Minnesota, 120 miles west of Rochester. At these clinics, school nurses would bring in children—sometimes a hundred a day—and Mayo Clinic doctors would do triage, referring them to nearby hospitals. When Dad began the drive to Fairmont, it was still just a snowstorm.

Chris's diary, March 23, 1966
We've had the biggest blizzard we've had in a long time. Trees are down everywhere. Dad's out of town at some work thing and his car stalled on the way home and he had to stay at a farm. He won't be home tonite either.

Dad's boss, Dr. Mark Coventry, 1992
He was scheduled to do a children's clinic in Fairmont, Minnesota, but simply didn't show up for it. He told me that he had to stay overnight in a motel on the way to the clinic because of the blizzard that had hit Minnesota. Of course, by then, I didn't believe him. He simply didn't show up at the children's clinic and of course the people there called me, asking, "Where is Dr. Sullivan?"

As it turned out, the morning he was supposed to be there he was arrested for drunken driving by the police.

From the files of the New Ulm, Minnesota,
Police Department, March 23, 1966
Nature of report: D.W.I. Man leaving motel. Seems to have too much drink to drive.
Report: I received the call by radio from officer Stoll. I went on Broadway and saw the car, an MG convertible, license 1 GI 275. At 7th N. & Broadway the car stopped in the left lane to make a left turn. At this time I approached the driver and asked him to step out of the car. He was unsteady on his feet. Also the smell of some sort of alcohol drink was on his breath. He said that he was on his way to Fairmont, Minn. to attend some sort of clinic for children but was caught in the snow storm and had to stay "at a farmer's house"

for the night. From that time on he has lost a few days and seemed confused as to what day it was.

How my father ended up in New Ulm is a mystery. It's fifty miles straight north of Fairmont and way off the direct drive from Rochester.

Police report, continued
Dr. Charles Roger Sullivan was taken to the station and given the usual tests, including the State Highway Alcohol Test. A urine sample was obtained and Dr. Sullivan was charged with driving a motor vehicle under the influence of intoxicating liquor. City Ord. 214 Sec. 4. Dr. Sullivan was placed in cell #3. A black bag and his belongings are in the gun locker. $51.00 in paper money & $2.15 in change. He made a phone call to his wife at Rochester, Minn. Dr. Sullivan bailed out at 7:15 p.m. by check and was OKed by the judge to appear in court on 4/2/66 at 10:00 a.m.

Mom said Roger called her at the Millstone with a story about how he'd been pulled over by the New Ulm Police. He said it was because he "didn't have a muffler and that he wasn't allowed to drive. That he couldn't make it home on the night he'd planned." Mom, having lived with a liar for so many years (plus the fact that it was a spectacularly shitty lie), guessed correctly, called the New Ulm Police, and discovered the truth.

When Roger got home he didn't bring up the arrest, of course. When Mom told him she knew about it and asked him—probing toward the hoped-for response of, "Maybe I need to go back to Hartford"—all she got was a clipped, "Well, I guess we'll have to pay more for car insurance now."

Mom's letters to her parents, March 23, 1966
We have had a serious set-back but a conversation by phone with the Hartford doctor encourages me to take it as typical and not to be discouraged. That—plus the blizzard—has kept my mind completely occupied. I'll begin writing again in a few days. Don't take a silence to be a desperate sign. It's just that situations like this drain away all my energies and interests and require so much of me to try to deal with everything to everyone's advantage. All is now well so do not worry.

Mom, 2006
Looking back, that conversation with the Hartford doctor now seems astonishing. How could he have just accepted news of a DWI and assure me, "Oh now, it's not the end of the road. No need to be alarmed"? He didn't stay on the phone with me very long, there was no back-and-forth, no question and answer. Just a curt, "Don't worry" and he hung up. I remember looking at the snow falling outside, wondering, "What am I going to do now?"

Soon, Dad no longer tried to conceal his drinking by hiding in a motel room a city away. We were back where we started.

Chris's diary, April 9, 1966
The whole family left for Easter vacation in La Crosse, Wisconsin, around 10:30 this morning. [The handwriting changes here, appearing angry.] God Damn it! Last night dad started drinking again. He was juiced the whole night. Mom and us left the motel with him still sleeping it off. We rented a car and came home. Things will be just like old times. SHIT, I KNOW RIGHT NOW NEVER TO EVER DRINK IN MY WHOLE LIFE.

Mom, 2006
That was a bad night, that one in La Crosse. I remember pouring a bottle into the motel sink. It didn't raise his ire; he was too drunk by then to care. I left him in our room and came next door and slept on the floor of the room where you four little ones were. I remember the next morning one of you asked, "What are you doing down there, Mama?" and I lied. I said I was "exercising."

Mom rented a car and drove us home, and a pall hung over the Millstone on Easter Sunday. After this incident the letters from Rochester stopped. In Grandpa's bound collection of letters, Myra writes only one letter in all of April and June, and not again until a week after her husband's body arrived back in Rochester.

Dr. Mark Coventry, 1992
Well, by then it was out of my hands. He was coming into work impaired from drinking the night before. The Clinic's board of

governors decided that with several warnings already, with his institutionalization, and now with him drinking heavily again soon after Hartford, they weren't going to put up with it any longer. They suggested he leave.

They said they "would do everything they could" to help him find another place, but that's always difficult with a history like his. Still, I helped him arrange a trip to the Southeast; he seemed particularly interested in settling there. And so we wrote letters to people in Florida, in Georgia. But of course those letters have to be honest.

And so the young medical student who'd aspired to be Albert Schweitzer was kicked out of the most prestigious medical center in the world. And it was clear they weren't going to give him a good recommendation. On May 24, my father began his final, frantic, and futile trip around the country looking for a new job.

Kip in the Millstone's dining room during his first visit home from college.

MELTDOWN IN
WEST PALM BEACH

ℐℛ

In Alcoholics Anonymous, they have a phrase for it: "hitting rock bottom." Few alcoholics recover without reaching this place, one that AA describes as a point of "pitiful and incomprehensible demoralization." By now Roger had racked up quite a few excellent candidates for rock bottom—publicly accusing his best friend of sleeping with his wife, jail time for a DUI, a fistfight with his son.

Getting just one of these wake-up calls would be enough to make most people tilt their heads and say, "I did *what?*" But to be noticed over the day-to-day insanity of an addiction, a rock bottom usually requires the kind of debauchery that would get you kicked out of the Rolling Stones. *(Cut to Keith Richards goin', "You bloody fucking LUNATIC! Get outta here! And leave the guitar!")* But Roger's candidates for rock bottom came and went, came and went, and still he plowed on.

One of the last bottoms occurred in West Palm Beach, Florida, where he'd gone looking for a job. He'd had something like an offer from an old medical school chum, made back in the days when he was one of the clinic's bright boys. *("You ever get tired of Minnesota winters, you come on down to West Palm Beach.")* Though it was more of an offhand compliment than an offer, it was all Roger had.

"Even though I knew the trip would be futile," Myra remembers, "I went with him. And it was humiliating from the start."

The man who'd made the offer, Dr. Phil Greenbaum, was downwind from the stink of Roger's career and had heard plenty about his being fired at Mayo. Too much of a gentleman to rescind the ancient invitation, Phil met with Roger and after the interview offered him a salary less than half what the clinic paid and a contract that my mother noted "might have suited a beginning intern. Phil certainly expected him to turn it down, but I'm not sure your father even realized how insulting the offer was."

229

After the interview was over, the Greenbaums abandoned their role of gracious host. They suggested Roger visit other clinics in Florida before making a decision, and then they simply left, disappearing for the weekend.

"I'm certain to avoid our company," remembers Myra. "Understanding how awkward and horrible they must've felt, I don't blame them."

The car was barely out of the driveway when whatever civilized veneer Roger had managed to maintain crumbled away. He looted the Greenbaums' liquor cabinet and stayed caveman drunk for the next two days.

Myra, 2006
Two nightmarish days. No day, no night. No time for me to eat or sleep. Just one long forty-eight-hour struggle to keep him from wrecking the Greenbaums' house. I left him asleep once, while I went to get food. Before I got back he'd managed to set fire to a corner of the bed in the guest room with a cigarette. He was simply gone. He babbled witlessly. He couldn't walk without falling against furniture. Occasionally he collapsed on the bed but never to sleep deeply. He'd lie there, muttering, fingering the bedclothes like a dying old man. He was gone. That's the only word I have to describe him—gone. Nothing in his eyes. No recognition of me nor his whereabouts. He was like a dog that's been run over, kicking around in the ditch, not quite yet dead.

When the Greenbaums returned Sunday, Myra met them at the door, humiliated. Suitcase packed, head down, she quietly asked Phil to please take her to the nearest bus station right away; to let her just *go*. With the Bourbon Zombie lurching about in the background, Phil quickly took in the situation, said he understood, and that he'd handle it from there. My mother fled north to her parents' apartment in Jacksonville.

Myra, 2006
I dropped the whole miserable disgusting seamy story on the shoulders of my sorrowing mother and father and left for Minnesota the next morning. We didn't see Roger many times after that. The disintegration from then till July third was rapid and probably irreversible.

Grandpa's letters to Mom, June 3, 1966

It doesn't seem possible. Were you really here, right in our little apartment this very week? All your Mama and I can talk about is our visit with you, and we go over it again and again. . . . Suddenly it was all over—our first visit with our daughter since 1962. When will the next be? We do not know. I refer again to my favorite Tennyson line: "And yet we trust that good will fall. At last far off, at last to all. And every winter change to spring."

From left: Roger, Myra, her best friend, Tacy Moore, and her brother, James Longstreet, circa 1942–43.

"DO I OWE YOU
ANY MONEY?"

ℐℓ

O n the phone is Myra Longstreet's best friend from Seabreeze High
School, class of 1941. Tacy Moore, now eighty-nine, is speaking
from her home, still in the Daytona Beach area, ten miles up the road from
R. J. Longstreet Elementary School.

"There was simply never a finer man than your grandfather," says Tacy,
long an admirer of the old professor.

Fine men were in fact hard to come by for both Tacy and Myra. Over
the years, Myra's friend had also suffered a horrible marriage to an alcoholic,
and the weight of those decades is evident in her thin voice today: one that
breaks occasionally, not with tears but the simple exhaustion of age and of
years spent worrying about things beyond her control. But beneath the rice-
paper words is also a kind of steel, the voice of a survivor. Like her best friend
from those impossibly long ago, impossibly bright days under the Florida
sun, Tacy has outlived her tormentor.

"Yes, your father did in fact come to see me after that incident at the
Greenbaums'," says Tacy, and this is in fact why I've called. After Myra fled,
Roger remained alone a few days longer in Florida, and it was during this
time he paid one last visit to Tacy.

"He just showed up at my door one night, around seven. I was holding
the baby," Tacy recalls. "I could tell he wanted to talk to me. And the way
your father was acting, it seemed whatever he wanted to talk about was
something . . . something important. But my husband at the time, Bob, he
wouldn't leave the room. He was very controlling, you know; wouldn't allow
me something as simple as a private conversation."

So the conversation between the three stayed light. Whatever it was my
father had come to talk about was nearly postponed forever when Tacy's husband suggested the menfolk head off to the nearest saloon to throw back a

few. Roger agreed Bob's proposal was an outstanding idea, but before the men left Roger managed to come back around to what may have been his original agenda. He asked Tacy one question.

"Do I owe you any money?"

Tacy had in fact made a loan, back when Myra and her new husband were living on a medical student's wages, but Myra had long since repaid it. Two weeks later, when Tacy heard Roger had died, the question gave her pause.

I ask if his sudden appearance, his question, if it all seemed a little strange.

"Well, yes, I do remember thinking that he was . . . how do you say it," she asks, searching for the phrase, "putting his affairs in order."

The conversation with Tacy turns at last to Myra. She asks how her old friend has been getting along, and as we chat I look at an old photograph of the two coeds sitting together in a booth at a diner. Sitting with them are my father as well as my mother's one sibling, Uncle Jimmy—but my eyes go to Myra and Tacy. They are both smiling for the camera, both unaware of monsters that wait for them in distant houses. Like an audience member at a horror movie, I want to stand up and yell, *"Don't go in the house! He's in there!"* But neither of them can hear me. The group calmly gets up from the booth in the ancient diner, hugs are given, and they walk off into the future.

Grandpa's letters to Mom, June 3, 1966
You may know that Roger called us mid-morning, June 1st. Your mother talked briefly with him. He said he "thought" he was in Norfolk, Virginia.

STATE OF GEORGIA
DEPARTMENT OF PUBLIC SAFETY
CRIME LABORATORY
GEORGIA BUREAU OF INVESTIGATION
BOX 1456, ATLANTA, GEORGIA

AUTOPSY OR REPORT OF EXAMINATION OF BODY   7 5 4 8 5 1

NAME OF DECEASED   Dr. Charles Roger Sullivan

DATE OF DEATH: MONTH July   DAY 3 19 66 COUNTY WHERE DEATH OCCURED   Richmond

Investigation revealed that this 45 year old medical doctor,who
lived in Rochester, Minnesota, had arrived in Augusta on June 30th
relative to securing a position at the Medical College of Georgia.
He had conferences with the Chief of Orthopedic Service at the college.
On the day he arrived he said that he had had the "flu", and was so
hoarse that he could not talk. It was known that he had been depressed
and had had difficulties at home, and with drinking. He was given
penicillin tablets by a local doctor, all of which he had taken. He
had finished his business and had purchased an airplane ticket to return home on July 3rd. About 12:30 a.m. that morning, July 3rd, he
had called Rochester and while talking he dropped the phone. The
Motel manager was aware of this but thought that he had just "passed
out", because of his drinking. The door of his room was opened at
9:30 a.m. and Dr. Sullivan was found dead crouched by his bed with
the telephone receiver off the hook.

Examination revealed that there was a broken ashtry under the body.
He was on his knees with his head down on the floor supported in this
position by the left side of his body resting against the bed. There
was vomitus on the floor and in his mouth and nostrils; it had a strong
odor of alcohol. There was a 1/4 inch laceration above his left eyebrow from which there had been a slight amount of bleeding. It is
thought that this laceration was caused by striking his head when he
fell on one of the fragments of glass on the floor. There were no
other marks of violence. There was definite flatness to percussion
over the upper half of the left lung posteriorly. There were no other
abnormal findings.

On his dresser there was a half empty fifth of whiskey and three bottles
that had been dispensed at Mayo Clinic on June the 8th. Two of these
bottles had contained 100 capsules each of Placidyl, 200 milligrams.
These two bottles were empty. The third bottle had contained 500 capsules of Librium, 10 milligrams. Only 442 of these remained in the
bottle.

Cause of death: Pneumonia involving the left lung; type undetermined.

DO NOT FILL IN THIS PART OF FORM
(FOR CRIME LABORATORY USE ONLY)

DATE 8 . 3 - 66   DATE   July   66

Report of the death scene.

THE FAMOUS FINAL SCENE

⁂

The addict loves drama.

"I'll show them," thinks the drunk as he leans over the bridge and looks into the swirling waters below. In the movie playing in his head, he writes the Famous Final Scene. It will be a scene so touching, audiences everywhere will weep and as they cry, they'll blame themselves. *"How could we not have known?"* An usher comes down the aisle handing out packs of Kleenex and still the people keen, *"Oh, Tortured Arteest! Please come back. Come back and explain again how your burdens were heavier than ours, your sadness deeper. We'll mix your favorite drink . . . and we'll really listen this time."*

The addict loves drama. His whole life has been drama. Did he not have the Hardest Job in the World? Did he not have the Meanest Boss Ever? And so at last he comes to the Famous Final Scene and it too must be the Most Dramatic Ever. Let the camera pull wide, let the music swell, and let our hero fall nobly into the swirling waters below.

But there is no bridge; no camera pulling wide; no music. And if there are swirling waters here at the end, it is a flushing toilet. The metaphor, though unpleasant, better captures the final horrible weeks of June 1966—a toilet—where the swirling waters go round and round in ever smaller circles, and in them all the sordid horrible stinking crap that floats in the wake of every narcissist and addict—the emotional debris of broken promises, of neediness, of poor-me poor-me—all of it orbiting the empty void at the middle of the craving heart, and in its final hour all the careless words and selfish acts of the reckless life take their last lap, going round and round pulled into the addict's dark star and his life ends not in the hoped-for bang, not even a whimper, but in a gurgle of plumbing.

Mom, writing eight days after my father's death, July 11, 1966
Roger did not come directly home. . . . He went to St. Paul and was
there nearly a week. There he stayed, doing nothing, calling many
times a day. . . . When he did come back, he spent most of the day
in the bedroom with the curtains drawn, sleeping most of the time
because of the drugs and the liquor.

On June 1, Kip flew in to Rochester's tiny airport, having completed his
freshman year at Pomona. It felt good to have our top lieutenant back in the
trenches with us, and before he could even set foot in the Millstone, Kip
was neck-deep in the same insanity of the summer before. "The minute I
got inside [the] car," he wrote in his diary, "all the brothers hit me with bad
news. Mom says dad hadn't resigned—more like fired. So we may not be
able to afford Pomona next year. Family's gonna have to move out of Millstone. Shit!!"

The summer of '66 was all set to outcrazy the fist-fighting summer of '65.
Where we once lived with the proverbial Elephant in the Room that no one
talked about, now we had the Retarded Zombie in the Room who did stuff
so crazy there was nothing to do *but* talk about it. One of these scenes was
reported to us by a neighbor, Mrs. Hallenbeck. She told us she'd come by the
Millstone to see Mom and lend what support she could. We were all out at
the time and she found herself standing in the doorway of the master bedroom. Roger was sitting at the end of the bed, disheveled and insane.

"He was talking just pure nonsense and then he started to curse at *me*,"
she told brother Jeff. "He actually thought I was Myra and continued to
curse me. I tried to orient him, to tell him who I was, but I gave up and left
feeling very scared."

It was as if the teeth had been removed from the monster. He still
prowled the hallways, still growled, but his ability to truly frighten was gone.
We gathered nightly to snicker at Dad's latest stunts and marvel at how far
from reality he had meandered. Noted Kip in his diary, "He denied drinking
even when I showed him the Coke bottle he came in with had the smell of
whiskey in it."

By now, Roger probably had some vague sense his life was going down
the toilet. He knew Mom was seeing a lawyer; knew she was going to have
a "separate maintenance" order served on him. But even as he circled the
drain, he lived in denial, making new travel plans to find a job that didn't

exist. He packed for a trip south on June 28, and before he left called his old friend, Dr. Tony Lund.

"We met at that place across from St. Mary's," recalled Tony in a phone conversation. "I didn't know at the time he was drinking again or that he'd run into trouble with the Clinic. It was an emotional meeting. I remember his eyes filling with tears when he told me, 'What a good friend you've been over the years.' Near the end of our lunch, Roger told me he was going south . . . 'to a convention.'"

I asked, "Did you get the feeling he was saying good-bye forever?"

"Well, I've thought about that many times since," Tony said, "and maybe, conceivably he was. But at the time? No, I didn't have that feeling. But he was very sketchy about that trip though."

I remember watching a stand-up comedian on a late-night talk show do a bit about suicide.

"What's the deal with suicide, people? I mean, we're all gonna die anyway, right? Do you really have to walk up to God and go, "You can't fire me! I QUIT!"

Maybe Roger did in fact "quit." That's two reports I've heard now, two final and fairly curious meetings with Roger: Tacy's encounter in Florida ("He was, how do you say it, putting his affairs in order") and his lunch with Tony Lund in Rochester. Yet if Tony or Tacy ever believed my father killed himself, they never shared the thought with my mother.

Kip's diary, June 30, 1966
Dad phoned. From somewhere, I forget. Says now he's going to Georgia.

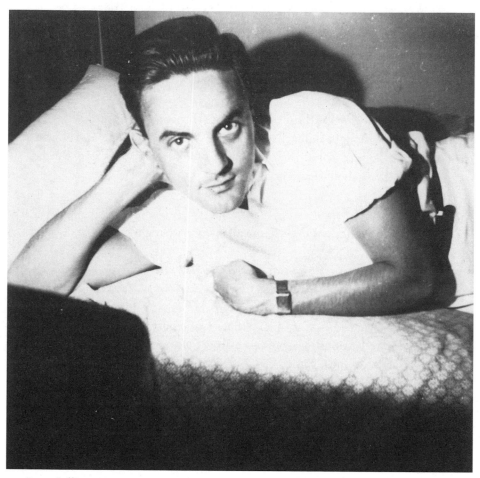

Roger Sullivan, circa 1941–42.

ZEE TORTURED ARTEEST

જી

Myra's letters home, 1958
[At a Mayo Clinic cocktail party, Mom had been introduced to a famous British surgeon.] According to legend he operates all day, spends the night at the Club drinking seven or eight double-scotches, and beats everybody to the hospital the next morning.

Back in May 1961, Mom was at the sink peeling potatoes when she saw Ernest Hemingway walk by the road out in front of the Millstone wearing his trademark turtleneck sweater and knitted cap. For a woman whose library included copies of the famous writer's best works, seeing one of the century's acknowledged literary masters stroll by her back window was worth a phone call to her best friend.

"I *thought* that was him," JoAnn Bianco confirmed. "He passed down here just a few minutes ago." The phone lines buzzed a few times around the neighborhood until it was established Myra had indeed seen Hemingway. He had first checked into Rochester's St. Mary's Hospital back in December 1960 under the name of his personal physician, Dr. George Saviers, ostensibly for treatment of high blood pressure and unofficially for psychiatric care of depression. After two months of sometimes twice-weekly electroshock therapy, he was released in January but was readmitted in April.

"He was friends with the Kjerners," Mom tells me, "who lived right across from the Biancos." She saw his short, stocky figure pass the Millstone's gates maybe ten more times that spring until he was released at the end of June, a week before he committed suicide in his cabin in Idaho. Like most alcoholics under traditional medical care, Hemingway charmed and bullshitted his doctors into releasing him; an assessment his wife, Mary, shared.

"The name's very mention brings to mind bullfights," reads one laudatory website, "barroom brawls, deep-sea fishing and daiquiri parties, big-game

241

hunting and booze binges; it is a legend as steeped in alcohol as it is in adventure." That sentence on the Hemingway mystique is full of the same kind of misguided admiration as my mother's letter about the British surgeon she met at the Clinic party—the one who'd had "seven or eight double-scotches and beats everyone to the hospital the next morning." Oh, marvelous. The doctor who is standing over you—with a scalpel and a hangover—arrived to work *on time*. Well, that's fucking great.

This mythical marriage of passion, creativity, and chemical dependency is a disease we pass down as a society through storytelling. For ages we've let our talented drunks cut wide destructive paths with impunity. If you have some sort of skill, be it word slinging or rock songs, the world waves you past the purple rope—*"He's with the band!"*—and you're allowed to become intoxicated, treat people poorly, and do whatever you want. This adulation has likely been going on since the first caveman crushed grapes. Some mead-guzzling schmuck named Thog probably did a great cave drawing and then spent the rest of his life barfing on the saber-toothed tiger rug and crying, "Village not *understand* Thog." Nothing's changed and we've simply moved on to applauding an obese Elvis or an emaciated Cobain as they slur their way through concerts while we all shrug and say, "Tortured genius."

If the Bullshit Police pulled up when we had one of these false heroes on our shoulders, we'd get the bullhorn to our ears and a loud reminder that behind every tortured arteest we celebrate are families and loved ones who suffer the actual torture. Behind every drunken high achiever is a trail of parentless and rudderless children, broken promises, broken teeth, cigarette burns, restraining orders, neglect, deceit, hurt, anger, shame . . . and for what? A nice song? A two-fisted story without adverbs? Whoop-dee-fuckin'-doo.

And when they're finished with "the work"? They slap a lip-lock around a 12-gauge and spackle the ceiling with their brains, leaving yet another in a long line of messes their poor families have to clean up.

Myra, 2006
I think of all those holidays he ruined—the Christmases, the Thanksgivings. Finally, on his way out, he wrecked the Fourth of July.

Dad's study at the Millstone in a happier hour. Just over Myra's shoulder is the phone that rang seventeen times.

PHONE CALLS
FROM THE DEAD

∽

July 2, 1966, Saturday

Mom, writing to her parents eight days
after my father's death, July 11, 1966
The last time I saw him was the morning I took him to the airport,
~~June 28th. Roger leaned in the car window to kiss me goodbye and~~
heaven must have been watching over me, for my last sight of him
was one which filled me with tenderness and the old love.

His first stop was Newport News. Mark Coventry phoned later
that first week to say the Newport News doctors had called to say
Roger was arriving for interviews intoxicated and irrational. A
three-way effort was made by Mark, me, and the doctors in Virginia
to get him to come home or go back to Hartford. But the expected
result was an intensified, hysterical denunciation of all of us—Mark
for following him across the country to "give him the ax," me for my
willingness to believe everybody but him, the Newport News doctors for being s.o.b.'s he wouldn't work with anyway.

So he went on to New Orleans—with much the same result: arriving full of confidence, leaving because the men there were dis-
courteous or incompetent. During this time I was in a constant
state of confusion and distress. The money was draining away
fast—with hotel bills, transportation, and constant phone calls. I
was getting too much advice—Mark saying, "You'll have to start
commitment proceedings," Dick Steinhilber saying it couldn't be
done, Tony pressing me to get funds frozen, the lawyer protest-
ing his inability to do much till Roger's return. In the midst of all
this, Tony and Mark Coventry were pushing to have the Clinic
put Roger on a disability basis, which resulted in me getting phone

245

calls from the Board of Governors, from the head of Psychiatric Department, Clinic insurance men, and the Orthopedic section heads. Even brother Jimmy called me during that last week—till my head was finally spinning.

Dr. Tony Bianco, 2007
Mark Coventry and I went to the board of governors and said, "Please, you can't fire Roger. He's sick." We asked that he not be fired, that he be reinstated so he could be committed and then put on full disability. And the board was very agreeable; they said yes. So we were ready to commit him when he returned—even against his wishes if necessary.

Mom's July 11, 1966, letter
Whenever the phone rang I was braced for bad news. Through all this was the dread certainty that doom was near. I feared he would meet with a fatal accident—or involve himself with the law since he always rented a car wherever he was. The Thursday and Friday and Saturday nights of July 1st through the 3rd were horrible. He phoned as many as eight times in one day—usually to berate me with all the old vituperation. I finally told him Friday night not to call again—that I'd hang up the moment I knew it was he. Those were my last words to him—a knowledge that will haunt me for a long time.

Kip, 2006
I remember Dad calling home from Georgia late the night he died. I answered the phone. His voice was weak and drunk. It pissed me off to hear it. I made small talk with him but only for his benefit. He asked to speak to Mom. She was upstairs and said, no, she didn't want to talk to him. I told him this and tried to end the conversation. When I said good-bye I wasn't sure he said good-bye back. So I waited a second, said good-bye again, and hung up. That was less than an hour before he died.

Mom's July 11, 1966, letter
At 12:45 a.m. I heard the phone ring. Kip and Jeff were down in the study and they answered it. He spent ten minutes complaining

to them about what was wrong with me. Kip says Roger fell silent many times and they had to speak to him several times before he began again. Then he drifted away and didn't even answer when they said goodbye. Kip came upstairs to tell me about it—and the phone began ringing again. "Let it ring," I told him. "You managed to be pleasant last time—don't let him antagonize you into a nasty answer."

Jeff, 2006

The phone was on the desktop to my right. We were watching TV in Dad's study. I was sitting on the big chair in the corner. At 12:45 or so, it began to ring again. I recall counting the number of times it rang—17, before it finally stopped. We all kept our eyes on the TV. No one said anything.

Mom's July 11, 1966, letter

So we let it ring—and that sound will echo in my ears forever I fear. Rationally I know that had we answered it, we'd have been subjected to the same accusations and perhaps have been goaded into angry retorts we'd have regretted even more. We'll never know. Unhappily, the medical report places the time of death at 1:00 a.m. This moment of time obviously is bothering me. I have been several days on this last page to you—unable to write all I'm thinking— equally unable to leave it and move on. This is a fact I must deal with. It is not easy.

CERTIFICATE OF DEATH   State File No.

BIRTH NO.		Militia Dist. No.		Custodian's No. **1149**

1. NAME OF DECEASED (Type or Print)	(First) CHARLES	(Middle) ROGERS	(Last) SULLIVAN	2. DATE OF DEATH (Month) (Day) (Year) July 3, 1966

3. PLACE OF DEATH (County)
Richmond

City or Town	In City Limits Yes ☒ No ☐	LENGTH OF STAY (in this place) D.K.
Augusta		

Name of Hosp. or Institution
University **MOTEL**   LENGTH OF STAY **D.K.**

4. USUAL RESIDENCE (Where deceased lived. If institution: residence before admiss

State Minnesota   County Olmsted

City or Town	In City Limits Yes ☐ No ☒	LENGTH OF STAY (in this plac
Rochester	D.K.	D.K.

Street Address or R.F.D. and Box No.
MR 72

5. SEX M	6. RACE W	7. BIRTHPLACE (State or foreign country) Ohio	CITIZEN OF WHAT COUNTRY? USA

15. IS RESIDENCE ON FARM? Yes ☐ No ☒	16. BURIAL ☐ REMOVAL XX CREMATION ☐	DATE July 1, 1966

8. DATE OF BIRTH April 27, 1921	9. AGE (In years) last birthday 45	IF UNDER 1 YEAR Months Days	IF UNDER 24 HRS. Hours Min.

NAME OF CEMETERY   Lakewood Crematorium   LOCATION (City or Town) (County) (State) Minneapolis Mi

10. MARRIED ☒ NEVER MARRIED ☐ WIDOWED ☐ DIVORCED ☐ SEPARATED ☐	If Married or Widowed Give Name of Spouse Myra Sullivan

17. EMBALMER'S SIGNATURE _[signature]_   LICENSE NO. 1738

11. USUAL OCCUPATION (Give kind of work done during most of working life, even if retired) Physician	KIND OF BUSINESS OR INDUSTRY Unknown

18. MORTICIAN
Elliott Sons Inc

12. WAS DECEASED EVER IN U.S. ARMED FORCES? (Yes, no, or unknown) (If yes, give war or dates of service)
yes   Navy 1943–1949   SOCIAL SECURITY NO. 277-22-5470

19. MORTICIAN'S ADDRESS
Augusta Ga

13. FATHER'S NAME Charles William Sullivan	20. INFORMANT R.F. Towey	Relationship None

14. MOTHER'S MAIDEN NAME Irene Compton	21. INFORMANT'S ADDRESS Rochester Minn

22. CAUSE OF DEATH [Enter only one cause per line for (a), (b), and (c).] PLEASE PRINT

PART I. DEATH WAS CAUSED BY:

IMMEDIATE CAUSE (a) Pneumonia involving the left lung, type undetermined.

Conditions, if any, which gave rise to the cause a, the under-cause last.

DUE TO (b)

DUE TO (c)

INTERVAL BETWEEN ONSET AND DEATH	DO NOT WRITE IN THIS SPACE
1.	2. 3. 4.
	5. 6.

PART II. Other significant conditions contributing to death but not related to the terminal disease condition given in Part I (a)

23. AUTOPSY? Yes ☐ No ☒

24. ACCIDENT ☐ SUICIDE ☐ HOMICIDE ☐	PLACE OF INJURY (e.g., in or about home, farm, factory, street, office bldg., etc.)	INJURY OCCURRED While at Work ☐ Not While at Work ☐

25. I hereby certify that I attended the deceased from
19___ to ___ 19___, that I last saw the deceas

(CITY OR TOWN) (COUNTY) (STATE)   TIME OF INJURY   (Month) (Day) (Year) (Hour)

alive on **not seen alive** 19___, and th
death occurred at 9:30 A.M., from the causes and on the date stated above
Found

HOW DID INJURY OCCUR?

26. SIGNATURE _[signature]_   Degree or Ti
Medical Examiner Richmond County Ga M.D.

27. DATE REC'D BY LOCAL REG. 7-23-66	28. REGISTRAR'S SIGNATURE _Earl W. Lewis_

ADDRESS 416-420 S.F. Bldg., Augusta, Ga.   DATE SIGNED 7/6/66

ADM-3.3

Georgia Department of Public Heal
Vital Records Service
Atlanta, Georgia 30334

This is to certify that this is a true and correct copy of the certificate filed with the Vital Records Service, Georgia Department of Human Resources. This certified copy is issued under the authority of Chapter 31-10, Vital Records, Code of Georgia.

Michael B. Lavoie
State Vital Records Registrar
and Custodian, Director, Vital
Records Service

County Custodian: _R.S. Adams_

Issued By: _[signature]_

Date: _7-29-96_

(VOID WITHOUT ORIGINAL SIGNATU
AND IMPRESSED SEAL)

The death certificate.

THIS MORTAL COIL

My father's autopsy
Charles R. Sullivan, deceased.

The body was embalmed by arterial injection. The heart weighed 310 grams. There were no congenital anomalies. The heart valves and myocardium were normal. The coronary arteries showed grade 1 arteriosclerosis. The trachea was filled with partially digested food material. There was no blood within the aspirated material. The right lung weighs 490 grams and the left lung weighs 515 grams. The pleural surface is smooth. Dissection of the bronchial tree reveals the entire tree of both lungs to be filled with partially digested food material. The stomach is normal and contains partially digested food similar to that found in the tracheal-bronchial tree. The liver weighs 1,950 grams. The surface is smooth. Examination of the brain reveals an intact skull. The brain in its entirety, is normal. Samples of blood and other tissues were not taken for examination. . . .

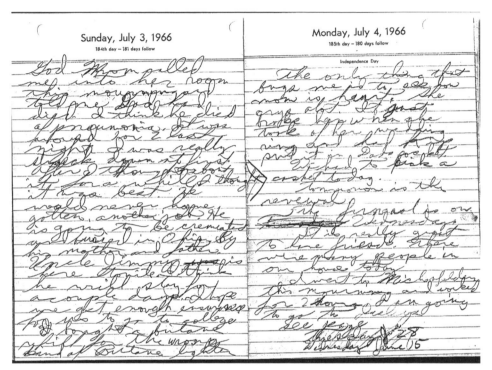

Chris's diary entry the day his father died.

ROOM 50

⚶

Report filed by the Medical Examiner
of Augusta, Georgia
Autopsy or Report of Examination of Body
   Investigation revealed that this 45 year old medical doctor, who
lived in Rochester, Minnesota, had arrived in Augusta on June 30th
relative to securing a position at the Medical College of Georgia. He
had conferences with the Chief of Orthopedic Service at the college. On the day he arrived he said that he had had the "flu," and
was so hoarse that he could not talk. It was known that he had been
depressed and had difficulties at home, and with drinking. He was
given penicillin tablets by a local doctor, all of which he had taken.
He had finished his business and had purchased an airplane ticket to
return home on July 3rd. About 12:30 a.m. that morning, July 3rd, he
had called Rochester and while talking he dropped the phone.

To learn what happened to my family in that hot July of 1966, my archaeology has taken me to some odd corners where the artifacts have come to rest:
the dusty boxes of letters in my mother's attic, the quiet stacks in Mayo's
Medical Library, and the wet char of my brother's ruined house. Today it
has taken me to Georgia, where I'm watching the young medical students
file out of a modern five-story building into the Augusta heat. I am standing
across the street, Laney-Walker Boulevard, looking at a building that's part
of the Medical College of Georgia. On that spot, back in July 1966, was the
University Motel and it was there my father died, in Room 50.
   I've come a long way to see a motel that no longer exists, but I can see all
I need to see from here. I see a sad little building, what you'd describe as the
kind of place you wouldn't want to be caught dead in if the irony wasn't so
thick. Yet, after Roger pushed the last person who cared about him out of

his life, the University Motel had everything any alcoholic wants—a place to be left alone, a room to hide in with his disease. Arguing with all who try to save him, the alcoholic is like a drowning swimmer who mutters insults into the ear of the lifeguard trying to keep him afloat. *("Fuck you and your little whistle.")*

Room 50 is a sad little room. It is where all drunks go to die. Rich drunks, poor ones, pill poppers, cokeheads, it doesn't matter; they all end up on the floor of Room 50. In the *Addict's Merriam-Webster's,* Room 50 should be defined as "any dinky shithole miles from the things that actually matter: wives, husbands, children, love, forgiveness, redemption. Room 50 is a place where the addict is free to concentrate on himself; to get a little '*Me* Time.'"

According to weather records, July 2, 1966, was in fact a "Rainy Night in Georgia." So if we were to open the door to room 50, it seems fitting to have Brook Benton's sad song playing somewhere, perhaps through the thin walls from a radio in the room next door:

> It's a rainy night in Georgia.
> Baby, it's such a rainy night in Georgia.
> I feel like it's rainin'
> all over the world.

Any song of self-pity will do really, as long as the singer's state of woe can be blamed on something: lost love, the weight of the world, or perhaps the classic "I'm too good for this world." Also acceptable is "I'm too bad for this world." In the end it doesn't matter, as long as "Me, Me, Me" is worked into the refrain.

Outside the window we might see the classic abbreviated "MOT" of "MOTEL," humming neon protest to the drizzle and, inside, a room art-directed to scream self-pity: faded wood paneling, avocado-colored drapes in a shiny fabric, and in the bathroom a cracked mirror into which Narcissus can stare at the fracture running through his broken youth.

Jim Morrison may have expired in the bathtub of a hotel in Paris, but he died in Room 50 same as my dad. Ernest Hemingway ate his shotgun in Room 50 and fell on the floor next to Kurt Cobain. John Belushi is over on the bed and Elvis is facedown in the bathroom. Room 50 is crowded with the bodies of people who have been thinking mainly about themselves for years.

Medical Examiner's report, continued

About 12:30 a.m. that morning, July 3rd, he had called Rochester and while talking he dropped the phone. The Motel manager was aware of this but thought that he had just "passed out," because of his drinking. The door of his room was opened at 9:30 a.m. and Dr. Sullivan was found dead crouched by his bed with the telephone receiver off the hook.

Examination revealed that there was a broken ashtray under the body. He was on his knees with his head down on the floor supported in this position by the left side of his body resting against the bed. There was vomitus on the floor and in his mouth and nostrils; it had a strong odor of alcohol. There was a ¼ inch laceration above his left eyebrow from which there had been a slight amount of bleeding. It is thought that this laceration was caused by striking his head when he fell on one of the fragments of glass [ashtray] on the floor. There were no other marks of violence. There was definite flatness to percussion[1] over the upper half of the left lung posteriorly. There were no other abnormal findings.

On his dresser there was a half empty fifth of whiskey and three bottles that had been dispensed at Mayo Clinic [pharmacy] on June the 8th. Two of these bottles had contained 100 capsules each of Placidyl, 200 milligrams. These two bottles were empty. The third bottle had contained 500 capsules of Librium, 10 milligrams. Only 442 of these remained in the bottle.

Finally, forty years after he died, I know conclusively what happened. For the first time I see what the maid and the police saw when they opened the door to Room 50. I finally know what happened in there.

And yet the report ends with the same startling non sequitur:

Cause of death: Pneumonia involving the left lung; type undetermined.

---

1. When you're getting a physical, the doctor taps your back while listening with a stethoscope, trying to determine how clear your lungs are. If they resonate well, or "percuss," your lungs are probably clear and you're in a good place. If the sound is flatter, the lungs are probably filled with phlegm. Or worse.

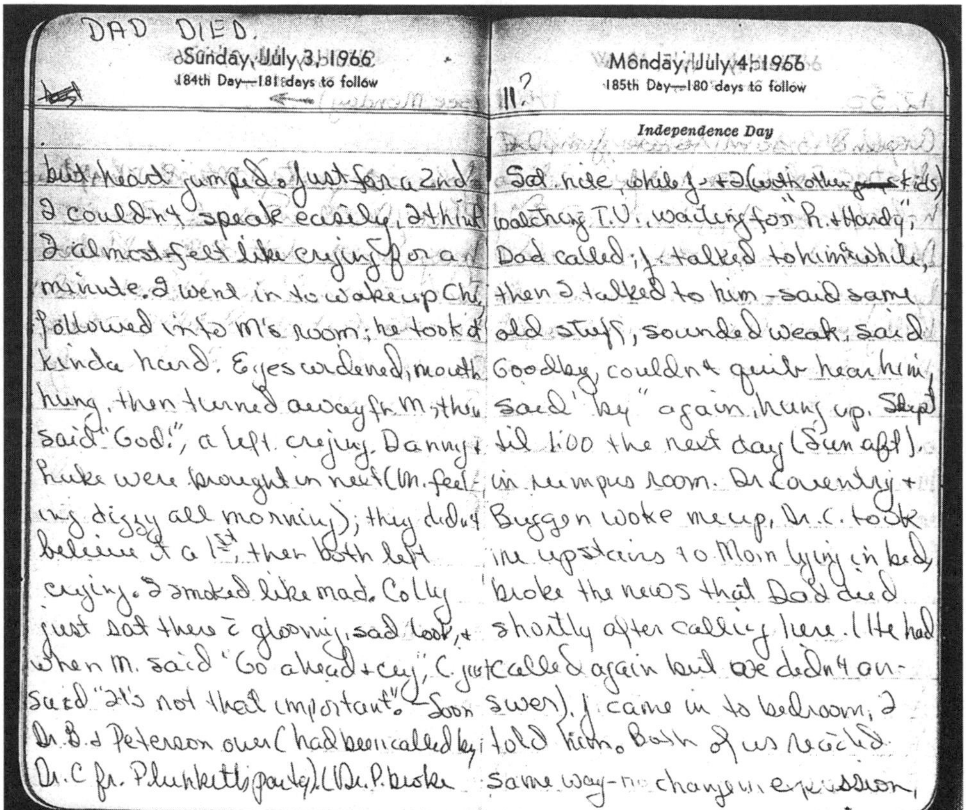
DAD DIED.

Sunday, July 3, 1966
184th Day—181 days to follow
(see Monday) ←

but head jumped. Just for a 2nd I couldn't speak easily. I think I almost felt like crying for a minute. I went in to wake up Chi, followed into M's room; he took it kinda hard. Eyes widened, mouth hung, then turned away fr. M, then said "God!", & left crying. Danny & Luke were brought in next (M. feeling dizzy all morning); they didn't believe it a 1st, then both left crying. I smoked like mad. Colly just sat there c̄ glooming, sad look, & when M. said "Go ahead & cry," C. just said "It's not that important." Soon Dr. B. & Peterson over (had been called by Dr. C fr. Plunkett's party). (Dr. P. broke

Monday, July 4, 1966
185th Day—180 days to follow
Independence Day

Sat. nite, while J. & I (with other kids) watching T.V., waiting for "L. & Hardy," Dad called; J. talked to him awhile, then I talked to him—said same old stuff, sounded weak. Said Goodbye, couldn't quite hear him, said "bye" again, hung up. Slept til 1:00 the next day (Sun aft), in rumpus room. Dr Coventry & Buggen woke me up, Dr. C. took me upstairs to Mom lying in bed, broke the news that Dad died shortly after calling here. (He had called again but we didn't answer). J came in to bedroom, I told him. Both of us reacted same way—no change in expression,

Kip's diary on the day his father died.

THE IRISH FLU

ℐℐ

O n the dresser of the room where my father died were three pharmacy-sized bottles of Placidyl and Librium, a total of 700 pills in a prescription filled, according to the labels, just twenty-six days earlier; 442 of the pills remained, leaving 258 unaccounted for. And the cause of death on my father's autopsy is "pneumonia involving the left lung; type undetermined."

Placidyl is the trade name for a depressant called ethchlorvynol, prescribed hesitantly by doctors as a short-term solution to insomnia; it's no longer even available in the United States. Librium is a sedative used for symptomatic relief of mild anxiety or tension. Neither should be taken with alcohol and both, says one medical text, "should be administered with caution to addiction-prone individuals or to those whose history suggests possible abuse."

On a medical website, I find this warning: "Taking an overdose of ethchlorvynol or taking alcohol or other CNS depressants *with* ethchlorvynol may lead to unconsciousness and possibly death. Some signs of an overdose are continuing confusion, severe weakness, shortness of breath or slow troubled breathing, slurred speech, staggering, and slow heartbeat."

So, 258 pills missing. And two bottles entirely empty. Even on the wild chance my father had limited himself to a steady number of pills per day since "prescribing" them, 258 missing pills means he averaged 9.9 pills a day—a lot, especially if you're chasing them with booze. That there are two empty bottles is also curious. Even in the unlikely event he was taking a measured dose of 10 pills a day, why were both bottles empty and on the dresser? Did he dispense pills first from one bottle then move on to the next? If so, would he really have packed an empty bottle back in Norfolk and taken it on to Augusta?

Now that I had read the police report, I wondered how the medical examiner could conclude the culprit was "pneumonia involving the left lung."

How could any rational person walk into Room 50, look around, see a dead guy on the floor, the half-empty bottle of booze, and three pharmacy-sized jugs of depressants with 258 pills missing, and go, "Mmmm, this looks like the work of a virus."

In the years since his death, we often doubted it was pneumonia that killed our father, and sometimes we suspected he simply took a fistful of pills and caused his own death. We also wondered if somebody—maybe a Mayo friend from behind the scenes?—had called in a favor and requested the doctor's cause of death be listed as "pneumonia." Suicide didn't look good in the newspaper, nor was it covered by insurance.

But my mother never questioned the medical examiner's stated cause of death.

"During the autopsy, there was no evidence of pills in his stomach," she says. "How can you suggest an overdose caused his death?"

Since I'm out of my depth here, I telephone an expert, Dr. Elizabeth Peacock, the deputy medical examiner of Travis County, Texas. A few days later I find myself in her comfortable suburban-Austin home watching her read the ancient police report.

"Well," she says, looking over the top of her glasses, "first of all, with overdose deaths you typically do not find pill residue. In order to work, the pills need to be absorbed, and to do that most drugs need to get to the small intestine."

"So, you think maybe it wasn't suicide?" I ask.

"Well, I see that they didn't take blood or run toxicology tests. So we're basically left here—as we often are in this business—with just the paperwork, from which we can only guess at 'intent.' Several things make me lean away from suicide here. There were lots of pills left in that bottle of Librium and suicide victims typically take the whole bottle."

I wrinkle my brow; it's not what I expected to hear. Maybe I actually prefer a cover-up theory, or I'm holding on to some of that Tortured Arteest crap; maybe I want my father to have purposely yanked his wheel to the left and crashed through the guardrail into the sea.

"It just seems like such a giant leap," I suggest, bringing her attention to the last paragraph before the cause of death. "Here you've got all these pill bottles, the booze. And a guy who's recently remade his will. And the medical examiner licks his pencil and writes down 'pneumonia involving the left lung.' Doesn't that just seem . . . strange?"

"Well, it is odd and it's certainly not where I'd end up."

She straightens her back and I picture her on the stand at one of the many trials where she's given testimony.

"I probably would've ruled this as 'accidental aspiration of gastric contents due to multi-drug toxicity.' But here's the thing. You have to understand forensic medicine was a fledgling science in 1966; there weren't even written standards for this business until the 1990s.

"The most you can say about this report is, maybe it was a little . . . 'lazy.' It was probably easier for the ME to write 'pneumonia' and move on to the next case. No one was going to dispute a claim like that."

Perhaps my mother is right that there was no suicide. Perhaps the final answer is banal—my father got into the booze and pills and they killed him. A story no different from one of those articles in the back of the newspaper: "Area Toddler Chokes to Death on Toy." The toy was on the floor, the toddler put it in his mouth; the booze and pills were on the dresser, the doctor took them. He simply screwed up the dosage and died.

In the end, whatever made the medical examiner list pneumonia as the cause of my father's death—a phone call from Mayo, a lack of facilities to run toxicology tests, or bureaucratic laziness—it put an acceptable face on an unpleasant story. The double indemnity clause in the insurance policy helped send Dr. Sullivan's six sons through school.

Interview with Dad's boss,
Dr. Mark Coventry, August 1, 1992
Later, the [insurance company's] lawyer called me and asked, "Could you confirm that this was an accident?" Well, I thought a long time about that. I said I really don't know legally the implications of that, but the drinking was not an accident. But if you can prove that vomiting was an accident incidental to drinking, that's fine. I would then agree that it was an accident. That made a great difference, as you have probably heard from your mother, because your family got double indemnity on the insurance.

Roger Sullivan, born April 27, 1921.

SUNDAY, JULY 3, 1966

Mom's July 11, 1966, letter to Grandpa

When I woke Sunday morning 10:00, I was sick. The room was whirling about me and when I stood on my feet I grew instantly nauseated, faint, and broke out in a clammy sweat. I sent one of the boys for a Dramamine (seasickness pill) and went back to sleep. Later I realized my trouble, affirmed by Tony Bianco, that it was heat prostration. Rochester had had unrelieved temperatures in the low 90s since the middle of June. I had conscientiously pressed salt on the boys everyday—but had not taken any myself. I began licking salt that Sunday afternoon and by evening was relieved of all the distressing symptoms.

Mom, 2006

So I was in my bedroom when Mark Coventry arrived, and before I could even consider where? here? there? upstairs? downstairs? to receive him, he was sitting in the rocking chair at the foot of the bed. No matter. Whatever the reason for his being upstairs, there he sat: Mark Coventry, handsome, proper, head of the orthopedic section, probably long a believer that your father had been "driven to drink" by me. I knew he could have been there for no reason except as the bearer of bad news.

Jeff, 2006

The morning of July third was dark—off and on rain. I had left the house early to go pick up my girlfriend, Bonnie, at about 9:30 a.m. When we came back to the Millstone around 10:00 or so, Dr. Mark Coventry's car was in the driveway and he was coming out, carrying an open umbrella. He was walking to his car as we came into the driveway. In a quiet voice, he told me to go talk to Mom.

Mom, 2006

The dread fear swept over me immediately, as it had so often with increasing frequency, that your father had, driving drunk, killed someone. Thank God, it wasn't that. That much Fate had spared him. He had already sacrificed wife, children, job, reputation. For a man who truly intended to be a healer, killing someone so mindlessly would have shattered him. My last remaining, barely perceptible shred of sympathy for him recognized that.

Mom's July 11, 1966, letter continues

I was in bed when Luke called upstairs to say Dr. Coventry was here. He came up to my bedroom and I babbled along, apologizing for being in bed. I knew he was here to give me some grave news. I did not ask him and we sat silently for a few minutes.

Finally Mark said, so very gently, "There's no easy way to say this, Myra. Roger died last night." Despite the years of violence and anguish and torment, it was still hard to take. As Kip later said, it wasn't a surprise or a shock so much as it was the wrap-up punch.

And so it was—the wrap-up punch. Kip and Jeff were sleeping in the basement because of the heat. Mark went down and woke up Kip and brought him up to my room—giving him the news in much the same way as he told me. I watched Kip. His eyes flickered—he swallowed hard—and then he looked at me. "You all right, Mom?"

Kip, 2006

I recall Dr. Coventry woke me up and asked me to come up and talk with Mom. She was sitting up in bed with the sheets covering her legs. Dr. Coventry got right to the point and said something like, "Your father died last night."

I think he said "passed away." I don't recall much of my immediate reaction. My recollection is I was relieved. Eventually I did experience a lot of anger toward Dad; several years later—when I discovered that old letter from him actually—I finally cried hard about him. But that morning I don't think I felt that stuff—not consciously anyway.

Mom's July 11, 1966, letter continues
Mark left then. He would have told the other boys—as would Kip—but it seemed right for me to do that. So Kip got Jeff and I told him. Then one by one, I told the other boys. It wasn't easy and I hope I did it in the right way.

Jeff, 2006
I found Mom lying in bed, covers pulled up, Kip was standing on the far side of the bed. Kip said it simply—something like, "Dad died last night." I remember going downstairs and joining Bonnie on the porch swing. Her reaction surprised me because she responded with a gush of how sorry she was. I didn't feel anything. It seemed to me that she was saying what you're "supposed" to say when someone learned ninety seconds ago that their father had died.

Kip's 1966 diary
J[eff] came in to bedroom, I told him. Both of us reacted same way—no change in expression, but heart jumped. Just for a 2nd I couldn't speak easily. I think I almost felt like crying for a minute. I went in to wake up Chr[is], followed him into M's room; he took it kinda hard. Eyes widened, mouth hung. He turned away from M, then said "God!", a[nd] left crying.

Chris, 2007
Kip retrieved me from my room on that Sunday morning. He told me Mom wanted to see me in her room. He preceded me down the hallway and sat by the bedroom fireplace. I stood at the front of her bed.

I have a recollection of having my right leg up on the bed when Mom told me, "Your father died last night." I do not remember if those were the exact words but I distinctly remember having a falling sensation combined with the feeling of getting punched in my solar plexus. The floor beneath me exploded and I said, "Oh, God."

I could see Mom had been crying but Kip seemed undisturbed. I do not remember crying then. The first moment I can remember crying was at the funeral.

Chris's 1966 diary
God Mom called me into her room this mourning and told me Dad had died. I think he died of pneumonia. It was around 1 or 2 last night. I was really struck down at first. After I thought about it for a while, I thought it was best. He would never have gotten another job. He is going to be cremated and buried in Ohio by his mother and father. Uncle Jimmy is here tonite. I think he will stay for a couple days. I hope we get enough insurance for us to go to college.

Kip's 1966 diary
Danny & Luke were brought in next. (M. feeling dizzy all morning); they didn't believe it a[t] 1st, then both left crying.

Dan, 2007
I was at the side of Mom's bed and I remember making a conscious effort to react "properly." I did an obligatory cry and then went to my room. Instead of grief, I felt shock. Sitting in there, I could hear people talking and crying and I was moved by the magnitude of the events.

But I didn't feel grief. In fact, I wondered how these events would affect my standing in the eyes of my eighth-grade peers. I had always thought it was pretty cool to come from an abnormal, dysfunctional family.

What I remember
I saw Dr. Coventry go upstairs and then after he left, somebody called me upstairs, just as I was pouring Cheerios into a little metal bowl. Up in Mom's room I stood in the sunlight, spoon in hand, chasing one of those little tan-colored Os around in the warming milk, knowing what I was about to hear, and then hearing it. There is a jump in the film and the next memory is buying a couple of cigarettes from Jeff and smoking one down in the Low Forty. I was not worried about being seen or caught or punished.

Kip's 1966 diary

I smoked like mad. Colly just sat there [with] a gloomy, sad look, & when M. said "Go ahead & cry," C. just said "It's not that important."

Collin, 2007

I was in my room playing with a little radio that had an alligator clip on an antenna wire. I was looking for something to clip the antenna to when someone, I think it was Kip, invited me into Mom's room. When I came in, Mom was lying on the bed looking quite somber. Kip was sitting at her side, facing the fireplace.

I don't recall word for word how Mom told me Dad was dead. She said something like, "He's not coming back."

Mom's July 11, 1966, letter continues

I don't have a very clear recollection of the rest of that day. Kip and Jeff stayed with the little ones, keeping them busy and under their eyes. Jeff's girlfriend Bonnie took care of everything—cleaned up the house, fed us all, answered the phone, and generally made the day easier for all of us. Mark had called Tony Bianco who was at a luncheon party. He came right over, shortly after Mark left, but did not tell JoAnn till after the party was over. She was here for me for the rest of the day, with Tony coming in and out as the affairs of the day demanded his attention. As usual, they both carried me through tough times I could hardly have done alone.

The moment Mark left I phoned my brother. As I reported to you earlier, his simple answer to my "Jimmy, can you come help me?" was "I'll be right there." He phoned back within half an hour to give me his arrival time—and from that moment a huge load slid away from my shoulders.

Chris, 2007

The pain was dulled for me on that first day, except for one particular moment, which came not long after lunch. We had a lot of visitors that Sunday and Mom received most of them on the screen porch. At least two people were already there when still more arrived. I was walking behind these new visitors—it may have been

263

the Biancos—and they preceded me onto the porch. Mom stood up and embraced the woman, laid her head on the woman's right shoulder so that I could see part of Mom's face from my position at the door to the kitchen. The arrival of her friend sprang Mom's tears again. Seeing her pain released a great swelling of pain in me, one that has been so familiar to me for as long as I can remember.

Jeff, 2006

Kip and I picked up Uncle Jim at the airport. We came home in the blue Falcon, taking the back way home. Just like Bonnie, Uncle Jim seemed to feel obliged to say things that would make me feel better. I have a vivid memory of him describing the body as a "shell that contains the soul." And even though the shell has died, the soul lives on. I was already a raging atheist by then, but didn't choose to argue the point with him just then.

Kip's 1966 diary

Picked up Uncle Jim at airport 9:00. Mom cried when he slipped in front door and hugged her. Jim got to work on papers, tried to make guesstimates of insurance. . . . Today, it looks like insurance payout of $155,000 + V.A. benefits + Social Security.

Mom's July 11, 1966, letter continues

Kip and Jeff met Jim at the airport at 9:05 Sunday night. By this time news was beginning to spread faster. Though most of the phone calls were mercifully made to the Biancos' house, there were still many calls here, and there was an increasing flow of good friends bringing food to us. . . . So I lack nothing that can be done for me. Let me go back to Ted Bliven, unknown to you, scarcely remembered by me, but to whom I owe much gratitude. He is the man in Augusta (an old medical school classmate) whom Roger went to see. And this man—fully aware of the situation—was willing to give Roger a chance. He gave Roger a three-year contract, beginning in a teaching capacity and returning him to surgery if he managed to get a hold of himself sufficiently. Again, much of this credit goes to Tony Bianco with whom Bliven talked at great length. Tony told him that Roger was eminently worth saving if Bliven was willing to take the chance. And Bliven was. Which meant that before he died, Roger had been given back his confidence, his self-respect, and we must hope, a degree of happiness. That Christian act cost Ted Bliven nothing but think of the joy it must have brought Roger in the last few days.

Inside the First Methodist Church on Fourth Street
(now Christ United Methodist Church) in January 2008.

PAGANS IN THE TEMPLE

Monday, July 4, 1966

And so Jesus said to the worshippers gathered at the foot of his cross, "Come closer." And they came closer.

"What is it, my Lord?" asked one.

And Jesus said unto him, "I can . . . see your house from up here."

This joke used to make us howl. We'd collapse to the floor, delighting in its blasphemy. Yet even as we professed active disbelief in God or an afterlife, we did in fact believe in an unseen world—ours was the one full of all the scary shit. We little ones believed in ghosts and monsters. We believed in the Horrid Light and the gremlin on the wing of Rod Serling's plane. Grandpa Sullivan may have thundered "Fear God," but it was monsters we feared. In fact, fear of monsters made us hedge our bets about God and adopt a sort of conditional atheism. We'd often find ourselves muttering conciliatory asides to God when we felt we were in danger and needed a backup plan. *("God, if you're there, please let me make it to the light switch.")*

Kip, being the oldest of us pagans, was the first to take his atheism public. He was on the debate team at John Marshall High School and in the fall of 1964 gave a podium thumper promoting atheism and hammering organized religion.

"It created a big stir," he remembers and said it led to an impromptu after-school discussion group that filled a classroom. "With the exception of a few people who spoke out with me, I was peppered by questions from irritated true believers. I remember feeling just great about the whole episode."

Looking back, the controversy wasn't surprising. In the 1950s and early '60s, there was no other strain of spirituality for sale in America except one-size-fits-all Eisenhower Christianity. So ingrained in the culture was this house brand of religion, it's surprising no one thought of putting it in the city water along with fluoride. Any child who had questions about subjects like death—or the soul, or wondered about existence, or mortality, or any fundamental life question—was anesthetized with party-line answers about crowns of thorns and bringing in sheaves and ancient tales of lost sheep and donkey jawbones, all of which were so incredibly boring we simply stopped asking questions about the things that mattered.

We grew up, like many kids of that era, never having a single conversation with an open-minded grown-up who might embrace our doubts along with us. We never had a discussion about what it meant to be human—or about death or the soul—with someone who might wonder as we did what it all meant. Without any form of spiritual apprenticeship we simply made our way into what seemed a harsh world carrying with us an anger toward anything remotely associated with organized religion.

In the days following our father's death, our anger was stirred by the assurances of well-meaning neighbors who took us aside to tell us, "Your father is now in heaven with the angels." Kip noted in his diary that "Mrs. Martin stopped by, drunk as hell, made blunders that hurt Mom. I walked her home. She nearly cried praising Dad." Worse than these blubbery eulogies for a man we were all angry with were the whispered admonitions from visitors that perhaps it was time for us six boys to forgive. This one just pissed us off.

Okay, so Dad's dead and he's forgiven? Is this how it works? Everybody gets to crawl sideways out of their sin like a crab and go skittering off to their grave and hide out in eternity? Like death is some sort of payment? "Sorry, everybody, I was an asshole, but I died so all bets are off. Paid in full. Ticket punched. Can't touch me 'cause I'm in the bosom of Jesus."

Forgiveness wasn't what we needed to hear just then. The wounds of his rages were still tender, the bottles still in the liquor cabinet, the image of Mom's big white sunglasses still lingered on the lawn out front. But the religious bromides came into the house along with the casseroles and we accepted both, guessing this was simply what grown-ups did when someone died. Harder to accept, though, was the pressure we were feeling to embrace the rituals and ceremonies required by a church we didn't consider ourselves members of. When Kip and Jeff began feeling railroaded into buying an expensive coffin, their anger began to surface.

"I remember having to go to the funeral home to pick out a coffin," Kip told me. "The whole idea of putting us all through a funeral pissed me off. Dad was to be cremated and a coffin seemed a waste of money. I tried to quickly pick a plain coffin and just get out of that place, but Uncle Jimmy called me farther back into another room to look at more expensive coffins, soothing me along the way with spiels about 'custom and society.'"

Jeff also remembered feeling anger while at the funeral home. Only hours before, Uncle Jim had been assuring him "the body is just a shell that contains the soul" and now his uncle was pressuring him to buy an expensive box to put Dad's "shell" in—a box they were only *renting*, given that Roger was to be cremated and only his urned ashes were to go beneath the sod near his father's grave in Ohio.

"I remember a cramped little basement display area with thirty or forty coffins," Jeff recalled. "Kip and I argued with Uncle Jim that we not blow money on an elaborate coffin. We favored the simple blue metal one, but Uncle Jim said, 'You must keep in mind that people at the funeral might judge us as being disrespectful.' This conversation happened more than once and I think Jim was getting pissed. Eventually we settled on an oak and brass one with white satin lining for a thousand dollars."

The tension grew again when Uncle Jim began double-checking the details on Roger's funeral clothes. Mom had provided Kip with Dad's favorite blue suit, but at the last minute, Kip remembered, "I couldn't find any of his ties. I had no tie for him when I got to the funeral home, so I wound up taking off the tie I was wearing and donating it to Dad, for him to be cremated in. I was so angry I think I came close to tears."

Kip, 2006

Having to deal with Dad's funeral angered me because it forced our family to deal with our incredibly mixed-up feelings in public. I just wanted the transition from Life with Dad to Life without Dad to begin immediately. I wanted to retreat to the Millstone and begin mending my psyche, and tending to the wounds of the rest of you guys. But the funeral forced us out into the public eye, where everyone could see us trying to cope with our pain and confusion. The fact that Jimmy wanted me to think about which tie Dad wore angered me. It was bad enough we were going to have to parade ourselves into a church and listen to formal blather about Dad from someone who didn't know him and didn't know us. Having to sweat the details—which coffin to buy, what shirt to put him in, which tie—it was more than I could bear.

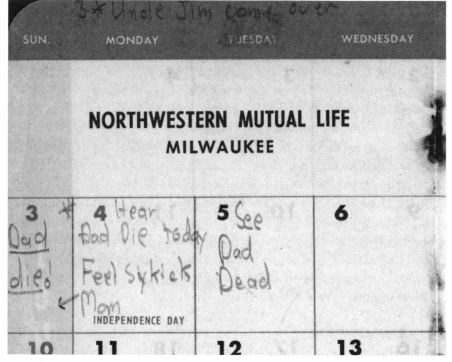

Luke's diary the month Dad died.

ONE LAST LOOK

ℐℐ

Tuesday, July 5, 1966

Chris's diary, 1966
The only thing that bugs me is to see how Mom is hurt. She crys a
lot. It just broke her when she took her wedding ring off and had
Kip put it in Dad's pocket. We had to pick a casket today. Tomorrow is the reviewal.

Death caused by a long illness often allows a family to prepare for the end.
At the Millstone, however, we had moved in one leap from alcoholic insanity to religious ritual, and we understood neither. One day there's a mad dog
foaming through its teeth and the next a minister is smiling in through the
screen door. All we really knew was that we were angry, and even our anger
we didn't understand.

If we could have had our way, there would have been no funeral, no viewing. We simply would have raised the drawbridge to the Millstone and retreated to its rooms. Was it not as if a cancerous tumor had been removed
from the family body? Was there really a need to go "view the tumor"? Is it
really "with the angels" now? We were ANGRY and in our fury and trauma,
the religious rites that were offered to us as comfort felt more like cover-up.

Anger, like lightning, needs to strike something and discharge itself in
the ground, but at the Millstone there was no target anymore—he was dead.
Anger could only crackle out of our scalps and the tips of our fingers, fly
around the empty room, and rebury itself in our chests. How could you be
mad at a body?

Roger's body was, in fact, now back in Rochester, delivered from Georgia
in the cold cargo hold of a jet. Jeff drove out to Rochester's small airport to
watch the plane land. "It took quite awhile to unload cargo onto a train of

three or four wagons," he remembers. "The people got off. The luggage was picked up. Finally I saw what was clearly a casket being lowered from the cargo door with two guys in the plane's hold and two on the ground."

With the arrival of the body came more details of how Roger had actually died. Kip wrote in his diary that Uncle Jim had confided some details: "Vomited (flu), evidently fell (bruise on forehead) unconscious, choked to death." This information was passed down to the rest of us, and as the day approached to view our father's body at the funeral home, our group anger curdled into a shared sense of anxiety.

That night, Kip and Uncle Jimmy dressed to make the trip downtown for the viewing, Kip bearing Mom's wedding ring and her instructions to slip it into the pocket of Roger's blue suit. "The poor dear man—who was so afraid of being alone—took something precious with him to the grave," Myra wrote to her parents. "For no logical reason, it makes me feel he didn't make the journey alone."

Dan and I, seeing these tribal elders dressed in suits and ties, guessed where they were going and, in Mom's words, "put up a clamor to go along. And so Jim and I found ourselves faced with a truly big decision."

From Mom's long July 16, 1966, letter to her parents
My first response was "No!" as was Jim's. I could see Jim was ready to explain it to Luke so I walked out of the room. But I realized that I was refusing Luke the last chance to see his father and that perhaps I hadn't that right. I went back toward my library and met Jim on his way to me. "Let's consider this, Jimmy. We're dealing with a finality here and we mustn't make a mistake." My dear brother stood before me with tears running down his face. "I've already decided," Jim said, "I asked Luke why he wanted to go and his answer was, 'Because I can't believe my Daddy is dead.'"

My 1966 diary
See Dad dead.

That was my last entry in my diary for the year 1966—three unemotional words: "See Dad dead"—written in a little calendar journal I'd begun to keep on my February trip with Dad to his mother's funeral. I have no memory of writing the three words, but there they are in number two pencil.

I don't remember the ride downtown to the funeral home either. I don't remember wearing a suit, what words were said in the car. I do remember that when we walked into the funeral home someone over my shoulder quietly said, "He's right in here."

I went around a corner and entered a dimly lit room. The walls were green. It took a minute for the image to come together, to understand that the box over there with the curved top was a coffin, that half of the box was open and that only the top half of my father was visible. There was no anger now—only awe. And a wondering: *What happened? What sort of trouble did you run into, Dad? You were just at home the other day. And now . . . look at us.*

The perspective in this memory is from a low angle, it being the summer after my sixth grade. The left side of my father's face is at eye level. I can see he's banged his head on something, a small wound the mortician's makeup can't hide. I stand with my hands at my sides and wonder: *Should I touch him? Shouldn't I? What if I do and it's only out of "Wow, a dead guy. What's that feel like?" It's bad to think that, isn't it? If I touch him I might get nightmares too, right? But in a few minutes I'll never see him again. This is it. So if I don't touch him, won't I get nightmares about that? What if I turn around and walk out of this green room without touching my father ever again, what about that?*

I reach out, up a little, over the edge of the casket and touch his . . . his cheek? his hand? I don't remember. I do remember a feeling of cool. The suppleness of skin was gone. There was a hardness that the living have only at their kneecaps or where the bone rides under flesh. The reaching out, that touch of cool, and then nothing. The film stops. No memory of turning my back on my father forever, no image of sidewalk under my dress shoes, no feeling of the hot summer night, no sound of car doors slamming. Just the good-bye hand reaching over the suit, the cool, then nothing.

My father's grave in DeGraff, Ohio.

SUNLIGHT STREAMS THROUGH
A HIGH WINDOW

᧞

Wednesday, July 6, 1966

Mom's long letter to her parents, July 16, 1966
After days of oppressively hot weather, Wednesday, July 6th dawned clear and cool. I wore a plain black dress, with ¾-length sleeves—white cuffs and a wide white horse-collar which I had pinned up from its low line—it was a favorite dress of Roger's. I had no hat but I wore that black lace mantilla that Mother gave me and white gloves. And as I dressed I knew I was dressing for Roger for the last time. At 9:30 the Towey Funeral Home limousine came.

Kip's diary, 1966
Jeff, Chris, Dan and I rode down in family car behind Mom, Jim, Col and Luke in funeral place's car. At bottom of Institute Road, we were crying with laughter; actually had to hang back from their lead car so they couldn't see us.

We were led into the Fireside Room. All of us were just convulsing inside. Led as a group into a pew up front: Jim, Mom, Col, Jeff, Chris, Dan, Luke, me. Chris let part of a laugh escape within a minute after sitting down (big crowd right behind us). Jeff and Dan said later they were in same boat.

Kip, 2006
Somehow we got into a hysterical, laughing mood just before driving to the church. I think all the jokes were about ridiculous events that might happen at the church. In our car, the one I was driving, the four of us were laughing so hard that by the time we passed Biancos we had tears running down our faces. On the county road, I

275

slowed the car down to put some distance between us and the front car. I was worried about how we would behave in the church. We were so off the deep end.

Chris, 2007

As we pulled into the parking lot, Jeff observed there was "quite a turnout," as if for a party or a celebration rather than a funeral. A renewed fury of laughter came over us. We convened again in a small lounge, all dressed in our jackets and ties. There was a strong conspiratorial sense in our little group. I remember feeling very separate from the crowd—even from Mom and Uncle Jimmy. In the car and in the lounge, I felt a bubble around the six of us. We brothers who had gone through so much, we six had a common experience. It was just us six, and beyond that the bonds stopped.

Kip, 2006

As we sat in the waiting room, I tried not to look at other brothers, one or two of who were trying to get us going again. As we sat in the pew I thought I was going to bust. Someone made a slight noise by barely shifting the movable foot rest in front of us. I thought that was going to get us all going again. Linda Wooner or someone later said she saw our shoulders convulsing and thought we were crying. My God. Emotionally, I was hammered. I lost twenty-five pounds that summer.

Jeff, 2006

We all cracked up and everyone behind us saw our shoulders shaking. The story we've all been tellin' since then—that the crowd behind us thought we were sobbing—I doubt that now. At least the people directly behind us, they probably knew we weren't sobbing.

Chris, 2007

Dan put his foot up on the kneeling bar at our feet and it creaked. That's what set it all off. Just that noise. It seemed as if there had been no sound before that one noise and everyone in the silent audience had been straining to hear some indication of where these six boys were emotionally. And now Dan announced to the whole crowd, as if with words through a bullhorn, "We are so indifferent to the death of this beloved ogre that I am casual at his funeral and I am about to put my feet up as if I were watching a football game on TV." The footrest creaked as if it could not circulate this piece of gossip fast enough, as if to condemn us for our casual attitude.

From the perspective of all these years later, I can see the hysterical laughter was a wild release from a severely tense family situation mixed with anxiety about the future and a whole lot of grief from our father's death. But at the time, laughter was laughter and I was scared Mom would see our laughter as scoffing at her pain.

My immediate response to the creak was to burst out laughing. The burst I could not control. But the church environment provided me with the motivation to overcome the laughter. There was a surge of terror through the six of us that we were just going to lose it and all break into gales of laughter.

Then I saw the casket. I hadn't been aware of it for the first half of the ritual. I had chosen not to go to the viewing the night before and the sight of the casket in its faintly humanoid dimension was the first real moment when I felt in my throat that my father's death was real. All of the hysterics drained out of me in that moment. I was no longer in danger of laughing. I felt only loss.

Dan, 2007
The only moment of grief I felt was at the end of Dad's funeral, when his coffin was wheeled down the aisle. The magnitude and finality of the event finally caught up with me at that moment.

The end of Mom's long letter to her parents, July 16, 1966
Standing there listening, I knew I'd not get through the ceremony without a crutch of some sort because I was already beginning to cry. I cast about—nearly frantic—for something to pin my mind on. The Greek alphabet saved me. I silently recited the Greek alphabet, saying the letters one by one. I cannot tell you what people thought of my conduct during the next half-hour. But it would have made little difference for I could only do as I did.

I cannot tell you how we sat. I know only that as we walked in, Jimmy went first, I second, Collin behind me, and Kip at the end. I never in my life stood straighter or taller or held my head higher. I wanted everyone in that church to know I was proud of Roger, regardless of whatever else they might have thought I felt. The moment we sat down Jimmy took my hand and never let it go till we rose to leave. I looked at nothing except that magnificent stained glass window which kept my head high and my eyes away from the casket. I cannot tell you what was first said by the minister, I did not listen to the prayer. I did not listen to his reading of the 23rd Psalm (Jimmy's choice), I only looked at that great window and went over and over the Greek alphabet. If that sounds callous, you must remember it was done only because I was feeling too much, too deeply to yield to it.

But I did listen attentively to his words about Roger. Jimmy will have reported to you that he spoke beautifully and said nothing untrue of Roger. When he was finished, the organist played Bach's "Come Sweet Death" and while it played, the sun came out and streamed gloriously down through the church windows. I had to go back to the alphabet. The minister then made his final benedictory remarks and farewell.

Till that moment I had not looked full upon the casket—but I watched as the ushers came up, rolled it into position and moved it up the aisle. I saw it disappear behind Jimmy's shoulder. At that moment the organ began the opening refrain, with bells only, of "Eternal Father." We walked out but I held Jim back just outside the door to hear the last notes. It was done. I had gone through it despite the fear I couldn't. When we arrived home, there were many good friends here—but I simply went to my room, swallowed that last Seconal and went to bed.

Grandpa, writing at the hour of the funeral
I am with you, this moment, in the First Methodist Church, Rochester, Minnesota—you, the six boys, and he whom you often called "Lil' brother." He does for you now what your far-away parents are unable to do.

It is hard to believe all those years of penury and intellectual achievement were to no avail. I refuse to believe they were. Perhaps only Roger knows now, more than we can on this side of eternity. I wonder if he is not there with you at this moment, weeping over his possession by devils.

One era in our lives has ended. What will be our future—your future and that of six boys? And what of the remaining time which shall be vouchsafed to me and your mother? How shall we continue our lives after this act of Providence? Shall we continue our Blue Books, with all the trivialities with which I load them? Shall we institute a new process of communication? And if so, what type? After this break in our common life, can we gather up the pieces and proceed again as once we were? I do not know. I shall be guided by your sentiments in this matter. It will probably never be as once it was.

Can it be richer and more full of understanding and empathy? Perhaps only succeeding weeks and months can tell. In the meantime, you know that we love you and are sorry only that we can do nothing to help you recover from the ravages of recent years. We stand in awe at your courage and indomitable spirit. I am persuaded there is indeed a force which shapes our ends.

Thus, for you, I anticipate a renewed devotion to things of the spirit—books, if you please—and ships and seas and birds and butterflies—and most of all the care and culture of guiding the growth of six boys—whose father was Phi Beta Kappa and whose mother is his equal, if not superior, in mind and spirit. Now the service is over. I had better pause, consider, and re-write.

Your loving Father.

I Believe in God Briefly

Oh how I wish there was a God, I think, sitting in a church.

And if there ever is one, I want it to be Grandpa Longstreet's God, not Grandma Rock's. I'd want a sunny god, with deep laughter like Grandpa's, a god who comes in at the last minute and makes everything right and tells me that if I look up into the dark rafters right now I'd see my dad's faint outline floating there like a firefly, friendly and clear, and then Dad would come down to me. As he descends to our pew he'd see my smile—my eyes like landing lights and he'd know right away all was forgiven, everything—the gun, the ax, the BOOM! on the library door—don't you see? None of it will count if you can just pull off this one trick and come down to talk to me one last time.

As Mom whispers her Greek alphabet and Uncle Jimmy squeezes her hand, the sun angles down from the high stained glass windows like a banister and down the stairs Dad comes, slowly, as if doubtful all he's done can be wiped clean with one fantastic appearance in a church but it is, Dad, it is, and he floats closer and I see he's skinny again and his eyes, oh they're so focused and clear and they're full of fierce love and then of tears as he surrounds me, the soft crackle of starched white shirt, the smell of Old Spice and a whispering, I'm sorry, so sorry for everything. I love you, I've always loved you, and he looks down the pew at a line of six little boys he once kissed on the head one by one in a sunny dining room long ago and finally he sees the beautiful Florida girl at the end, no longer in her black funeral dress but in the bright citrus colors of her mama's homemade clothes, sees her big white pearly button earrings, and remembers how brightly the "Gypsy" stood out on that drab midwestern campus of 1942. He whispers, tell your mama I love her. And tell all your brothers, each one, I love them all. Tell them I'm sorry, for everything.

And presently the scratch of his cheek eases and he's up the sun stairs again, waving, says he's going back.

"Back to a place I know where the sand is white, the sun is hot, the palm trees whisper, and the Gulf of Mexico is green and clear. Your mother and I went swimming there thirty years ago. I might even dig up a fishing pole."

You tell them now, don't forget, tell them, okay?

In the dining room sometime after Dad died. Clockwise from front: Collin, Chris, Kip, Jeff, and Luke.

THE BIG BAD WORLD

◈

Mom, July 31, 1966

Dearest Mother and Father: Four weeks have passed—and it's still July. I'll be glad to be rid of this month. 1966 is more than half over and has not turned out to be the year we expected it to be. The long struggle is over (for both Roger and me). And my problems have been reduced to two—one an old one, one new. The new one is to learn to live on much less money; selling this wonderful old house will help with that. The old one is the harder—to raise to manhood six boys whose lives have been full of violence, uncertainty, hate and neglect. It won't be easy.

Being twelve years old in Rochester, Minnesota, in the summer of '66 was a good thing. There had been family trauma for nearly ten years, yeah, but nobody'd died. Well, not counting my dad, but the point is we were all alive, the seven of us—the ten actually, if you count Pagan and my hamsters.

On one level, it was kind of cool having a dead dad. At school, I was able to strike some seriously sad poses for Debbie Laney, leaning against the bike rack with a look that said, "Yep. My dad died. Pretty sad. Me? Nahhh, I'll be all right. Maybe I'll see ya 'round then." I'd walk away (in slow motion, of course) employing the Lonely-Guy-on-Cold-Street walk. Lonely Guys aren't supposed to turn around to see if they're being watched, but if they were, I would've walked backward for blocks yelling back to Debbie, "STILL DEAD, MY DAD IS. YEP. FEELIN' PRETTY SAD!"

The Beatles' new album *Revolver* was number one on the charts and all the films of my fantasy life were now scored with Harrison's "Taxman." Paul McCartney's joyful numbahs "one-two-three-FAH!" had matured into George's deadlier count-off, intoned like a mortician and followed by a guitar riff a Lonely Guy could nicely time his steps to as he walked down the hallways of Central Junior High School.

I turned to smoking cigarettes full-time and posing for effect at every opportunity. For my birthday, Mom bought me my first bike, a Sting-Ray with Banana Seat and Ram's Horn Handlebars. I would ride this fantastic machine to the YMCA downtown and Lonely-Guy my way around the edges of seventh-grade mixers hoping to be noticed. If only Debbie Laney had read the script I'd written for her.

"Hey, Sue, look, it's Lonely Guy. Walking alone down the street, threadbare collar turned up to the cold November wind. Suddenly I feel so shallow."

My fantasies were becoming self-conscious and were harder to sustain. Still, I never had the courage to just talk to Debbie Laney—until the day I was beat up. On that day, I was riding my bike to the YMCA across a footbridge on a golf course where three "hoods" blocked my way. When I asked them to move, they blocked the footbridge completely.

I said, "Don't be such pricks."

"Lonely Guy" Beats Up Three Hoods

With one slow-motion roundhouse kick, I ruin the lives of three . . .

POW! Right after I said "pricks," one of the hoods hit me hard in the face; I fell off my bike and began to bleed. The hoods rode off laughing and I lay there measuring my options. Since I couldn't go into the Y with blood all over my face and shirt, there was clearly only one alternative—let the blood dry on my face and then pedal to Debbie Laney's house. When I got there, I would park my cool Sting Ray bike with Banana Seat and Ram's Horn handlebars, ring the doorbell, and give 'er an eyeful of the rough-and-tumble life we Lonely Guys lead. I wouldn't even mention the injury unless she brought it up.

"There's what? Blood, you say?"

Twenty minutes later, the look in Mrs. Laney's eyes when she opened her door suggested my fantasy wasn't playing out as scripted and the soundtrack of "Taxman" came to a scratching halt. Debbie wasn't home and never saw Lonely Bloody Guy. Mrs. Laney did, but just cleaned me up and sent me home. As I prepped my cool Sting-Ray bike with Banana Seat and Ram's

Horn Handlebars for flight, I looked back at Mrs. Laney and said, "But you'll tell Debbie about . . . you know. Okay?"

Back at the Millstone, the six of us dealt with Dad's death privately, each of us retreating to our rooms—to play a guitar, to build a model plane, to draw comic book superheroes. With Dad no longer our common enemy, fights among the four little ones became worse.

Chris's diary, August 26, 1966
Dan and Luke have been fighting so much. There are, on the average, 3 free-for-alls a day. Both demand full rights. Luke's a Goddamn needle and Dan's a Bull. Luke is worse even than Collin. He smokes. He spends all his time in the basement. He has big plans for his stupid comic book career. He likes his hamsters more than anyone.

When Dad was alive, at least we all knew what was wrong with us. Now the house seemed to be unraveling and we weren't sure why. With Kip back at college studying pre-law, Jeff and the remaining Pagans limped along through the fall and finally disbanded. Everything was just different. There was no Kip, no Pagans, no Dad; even the Millstone was up for sale. The dark star we'd revolved around so long was gone and we became aware of a big bad world beyond the gates of the Millstone and saw things were just as shitty out there.

Barely a month after Dad died, Kip noted in his diary: "Sniper in Texas killed 12 people, wounded 33. They said he was an Eagle Scout and worked at a bank . . . like me." This was the summer Richard Speck raped and strangled eight nurses in Chicago and Capote's *In Cold Blood* was a best seller. Even my Beatles were in trouble, with John's controversial statement, "We're more popular than Jesus." We saw these things on TV and on the cover of Mom's *Life* magazines and felt our frying pan give way to fire. We wondered if our troubled childhoods were just the cartoon before the movie.

Troop strength in Vietnam leapt to nearly half a million in '66 and the military draft was sweeping through neighborhoods. Without Dad around to dominate the political conversation, Mom's liberal views flowered; books like *The Anti-Communist Impulse* and authors like Noam Chomsky became dinnertime conversation. When Jeff's reading began to convince him that joining the navy meant "barbecuing farmers," he requested to withdraw from officer candidate school and "to my great relief," he said, "the navy just dismissed me without obligation." After several different college majors, he applied to and graduated from medical school.

Chris, too, could see revolution was in the air and discovered he had a lot more to be mad about than just three little brothers. With the war, civil rights, and women's liberation on the *Huntley–Brinkley Report* every night, he could now smolder over a different injustice every day and not repeat one for weeks. His anger and emotion on occasion surprised even him.

Chris, 2007

I didn't understand what happened to me in Mr. Mason's history class in September of that year. One day he rolled the projector into the room and played a pulp anticommunist film, something that looked like it was written by the Pentagon. When the lights went back on, I raised my hand and said the film was propaganda and its use in a public school was inappropriate. He scolded me in front of the class, said I didn't know what I was talking about and that I wasn't entitled to make judgments about his pedagogy.

The next day I retaliated. I remained totally silent and sat sideways in my chair staring out the window at the Mayo High School parking lot. At the end of class, he asked me to stay behind. He was friendly and conciliatory, saying he wanted me to continue participating in class and that he didn't mean to jump on me the way he did.

I have no idea how much he knew about me personally. Dad's death had been mentioned in the newspaper a few weeks before and so he may have known I was raw. In any event, his kindness gave me permission to feel my sorrow. Mr. Mason felt soft to me; warm and human. I may have seen in him the father I needed. Here was a big, friendly, centered, sober and non-screwed-up man; and he was concerned about me. He probably thought he was just patching things up with one of his students, but what he got for his efforts was a flood of tears.

In the empty classroom, I collapsed and just came apart completely. I remember weeping so hard my diaphragm and ribs hurt. He let me have my cry without shaming or limiting me and then gave me a pass to go to the bathroom to pull myself together before my next class. Years later I could see the tears of that day were part of a deep pain that had started a long, long time ago.

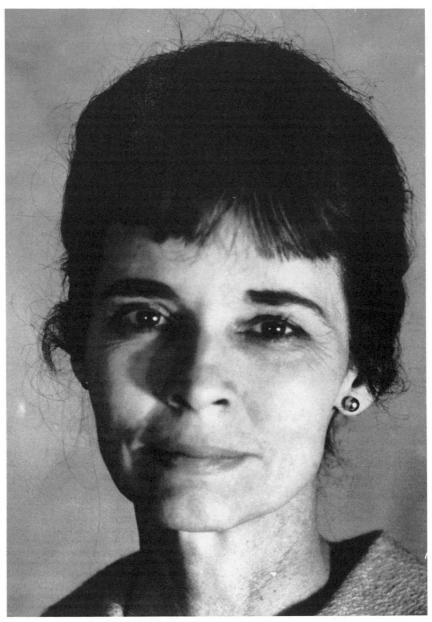

The photograph of Myra that RJL so loved.

TAKE A SAD SONG AND
MAKE IT BETTER

ঞ

Mom's letters, August 1966
The deep unhappiness that occasionally overtakes me has two forms: one, that Roger's life was such a misery to him—to him who seemed to have so much. The other, that the boys have not had in the last ten years a father—and never will have. Related to that, I have not and, at my age, never will have a husband who is rock and oak in life's storms and a joy in life's sunshine (you recognize the Ingersoll). In my life, I had such a short time of true love that I look with a wistful eye on other marriages. I am going to miss one of life's greatest joys—and this often grieves me.

My dad died of "pneumonia." It's on the record. But if *I* ever turn up dead, bring my Mom in for questioning and grill her about what little bastards we were when she tried to start dating again.

After ten years of life with the Volcanic Thunder Bourbon God you'd think pretty much anybody Mom brought home would look like a fucking Ken doll. But for some sad reason we weren't ready to be friendly to anyone Mom invited to sit in Dad's seat at the table. Of particular note was a good man named Dick Swanson, a contractor Mom met while building the new house we moved into after the Millstone. He didn't drink or smoke and there wasn't a cynical bone in his body—which may have been the problem. We were dark little critters by then, Orcs with braces, and his avuncular knock-knock jokes didn't fly with us. His stutter didn't help matters either.

Have the cops ask Mom about that time I said, "Hey, Mom. You goin' out again with D-D-D-D-D-Dick?"

. . .

There's truth in that strange old saying, "You can shoot the horse, but it won't fix the leg."

Yes, Dad was dead, but our family was still broken. There followed a few years of conflicts between Mom and the four of us who remained at home, but most of these skirmishes worked themselves out as our adolescence passed. We began to have great times there in the house on the hill, a home Mom designed herself.

She built the entire house around a library—her dream library: two stories tall, with catwalks and ladders to reach the high shelves; a stone chimney rising 40 feet; and books—books everywhere. Her hobbies and her reading no longer had to be hidden up in the Tower Library or tucked away in drawers at five o'clock. The Hill House spilled over with her interests: pictures of her beloved ships on the walls, dictionaries set open on pedestals, and a bust of Shakespeare looking down over her peaceful kingdom.

She began to do things for us she couldn't when Dad was alive. For his fifteenth birthday, Dan asked for a "Viking dinner"—a dinner without a table or chairs, with the food served on the floor and no plates, no forks, spoons, or utensils of any kind—just the food. Mom loved the idea provided we spread our feast on a tarp of clean plastic. So the sheet was rolled out, the brothers sat on the floor and Mom came in with the steaming tray of meat loaf and plop! it went on the mat. Hot mashed potatoes were scraped from pot to floor, followed by a green waterfall of peas and our feast was set. We made Neanderthal grunts as we dug our fingers into the meatloaf as if it were a bison with the spear still sticking in it. Peas took some chasing around to get a decent mouthful, and all agreed sinking your fingers into a hot mound of the mashed potatoes was a rare culinary delight. At the very end of our Viking dinner, Chris scraped the "leftovers" with the flat of his hand into an urpy-looking pile in the middle.

"Anybody who's a real Viking will eat a handful of *that*." We all took the challenge and had our first, and last, taste of Tarp Goulash.

When the last of the brothers left the Hill House for school in 1972, Myra moved out of Rochester to a small town an hour north and become a "farm lady" (her description). She also took training to teach dyslexic children how to read. A love of books and the RJL-professor in her combined to make her an extraordinary, sought-after tutor. After teaching hundreds of kids how to read at the kitchen table in her farmhouse, she was awarded "master" status and began training teachers to help children and young adults all over southern Minnesota. Along the way she raised chickens, wrote poetry, and cried at *When Harry Met Sally* (the part when Billy Crystal runs up the stairs at the New Year's Eve party looking for Meg Ryan). And though it was clear to the six of us she hoped one day to get married again, it never happened and she made her peace with it.

She continued her weekly letters to Grandpa and Monnie through the Hill House years, and though Grandpa was by then too old to travel, she finally got her trip to Gettysburg. Chris and I accompanied her on the train to Pennsylvania. The happiness on her face as we picnicked by the infamous Copse of Trees—a moment years in the coming—was complete.

"Right there, boys. *That's* where General Armistead made it to the Federal cannon."

In the fall of 2005, my mother and I took a vacation at an old lake resort in Wisconsin; Kip and his wife, Georgia, were there, too. They had room 8 and Mom and I shared 7 next door. It was 10:00 p.m. and we were both in our beds reading. She finally called it a night, placed her bookmark in its spot, and rolled over to sleep. After a little while she sat back up.

She was crying. And she asked a question that still astounds me.

"Was I a good mother?"

"What are you *saying,* Mom? 'Was I a good mother?' Of course you were. What is it . . . what can you be thinking?"

"I should have taken you boys out of that house sooner. Just taken you all away."

This was what was on my mother's mind as she tried to fall asleep thirty-nine years after it had all ended: "I should have taken you out of there sooner."

"Mama, leaving was never an option," I tell her. By now, I've come over to her bedside and am stroking her head. "We all know divorce laws then . . . they were medieval. And it doesn't matter anyway because . . . you *did* save us, Mom, you saved all of us.

"We're all fine, Mama," I assure her. "I'm proof. I'm right here. Kip's right in the next room. We all made it, Mama."

As earnestly as I spoke those words, as hard as I looked into her eyes, I don't think I reached her. After a while, she simply stopped crying, patted my hand, said "I love you," and rolled back over to go to sleep.

My mother is eighty-eight as of this writing. Even in middle age she was a small woman, but that night, under the covers in her cabin bed, she seemed positively teeny. As I looked at her sleeping form I remembered how she saved all six of us. And then it occurred to me, forty years too late, that no one had saved her.

No one had saved her.

She made it through all those years, had protected us, shielded us, and tended to our wounds, but no one had tended to hers. She rebuilt the family, created a new house, got us through our dangerous adolescent years, and sent us into the world as a group of fairly normal young men. Yet even while the family stitched itself back together, for years after Dad's death it seemed there was sadness behind her eyes.

In November of '65, while Dad was hospitalized at Hartford, Jeff captured this sadness in a portrait he took of her. Whether Mom knew how poignant and telling the shot was I don't know, but she liked it enough to frame the picture and send it to her parents as a Christmas gift.

Grandpa's letters, December 24, 1966

It is noon. What do I see on opposite side of room? A fascinating photo of my daughter!! I sit here and gaze at it, trying to decipher what was in your mind as the camera snapped. I said to your mother, "There is maturity beyond any hitherto shown." To me, there are vague lines of grief, deep trial, sadness, overcome by a philosophy akin to that expressed by Tennyson in those words I so often quote: "And yet we trust that good shall fall, at last far off, at last to all. And every winter change to spring."

I look at the photo and see intelligence, beyond any I ever possessed. I have been a doer rather than a thinker. But you, you have the philosophical mind. Otherwise how could you have survived these recent years? But they may have left their mark upon you. I think I see it in your face—serene, untroubled now—but still, how shall I say—aware of tragedy.

Is it my imagination which leads me to say there is a Mona Lisa touch of a smile? Perhaps I am imagining things. I confess I am unable to arrive at an analysis. I lay pen down to let impression ripen.

[Later:] I look across room again at your picture, which now is in the shade of Christmas Eve. There is a slight smile—and do I discern a bit of the quizzical in the eyes? Well, I confess, I love this framed photo of you, my only daughter.

On a visit to the Millstone many years after our family moved out.

THIS VERY ROOM

There are places in the world where bad things happened. In these places the illusion of time grows weak and if you stand still enough you can hear what happened there, lingering like the last notes of a sad song. If you go to Dallas and stand in Dealey Plaza where Mr. Zapruder stood, you can fade back to November 1963 and, at the sound of the shots, throw yourself to the green grass and weep.

In the summer of 2007 I went to Rochester and visited the Millstone. I should say I went to visit the nice family who lived there, but it was the house I'd come to speak with. Driving up Institute Hills Road, I could see the water tower still keeping its watch over Bamber Valley, though today there are no boys standing on its red conical top. Coming down the last bit of road, the same eighty-foot fir trees keep the Millstone from view until you come at last to the stone gateposts, which still announce your entrance like a guest at a ball. Another Mayo Clinic doctor answers the door and after hearing again the story of my connection to the house, he and his wife kindly allow me and my camera to wander the rooms while they go grocery shopping. I am alone in the Millstone.

From the front door I can see the spot in the pine grove where a good dog named Caesar has been resting all these years. I think, "Stay, Caesar, *stay*," and the dark humor brings water to my eyes. But that's what we did here—dark humor.

The new owners have tried to make the space their own, but decorating the Millstone is like sprucing up the Pyramids—it is what it is, and the rooms want things where they belong, and so their living room couch is where we had ours, chairs where we had them. Even the stereo is in the same place, now with computer chips instead of the warm tubes that glowed orange in back of the wooden cabinetry of our "hi-fi."

I walk through the dining room, where our father returned from work and kissed each boy on the cheek, move into the kitchen and—well, I'll be damned—the liquor's found its natural habitat, stored in the same kitchen cabinet. Ah, a refrigerator, I see, with no dent marks. *(Their kids must've scored well on their months-of-the-year quiz—alriiiight!)*

There are small things here too, details only a brother would know to look for. In Dad's study, where the wall-mounted pencil sharpener was, three discreet screw holes mar the wood. The dent in the thin wood panel over the fireplace is there too, right where Mrs. Buttert leaned against it. (This is not a Mrs. Buttert joke; it happened.) Even the plumbing pipe in the basement where one of my hamsters disappeared is there, still open for business.

And around the corner, here's my old room in the fallout shelter. The national boogeyman—the Communist—has been dead for years, and the bricks over the windows probably came down long before the Berlin Wall. Our family boogeyman, he too is long gone and accordingly my old hidey-hole is awash in summer light again; there's even a small breeze. Out the open window, I can see the back yard from an angle I haven't seen since October 1962.

The owners have returned from the store. I greet them, and thank them for their trust and hospitality. Time for one last stop.

I go up two floors to stand outside Mama's Tower Library. The door is open now; no need to pound on it this quiet August afternoon. Come on in, and I do. It is still an oval room and its shelves still wrap around you like arms. But there's no literature or history here today—no Elizabeth Barrett Browning, no *Lee and Longstreet at Gettysburg,* but a mixed bag of how-to books, novels, cookbooks, old magazines. Overhead I see they've painted over Mama's constellations; and the wall's yardstick markings of six growing boys are also gone. It is different now, this room, yet it is the same spot, the very place where Mama took my face in her hands and said, "Honey, do you think you can make the climb down from the balcony and go get help at the Martins'?"

The French doors are still there. Looking over the edge of the balcony, I can see the first stone I set my foot on in descent. The very stone, used by Spider-Man himself. And on the ground below, the spot where the little boy runs off into the July heat to look for help that won't be there.

It strikes me at this moment: Why didn't we turn on him? The seven of us, turn and with locked arms say, "No, Roger. No, you cannot do this. You cannot treat us like this"? It was seven of us—one of him. There was no reason. It simply didn't occur to us we had the power.

But Spider-Man had the power. And he saved me, in his way. As did Quiet Man, Lonely Guy, and Suave Ghost. The Pagans and the Beatles saved me, too. And of course our laughter—our constant, inappropriate laughter—at the wrong times and the wrong things, it saved us. We laughed at victims, at ourselves, and at Dad; we laughed in the face of tornado weather, at fifteen-story falls from water towers, at death, and at funerals. Even to the hour we moved out of the Millstone, we were laughing.

We made another Ridiculous Film that bright sad day in the summer of '67, when the big moving truck was in the driveway. Here comes Luke out the front door carrying Mom's delicate model-ship-building kit (secretly emptied of its fragile contents); he cavalierly tosses it in the car. (Mom gasps a month later when she sees the film, then laughs.) Here's Chris, hauling something incredibly heavy, followed by Collin carrying a saltshaker. Kip emerges, carrying Collin, stiff as a board, and throws him on the truck with the rest of his stuff.

We were just screwing around. Screwing around to the very end.

As I leave, I stop at the stone gateposts at the end of the driveway. Turning to take a last look at the old house, I think of the many places I've searched to find the original memories of my childhood—the photographs and films, the letters and diaries. But the living memories are right here, on these grounds, stored right where they happened, each one buried like Caesar in the grove. With memories embedded in every curve of stone, in the light hitting a high window, the house remembers itself for you. I've stepped through the black-and-white photographs into color, reached through the amber and at last touch the actual thing. Every memory, good and bad, is right here.

And today, at the end of this driveway, the bad memories, they don't seem so scary anymore. They're bullies, bad memories, and they take up more room in our heads than they ought to. For every bad moment, the house has a thousand memories of joy and teems with happy ghosts. Just look at it. There in the front yard a collie dog chases the ghosts of six little boys through the deep snow, and on the back porch the Pagans are warming up—there are ghosts down in the fallout shelter building forts out of the canned food stored away for Armageddon—there are ghosts up on the pitched red slate roof doing things dangerous even for ghosts—there are Halloween ghosts too, still noisily counting out the night's take of candy at the dining room table, and down the hall from the living room hi-fi comes the ghost of John Lennon and the lyrics of *Help!*—our soundtrack for the years of romping through the great house. And everywhere there are boys—boys rolling and tumbling, singing, laughing, fast and slightly out of control.

The family rebuilds at Hill House. Top photo from left: Chris, Jeff, Luke, Myra, Collin, Dan, Kip, and Pagan in front. Bottom photo: running back to the house after the shoot.

"AND EVERY WINTER CHANGE TO SPRING"

∿

Grandpa writing on his birthday, September 28, 1966

Well, I look over these 74 years and consider myself fortunate, a child of Providence, that I have been granted 74 years of life on this interesting planet; that I found a wonderful woman to take care of me and give me two wonderful children; that I have had many friends who out-numbered my enemies; that I was able to get a good education; that I had work of an honorable sort my entire professional life; that I came unharmed through World War I; that I was never tempted to use alcohol or to gamble; that I had excellent teachers in my little Florida college. Oh! I have so much to be thankful for! Even if my 74 years produced no great work. I just was not endowed with the brains to do great things.

Grandpa Rubert James Longstreet, a man who did many great things, died on October 9, 1969, at age seventy-seven. Monnie was with him in Florida when he passed after a short illness. My mother took the train south again and attended the funeral with her little brother, Jimmy, again at her side. In Rochester, a family friend stayed with the three of us still living at home, and when Mom returned a week later she bore with her several boxes full of green books bound by Grandpa. They were the letters—a conversation of thirty years. She never went back to Florida.

I did go back, as I traced this family history, to see the house where my mother grew up; it's still there in Daytona Beach on Braddock Avenue. I went also to Mt. Dora, Florida, to see Grandpa's and Monnie's graves (Monnie lived to age ninety-three). During my visit I made a grave rubbing of that grand name—LONGSTREET—and it hangs here in my study as I write. Next to it is a rubbing of my father's headstone.

I visited my father's grave in November of 1988, twenty-two years after he died. I was driving from Richmond, Virginia, to take a job in Minneapolis and planned my route to take me through Ohio. Dad's grave is there, in the cemetery of a little town called DeGraff, near his father's and mother's headstones. My map said the town was just an hour's jog off the main highway and, once I found the cemetery, my map became a 1966 photo of the gravesite. I used the silhouette of the horizon in its background to find the plot.

I was videotaping this pilgrimage to show my brothers the final resting place of our father. As I approached his grave, I was giving a matter-of-fact description of the surroundings and when I was finally close enough to read my father's name on the gravestone, I stopped short and began to weep. The videotape stops there and when it resumes you can see the headstone is wet where I'd laid my head.

This for a man who terrorized us?

Betrayed us? Belittled us? Left us?

I didn't understand the tears. I still don't.

Over the years since his death, everyone in the family has gone through phases of anger, of sadness, of bewilderment, and back again, buffeted by contradictory emotions. There were days in the '70s when I asked Mom about the things Dad did, she'd wrinkle her face and say, "Why do you want to know such terrible things?" By the '90s, she was pulling Grandpa's old letters off her shelves to clarify an answer. There's no finality to it. Only, "This is how I feel about it today."

We all lived it. But not one of us understands it.

Dan, writing in 2005

Even though I can't think of one single incident when Dad made me feel good about myself, for some reason I can still feel sad about him and feel his loss. About three weeks ago, I had this dream about him, which was surprising because I've never had a sad dream about Dad.

In the dream he had that young, clear face of his early days, with none of the puffiness that came with the booze, and of course he had on one of those starched white shirts I always remember. And he was leaving.

To where, I don't know, but there was a bus he had to catch. He was looking for me because he wanted to say goodbye. But for some reason I avoided him. As he was getting on the bus and waving goodbye to everyone else in the family, all you other guys were calling for me to come, come and say goodbye. But I stayed back, hidden in some sort of place where I could still see all that was happening.

Finally I grudgingly came out of whatever place I was hiding and went to his bus window to say goodbye. But I had come too late. It was somebody else in the window by then and Dad had moved forward. He didn't see me standing there waving. The bus left and I waved and waved but it just pulled away.

EPILOGUE

"My name is Luke and I'm an alcoholic."

I'm in an Alcoholics Anonymous meeting in Austin, Texas.

I'm not visiting. I'm not here trying to learn what my father was like. I'm here because I'm a member of AA, in recovery, and I belong here. I'm an alcoholic.

I grew up promising myself that no matter what else I became, I wasn't going to be a drunk like my dad. And yet I became one.

How I became dependent on booze and drugs will have to be a story for another day. As for this story—about the years I spent wondering what my father was like—it turns out he was like me.

Acknowledgments

My gratitude to Dr. Tony Bianco and the entire Bianco family, Anne Brataas, Maria Carvainis, Dr. Mark Coventry, Mike Ferrer, Karen Gregory, Karen Jacobs, Mike Lescarbeau, Dr. Tony Lund, Jill Marr, Evan Mathews, Andrea McAlister, Tacy Moore, Bonnie Mulligan, Maxine Paetro, Dr. Elizabeth Peacock, Chris Raymer, Colonel W. P. Reed, Curlin Reed, Senour Reed, David Smyrk, Jackie Warner, Alexis Wilson, Steve Wolff, and of course my family: Mom, Kip, Jeff, Chris, Dan, and Collin, as well as Monnie and Grandpa RJL. The photograph at the beginning of "This Very Room" was taken by Shelley Aubin, and the two photographs with "'And Every Winter Change to Spring'" were taken by Susie Blackmun.

Author's Note

There's no fake stuff in this memoir. All the events in this book happened as depicted. Some quotations from the diaries or letters have been edited for readability. Many of the original documents are available for review online at thirtyroomstohidein.com. Names of a few family acquaintances were changed to preserve their privacy.

The author is unable to attribute the description used on page 1 of the Mayo Clinic as a "gray marble slab of medicine."

About the book's title: as children, we always said our home had thirty rooms, but looking at the original blueprints of the Millstone today I count only twenty-six. To me, thirty sounded better.

LUKE LONGSTREET SULLIVAN worked in the advertising business for thirty years and is now chair of the advertising department at the Savannah College of Art and Design. He is the author of the popular advertising book *Hey Whipple, Squeeze This: A Guide to Creating Great Ads* and writes the blog heywhipple.com. He lives in Savannah with his wife and two sons.